D1358079

C.1

BOOK STORAGE

B
G795l Greenbaum, Edward S
    A lawyer's job; in court, in the army, in
the office. [1st ed.] Harcourt [c1967]
    246p. illus.

MOUNT CLEMENS
PUBLIC LIBRARY

1. Lawyers. I. Title.

A LAWYER'S JOB

Mt. Clemens
Public Library

EDWARD S. GREENBAUM

A LAWYER'S JOB

IN COURT · IN THE ARMY · IN THE OFFICE

HARCOURT, BRACE & WORLD, INC., NEW YORK

Copyright © by David S. Greenbaum and Daniel W. Greenbaum
All rights reserved. No part of this publication may be reproduced
or transmitted in any form or by any means, electronic or mechanical,
including photocopy, recording, or any information storage and
retrieval system, without permission in writing from the publisher.
First edition
Library of Congress Catalog Card Number: 67-20328
Printed in the United States of America

To Dotsy,
whose love, encouragement, and help
have made possible both my life
and this record of it

CONTENTS

LIST OF ILLUSTRATIONS

A LAWYER'S JOB

PROLOGUE

THE particular Greenbaums to whom I belong began their life together soon after the Blizzard of 1888. My parents were married in my mother's home on the downtown side of Seventy-third Street between Lexington and Third avenues in Manhattan, just back of the house on Seventy-fourth Street which my wife and I bought many years later.

The snow of that famous blizzard drifts higher every year, especially in reminiscence, and naturally furnished the material for many stories told to us as children. A letter from my mother's older brother Joseph Ullman describes how my parents managed on their wedding day to make the snowy, icy trip all the way down from Seventy-third Street to Fiftieth Street. He says that they had ordered a coach from Dan Phelan's livery stable down the block near Third Avenue. The coach was there at nine o'clock as ordered, but, Uncle Joe writes, "There was no hurrying the happy couple (you know your mother), and when they were ready, the coachmen, to say nothing of the horses, had nearly frozen and had gone home. There were no telephones in those days, so the couple had to walk to Seventy-sixth Street and Third Avenue and get on an elevated train, probably after

a long wait, to Forty-seventh Street, and then walk to the Hotel
Buckingham at Fiftieth Street and Fifth Avenue, where they
spent their wedding night."

After a honeymoon in St. Augustine, Florida, they bought 131
East Eightieth Street, a comfortable little house on the uptown
side of the street between Park and Lexington avenues. The
following January, my brother was born. He was named Lawrence, but was always called Laurie except by my father, whose
speech was notoriously formal. I arrived in April of '90, my
sister Grace in June, '94, and Isabel in December of '97. We
were all born at home—childbirth at hospitals was unknown
then—and my mother's uncle, Dr. Mark Blumenthal, ushered
us into the world.

Eightieth Street was far uptown then, and there were open
lots all along Lexington Avenue. There was one just south of us
on the east side of Lexington, running down to Seventy-ninth
Street. It was a pleasant place, with trees and bushes, a wooden
house in the center with sheds around it, and goats and hens
wandering loose. Mother used to walk down Lexington Avenue
with my brother and me to visit her parents on Seventy-third
Street. Cable cars ran along Lexington Avenue, and in warm
weather they were open, with a long step running along the
side nearest the sidewalk. The conductor on one of these cars
took a shine to my brother. He waved to us when his car went
by, and he used to visit us on his day off. His name was John
Kelly, and he became practically a member of our family. Later
on, when my father became a judge, he selected John as his
court officer.

Father, who was born in London, was distinguished looking
and elegant in speech and manner. He seemed predestined to
be a judge. Besides being a busy lawyer, he was also active in
many communal affairs, including the Educational Alliance,
which he became president of after Isidor Straus, of R. H. Macy
and Company, was lost on the *Titanic*. Father was fourteen years
older than my mother and much more serious. She was gay,
handsome and witty, and active in literary and philanthropic
work, along with being president of the Jewish Working Girls

Vacation Society, which had houses in Bellport, Long Island, and in Margaretville in the Catskill Mountains.

My mother was next to the youngest of four sisters. Aunt Rosie and Aunt Jennie were older, and tiny Aunt Hannah was younger than my mother. Aunt Rosie married the piano manufacturer Leopold Peck, head of Hardman, Peck and Company, who made the official piano of the Metropolitan Opera and whose business connections filled his parties with opera and concert stars. The only one I remember meeting there was Caruso.

Aunt Hannah was unmarried when we were children. She spent much time with us, helping to take care of us and generally fitting in with our generation as much as her own. She was a perfect darling—and even in her old age she had a wonderful sense of humor and the most delightful giggle. She remained our pretty maiden aunt until she was about thirty, when she married George H. Newman, a cousin of Father's, and moved to Pittsfield, Massachusetts. Laurie and I spent boyhood holidays with them and they took us on visits to Williamstown.

My parents' closest friends were "Aunt" Rachie and "Uncle" Cyrus Sulzberger. We spent summer vacations together sharing a cottage—no mean feat, since two sets of parents each with four children made a household of twelve. (But we must have surmounted our difficulties, for our friendship continued as we grew older, and Arthur, later the publisher of the New York *Times*, is still my oldest friend.) There were hazards to this arrangement but also advantages, since one pair of adults could go off on a trip while the other pair "babysat." One of these excursions almost ended in disaster for my parents. In 1893 they took a steamer from Atlantic Highlands in New Jersey to New York, as the first leg of their trip to the Columbian Exposition in Chicago. There was a collision in the fog. As next day's newspaper testifies, it might have been a very serious accident. My mother was badly shaken. In her fine Spencerian handwriting, she wrote this sentimental, prayerful letter to her two infant sons after she got to New York:

My darling sons, Laurie and Eddie,

Your dear father and I, your fond mother, came to town this morning from the Highlands, to go to Chicago, to the great World's

Fair this afternoon. It was very foggy and, in spite of great care on
the Captain's part, there was a collision. God be praised, nobody was
hurt, but the danger was great, and all on board felt that the escape
was a very narrow one. In that moment—those moments, for it took
some little time for us to learn the amount of the damage—need I say
that our prayers went up to God on high for you, our own beloved
boys. And now, I cannot resist the impulse to write these lines to
you, tho' you are but babies now—you, my sweet first-born, but four
and a half years old, and you, my pet, my precious Eddie, but a
little past three, as though you were great boys with full understanding. If it should be the will of God that I should never see my sons
grow up, I want them to know something of their mother's love for
them, and to believe that always, always, *love* lives and that, though
my body should be dust, my love is undying.

My dearest wish, my most fervent prayer, is that they should be
like their dear father. He was ever, and is now, gentle and true,
loving and faithful, upright and noble. To know him is to love him,
and his name is highly respected wherever it is known. Lawrence,
beloved, be noble and true, good always. Edward, dear heart, be the
same. Love each other, dear sons, and be true to each other. May
God bless you with the three-fold blessing mentioned in our Law—
The Lord be merciful unto thee and bless thee. The Lord lift up his
countenance upon thee, and be gracious unto thee. The Lord let his
face shine upon thee, and give thee peace. Amen. Receive the loving
blessing of

> Your devoted mother
> Selina Greenbaum

At the bottom of the letter, my father wrote this:

My precious little boys,

Your darling mother has received such a shock today in the accident that her and my thoughts went out to you and brought to us
the feeling that at any moment we may be snatched away from you
and leave you to work out your life's duty without us, and without
being near to aid and encourage you.

You are so very young yet that it seems idle to write to you today,
but when you are older, you will understand the feelings of your
loving, devoted and affectionate mother and of your father. Think of
your darling mother as a bright, loyal, life-inspiring woman. All I can
say is be honest, God-fearing men and you will have as much happiness as life on earth can bring. God bless you.

> Your father

Father must have given me that letter and I still have it in
my desk drawer.

A later vacation we spent at a hotel at Long Beach on Long
Island. As usual we were with the Sulzbergers. Their older
cousin Frank from Chicago was visiting them. We were quite
a gang, and when one day we discovered an abandoned railroad
turntable on the dunes we decided it would make an ideal
battlefield. After collecting ammunition and lining up into sides,
we happily hurled rocks at one another until they were all used
up and then sent Arthur, the youngest, to the center of the arena
to collect more for the next round. But communication of the
"cease-fire" order must have failed: a rock knocked Arthur out
cold. His head was covered with blood and we were scared to
death. Somehow we got him to the hotel doctor, who patched
him up and put a huge bandage around his head. The doctor
must have had a sense of humor, for he didn't smile when we
asked him not to tell our parents about the casualty.

After we had lived there about eight or nine years, the house
on Eightieth Street became too small for a family with four
children and we moved to Two East Ninety-fourth Street, where
I lived until I was married twenty years later. This was one of
a row of houses built by a client of my father's and was the
usual high-stoop brownstone of the period. But it had a special
feature. Because an open lot adjoined the house to the west, the
view overlooking Central Park was unobstructed, and as there
were no houses north of us on the east side of Fifth Avenue, we
could see all the way to High Bridge. The adjoining lot was
owned by Jacob Ruppert, the brewer, who lived in a "chateau"
on the corresponding corner of Ninety-third Street. The open
space was a boon to active children. The lot was completely
fenced in, but we had a key to a door that opened to our backyard. This became the home grounds for our baseball team,
which, for some strange reason, was called the Homestead. We
had uniforms with this name proudly inscribed on them, and
we felt very professional. I played shortstop and our first base-
man was Reed Kilpatrick, a school friend who lived on Ninety-
third Street. Later, as president of Madison Square Garden, he
was our host at track meets, hockey games, and all sorts of
athletic events. My sister Grace, the only other remaining member of our immediate family, is jogging my memory in these
recollections, and she says that there was a tennis court too, and

that boys sometimes annoyed us while we were playing by throwing stones and breaking windows. Juvenile delinquency is evidently not the product of the present age exclusively, for gangs came over from east of Madison looking for trouble, and I remember my father falling down and tearing his trousers when he tried to chase them off the block.

The square block between Ninety-fourth and Ninety-fifth streets on Madison Avenue was occupied by the huge turreted armory of Squadron A and the Eighth Regiment of the National Guard. As I write, the old building is being demolished and there is a battle raging between the group that wants to "improve" the city by putting high-rise apartments on every corner and those who want to save at least one of the old turrets. The Eighth Regiment was infantry and inspired moderate enthusiasm in us, but Squadron A was cavalry and provided glamour and excitement for the neighborhood. On Memorial Day and other holidays the streets echoed with the sound of prancing horses lining up for parade, the riders and even the horses seeming to look down on us with disdain. But the Eighth Regiment was not so high-flown and even allowed us to attend their track meets.

While we lived on Eightieth Street, we first went to the Park Avenue School, a private school on the northeast corner of Eighty-fifth Street and Park Avenue. I remember very little about it—and nothing about anything we learned there. Indeed, all I seem to remember is walking home after school along the east side of Park Avenue. After that we went to P.S. No. 6 on Eighty-fifth Street and Madison Avenue for several years, and when I was in the sixth grade we went to Horace Mann, a modern coeducational school on 120th Street at Broadway. To get there we usually walked across Central Park and then took the subway or a streetcar up, and on fine days we walked the entire distance. After college we walked the same route with our sisters, while we went to Columbia Law School and they went to Horace Mann and then on to Barnard College.

We were a religious household. My parents were Reformed Jews, and their observance of the Sabbath and the holidays has left me with a feeling of respect for and pride in my religion.

On Friday nights the family was always together to give thanks for what we had received that week. Washed and combed and dressed in our best clothes, we would gather in the library, where my father conducted a short service. At its end we four children lined up before him, and he put his hand on each of our heads in turn, said a brief prayer, and gave us a kiss. Arthur Sulzberger says he used to slip in sometimes to steal a blessing. The Friday-night candles and silver candleholders, which were used on that night only, were set on the best white tablecloth and lighted, and wine was served that even the children were allowed to drink. It was an evening of thanksgiving and close family communion, and one of the loveliest recollections of my childhood. As we grew up and married, the table expanded, for as many of us as could came to have dinner together during the lifetime of my parents.

When the weather was good on Saturdays, we walked to our synagogue on 120th Street and Lenox Avenue. This was Temple Israel of Harlem, whose president was Daniel P. Hays, "Aunt" Rachie's brother and my father's law partner in the firm of Hays & Greenbaum, which later became Hays, Wolf & Sklar. Our rabbi was Dr. Maurice H. Harris, a simple, lovely human being who spoke to his congregation with a sincerity that was totally devoid of histrionics. He and his English wife were good friends of my parents, and when I was married he and my father stood side by side and performed our wedding ceremony. When Dr. Harris got older his sight began to fail, and although he wore very thick glasses, he still had trouble navigating. One day he was brought home by a taxi driver who had knocked him down. He was not really hurt, but shaken and dirty, and he got out unaided. Then to the driver's amazement he took out his wallet and not only paid his fare but added a large tip "because he was so nice to me"—probably the first time that anyone had ever been paid and tipped for knocking a man down.

Just before I was thirteen years old, I went to Dr. Harris to be prepared for my Bar Mitzvah, which takes place in the temple on the Saturday nearest the day a boy becomes thirteen. I was supposed to recite the blessing before the reading of the Torah and another blessing after the Torah was read. These were both in Hebrew, and though I understood the meaning of what I said, it took great effort for me to memorize the words. That's all the Hebrew I have ever learned.

On the east side of us, at Four East Ninety-fourth, lived "Uncle" Marcus and "Aunt" Esther Marks with their four children. We were all about the same ages and were in and out of each other's houses all day long. Laurie and I kept pigeons in our backyard, and this led to complications. The Markses were giving a dinner party one warm summer evening, and their dining-room table was festive with gleaming silver, lace tablecloth, and flowers. The maid left the window open, and the pigeons came in before the guests did. The table was a shambles and the Markses understandably irate. My father delivered the sentence—no pigeons! We sadly gave them all to our Dottenheim cousins, who were then living way uptown in Washington Heights, but true to their homing reputation the pigeons were back in no time. Either our joy at their return or their smartness so impressed my parents that the sentence was revoked and we were allowed to keep them.

"Uncle" Marcus was a reformer in politics, and daylight-saving time was attributed to him. I guess he can be called the father of it. Doris, the youngest Marks child married Henry Dreyfuss, the industrial engineer, and although they live in Pasadena, they are among our closest friends.

The great William Jennings Bryan spoke to us one day at Horace Mann. The whole student body was there and he was wonderfully impressive. I went home all excited, and could hardly wait for my father to come home so that I could tell him all about it. Father was a loyal Democrat and had voted for Bryan. He had also been a delegate at the convention which had nominated Bryan. Anyway, after I had excitedly told Father our great experience, he asked me the simple question, "What did he say?" That floored me. I tried hard but couldn't recall a thought that he had expressed. It made a deep impression on me. He had thrilled me along with everyone else, and yet I couldn't remember a single thing he had talked about.

When I was eleven my father was nominated for the New York Supreme Court. It was a great experience for me and an important one for the City of New York. There was a strong feeling among the voters that Tammany Hall had gone too far under Boss Croker's leadership. Robert Van Wyck had been mayor, Bill Devlin was the chief of police, and there had been some scandal about ice that gave rise to the slogan "Ice and Vice." Hope ran high that at last Tammany Hall could be thrown out, but a strong ticket of independents would be needed to do it. Seth Low, the president of Columbia University and one of New York's most distinguished citizens, agreed to become Fusion candidate for mayor, and the ticket was strengthened by nominating the popular William Travers Jerome for district attorney. Along with my father, an independent Democrat, John Proctor Clark and James A. Blanchard were selected to run for the Supreme Court. Samuel Seabury, a young lawyer, was chosen as the City Court candidate, and in our district, Bainbridge Colby, later Secretary of State, was nominated for the Assembly. It was a strong ticket, and after a vigorous, hard-fought campaign, the Fusion ticket won. Long before Fiorello LaGuardia or John Lindsay were heard of, it was proved that Tammany Hall could be licked.

On Election Night the lot next to us on Fifth Avenue was put to a new use. A brass band appeared to help in the celebration and put on a lively performance. There was much joy in the household that night. Now Father had become a justice of the Supreme Court. That election made a tremendous impression on me as an eleven-year-old boy. My father was chosen not because some boss had selected him, but because the people had wanted him. I believed then, and still believe, that if citizens really want to override the boss's choice, they will do it.

My father's own campaign, although part of the larger campaign, was a personal one, with such people as "Uncle" Cyrus L. Sulzberger and "Uncle" Marcus M. Marks taking part. (Later when Seth Low was not re-elected mayor, "Uncle" Cyrus was defeated for borough president, but when John P. Mitchel was elected mayor, "Uncle" Marcus was elected president of the Borough of Manhattan.)

Our Ninety-fourth Street block seemed to become a block of judges. On the other side of the Markses, at Six East Ninety-fourth Street, lived another New York Supreme Court justice, Vernon M. Davis. Up the block across the street was Supreme Court Justice Daniel F. Cohalan. They were both friends of my father's and frequently walked downtown together in the mornings. Because of Judge Cohalan's close connection with Tammany Hall before he became a justice, he was later impeached. Proceedings were brought against him up in Albany, and Father was called as a witness on his behalf. He testified to the fine record Justice Cohalan had made while he was on the Supreme Court, and he was eventually cleared because nothing had been shown that in any way reflected on his conduct while he was a justice. Later on, I had the firsthand opportunity of knowing Justice Cohalan and was able to see how well he conducted his work in court. On the day that I got married I was trying a case before him. Fortunately it was finished in time for me to go to my own wedding, and when court adjourned that afternoon, the Judge told the clerk to note on the record that court stood adjourned in my memory.

When I was fourteen my parents took the four of us to Europe. Being a judge allowed my father a long vacation, but I'm surprised that he could afford Europe, even though the dollar went much farther then. After spending the night before we left at the Hotel Seville on Twenty-ninth Street we set sail on the *Moltke* of the Hamburg-America Line and eight days later arrived in Plymouth. We spent three weeks in London, where Father was born, seeing all the usual sights, including the law courts and offices at Chancery Lane, which I found "extremely interesting" according to a diary I kept. My diary also tells of a visit we made to a friend of Father's in the country at Hadleywood, "where they have a large house and beautiful garden, cats, dogs, twenty horses, birds, mules and cows." Crossing the Channel from Dover to Calais, "we were in three countries in one day, viz, England, France, and Belgium," where we stayed in Brussels. We spent the next month visiting Scheveningen and traveling up the Rhine into Germany and Switzerland, where we took a trip on a "phenicular." We ended what seems to have been a well-planned trip with a week in Paris and then came back home on the *Moltke*.

Three summers later we made another trip to Europe and I had further opportunities to explore places that until so recently had been just names in a book or newspaper to me. This three months' trip, again including London and Paris, rounded out my bowing acquaintance with Europe. Laurie and I finished off the trip by meeting John Kelly on the steamer and coming home with him, so that I could get to Williams in time for the beginning of my first year there.

Laurie had graduated from Horace Mann in 1906 with enough points on his college entrance examinations to enter as a sophomore. I did the same the following year. So we both graduated from college in three years. One of our teachers at Horace Mann, Miss Helen Baker, believing as she did in the virtues of the small college, had plugged hard for her students to go to Williams. Because of our visits to the Newmans in Pittsfield and the side trips they took us on to Williamstown, we were fertile soil for this propaganda. Miss Baker's other converts included Morris Ernst, who later became our law partner; Heywood Broun; Belvedere Brooks, captain of the football team, who was later killed in World War II; his brother Bruce, who went to law school with me; and George Carrington, another lawyer and lifelong friend, and one of the wittiest men I have ever known. Williams was a wonderful experience for me. The fact that the college was small enabled us to have a close relationship with some of our professors, whom we even visited in their homes. I think that the professor I learned most from was Carroll Lewis Maxcy, who taught English. His personality and his clear, crisp teaching were unforgettable. Professor George M. ("Dutchy") Wahl was another favorite, but entirely different. I took two semesters of Goethe's *Faust* with him. One day a student translating a particularly romantic passage said "pigeons" instead of "doves." That was too much for Dutchy. Plaintively he said, "No. No, Mr. Claussen. It is doves. Not pigeons." In despair he hit a small pane of glass with the window stick, and after again muttering, "Pigeons, pigeons," he said in disgust, "The class is dismissed."

Another one of my favorite professors was Edward M. ("Ted") Lewis, who had had a fabulous reputation as a Williams pitcher when he had been an undergraduate. He gave a course called "Argumentation and Debating," and after hearing a student say a few words at his first class, he could tell whether he came from Bangor, Maine, Redwing, Minnesota, or Brooklyn. We suspected that he had taken a look at the admission records before he performed this feat. In junior year the Van Vechten Extemporaneous Contest was held. Trials were held once a week on five consecutive weeks. The contest carried what we all considered a very large prize—$125, I think. A subject was assigned to each entrant, and after about five minutes to prepare, the student had to give his talk. The big prize attracted about a dozen of us to the contest, and at the suggestion of my classmate George Carrington, five or six of us agreed to split the prize equally among our group if any of us won. This included all those we thought had any chance of winning. As George said, "Why should we do this for nothing every week?" But we did; none of us won. Our big deal was discovered before the prize was awarded, and at an investigation, we all admitted it but denied that we had done anything wrong. The prize went to the guy we suspected of turning us in.

Anyway, thanks to Ted Lewis, I made the debating team and was captain of it in my senior year. We were in two triangular leagues: Brown-Dartmouth-Williams and Amherst-Wesleyan-Williams. In my senior year, we won both debates in both leagues. That was the year we won all our athletic contests, and I guess we would have been murdered by our classmates if we had lost. After an athletic victory, the chapel bells were rung at midnight in Williamstown, and that year for the first time they rang the bells for a debating victory.

I loved athletics and was an ardent rooter at all games. I played basketball and golf, and although I wasn't good enough to make either team, I was on the basketball squad that worked out with the varsity every day. The team was really awfully good that year. We won every game we played—the official New England Intercollegiate Championship, as well as the unofficial intercollegiate title.

During a scrub basketball game one afternoon, I was playing against Bel Brooks, when as a result of one of his bearlike hugs, my nose was broken. Bel was overcome with guilt and remorse, and spent the night in my room putting ice packs on my nose. The whole business wasn't too good for my physiognomy, since I'd broken my nose twice before, once playing basketball at Horace Mann and once when Laurie had pulled a folding-bed down on me. The third break didn't help.

I played golf whenever I could get out to the club. Laurie was on the team and played in the seventies. He was really good, but I was only good enough to play when one of the regulars couldn't show up. But once, in this very meager role, I won for dear old Williams against the Albany Country Club. Our captain, Richard L. Jackson, was then Connecticut state champion, and played the Number 1 position on our team. The other players followed along, down to me in sixth position. After the first five matches had ended, the team score was tied and the players, including Captain Dick, were all lined up around the eighteenth green to see me get licked. I was playing against an old guy who drove about 170 yards straight down the fairway on every shot. He was lying three, just a few inches from the cup. I was lying two, but was about ten feet off the green. Our captain sized up the situation and signaled me not to play until he could come over. He whispered some secret instructions in my ear. I took out my seven iron, then called a lofter, and dropped the ball in for a three. Dick, smiling all over, said, "Just what I told him to do," and walked to the clubhouse. His secret instructions were "Sink it."

The last semester of his senior year, when I was a junior, Laurie and I took a course called Astronomy II. I do not know what made me choose it, but I always had a feeling that what was behind Laurie's interest in that course was the proximity of the golf course to the large tract of land in which we did our field work. After an hour's surveying in the lovely spring weather, Laurie would slip away to a round of golf, leaving us to our tape and sextant. Our professor, Willis Isbister ("Lizzie") Milham eventually got wise and warned Laurie that his dereliction would be reflected in his marks. However, the course ended with Laurie getting an A and me a C, and to this day I think Lizzie mixed up our marks. But I may be wrong, for Laurie

later took a course in surveying at a business school in North
Adams, took the state examination, and got his Massachusetts
surveying license—all with his hands behind his back! Laurie
readily absorbed any subject with the greatest of ease. Although
he also took a course in constitutional law in his senior year and
got an A in it, he still did not know what profession he would
follow when he graduated in 1909 with a Phi Beta Kappa key.

He was intrigued by physics, mathematics, and engineering.
He knew a great deal about them without ever seeming to study
and always carried a slide rule in his pocket. Ever since he was
a boy he could fix toys and clocks, while nails flew out of my
hands and hammers dropped on my toes.

There were only fifteen months between us, and while we
were always very close, we were as different as we could be.
He was blond; I was dark. He was mechanical; I was clumsy.
But the prime difference lay in our social lives. Laurie was a
ladies' man. He danced beautifully, was in great demand at
parties, and lovesick girls rang him up from morning till night.
I was the shy type. His intimates included the garageman, a business tycoon, a notorious public character, an outstanding judge,
and a little nobody. Any two or three of them might spend the
day together, fishing with Laurie on his boat. He treated them
all alike, with affectionate abuse. His secretary was often reduced
to tears by his abuse, but she adored him and called him Laurie.
He was thoroughly involved in the law, but he came to the
office and left whenever he liked, and somehow found the time
to manage a local law office in White Plains as well as helping
to organize the Quaker Ridge Golf Club and to create the Beach
Point Club, serving as the president of both, while being active
in local Democratic politics and chairman of the State Board of
Social Welfare under both Governors Lehman and Dewey. He
was a "character"—and one of the most gifted people I ever met.
It was not until after I went overseas in World War I that I
emerged from the impact of his towering personality.

When I wanted to take that constitutional-law course that he
took in his senior year, my wise father interfered. Although I'd
never discussed it with him, he knew that I would be a lawyer
and wanted me to take advantage of the other things college

offered since he was sure that I'd spend the rest of my life studying law. And was he right! After graduating from Williams in
1910, I followed Laurie to Columbia Law School.

I

STUDYING LAW

FROM the start I liked the work at law school. In our first year, we had the good fortune to take Terry on contracts. This course came late in the afternoon, after Professor Charles Thaddeus Terry had done a day's work in his law office downtown. It was given in a large classroom in Kent Hall. There must have been about 150 students taking the course. When Terry came in the excitement began.

He was short and thickset. He had a slight limp, and his uneven face, which was often lighted by a charming smile, gave the impression that he suffered pain. His mind was brilliantly alert and he spoke with great clarity, both of content and of tone. Indeed, he impressed me as being the best teacher I ever had anywhere. He started right in by calling on a student by name. Something in the Socratic style then took place:

> TERRY—Mr. Smith, A said to B, "I'll give you five dollars if you
> will walk across the Brooklyn Bridge." Is that a con-
> tract?
> STUDENT—Yes.
> T.—Why?

S.—Because A made an offer for consideration.

T.—Was there any acceptance of the offer?

S.—No. I mean it would have been a contract if B had accepted the offer.

T.—When was the contract made?

S.—When B said he'd accept.

T.—That was a bet, not a contract, wasn't it? It's the same as if A said, "I'll bet you five dollars you can't walk over the Brooklyn Bridge."

S.—But when B said he'd walk over the bridge, he made a contract.

T.—When would he get his five dollars?

S.—After he walked over the bridge.

T.—Suppose he walked only halfway, would he get two-fifty?

S.—No, he didn't keep his contract.

T.—Suppose he walked all the way, except the last five steps, would he get it then?

S.—Yes.

T.—Why?

S.—Because he had substantially performed.

T.—Well, suppose he'd walked all the way but six steps, was that substantial performance?

S.—Yes.

T.—How about seven steps?

S.—I think that's substantial performance.

T.—Well, suppose he was only twenty-six steps away. How about that?

S.—No, I don't think that's substantial performance.

It would end up with the poor student trying to find some place between seven and twenty-six steps where performance was substantial and Terry asking whether that last step completed the contract. The whole class was just as excited and confused as the perspiring student, and each one was scared that he would be called on next to solve it all. After taking on one or two more students in an electrified atmosphere, the hour would suddenly be over. We would all remain around, still talking about walking across the Brooklyn Bridge.

At the beginning of class the next day, Terry might call on yesterday's student, who had thought that the odds were about 150 to 1 that he was off the hook. Or maybe Terry wouldn't call on that student again for the rest of the course. Sometimes we felt as though our entire future careers depended upon how we answered his questions. And we were scared stiff to miss a class because that would be the day he would call on us. But there was something very puckish about him; at other times we were really sure that he never even noticed what happened in the classroom.

One afternoon in the spring I met him on the subway going up to class. He was a Williams alumnus and asked me what kind of baseball team we had this year. I told him I thought it was going to be very good and said Williams was going down to play Princeton tomorrow and that I'd like to see the game. He told me I should go. I did so. The next day, as soon as I got back, everyone at law school told me that Terry had called on me the minute he arrived.

After two or three days of his classroom exercises, Terry would start to sum up. In a short time we knew what was an offer, acceptance, consideration, and substantial performance. What we learned has remained with me ever since.

Dean Harlan F. Stone, who later became Chief Justice of the United States, taught us criminal law. The only time I saw him fussed was one day when a Negro student asked, "Professor, is fingerprints good law?" Another student, who was short and heavyset like Stone, praised him as a teacher because "he has the build." I admired his teaching ability for other reasons. He was a fine teacher, although a little too judge-like in the classroom. His class was not exciting like Terry's, but it moved right along and I was never in doubt about a subject after Stone had explained it.

Gregory Mason, another Williams graduate, and I got out a "Constitutional Law Service," which we sold to students for $25. Every week we gave each subscriber a summary of the cases that our professor had assigned for discussion at the next session. The professor was William D. Guthrie, who had been the winning lawyer before the Supreme Court in 1895 when it had decided that the recently passed income-tax law was unconstitutional (*Pollock* v. *Farmers Loan & Trust Company*).* Near the end of the term the Dean sent for Mason and me and wanted to know if we had supplied this "service." We told him we had and that we had advertised it on the bulletin board downstairs. He said this was against the rules and thought we should return the money we had collected. We told him that we had never heard of "the rules," and innocently asked if our customers had also violated them, adding that we hadn't known we were doing anything wrong, that the course was almost over and the "service" was almost finished—and besides, we had spent all the money. The Dean decided to do nothing about it.

Professor Nathan Abbott taught us property. He was a fine teacher, though not at all like Terry or Stone. He was slow and dreamy, but we learned a lot from him in a strange kind of way. Among other things, he taught us the law in Shelley's case and in Dumpor's case. The famous rule in Shelley's case established that if A acquires land to be his for his life, either by gift or by sale, and if at the same transaction, it is provided that A's heirs get the land after A's death, then A owns the land outright. Dumpor's case determined something else, but I've forgotten what it is.

One fall day he told us about a pub he found in England the summer before. He used to go there and linger over his beer

---

* Whenever a lawyer tells what a court decided, he must cite the name of the case, as I just did. But he must also give the volume and page of the book in which this is reported. Presumably this is to show that he hasn't made up the case—and to indicate the scholarliness of the author. The citation is 157 U.S. 429.

Telling something in a footnote is also very fashionable among legal writers. For instance: Years later Mr. Guthrie became president of the Association of the Bar of the City of New York. An effort was then being made to liven up this august body, and Newman Levy was asked to write a play for performance before the Association. He did so and Mr. Guthrie asked to see it. Newman was with our office at that time and I was in his room when Mr. Guthrie called. He asked Newman if he thought the play held law up to ridicule. Newman replied, "Well, sir, that was its general purpose." It was years before the play was produced. Harrison Tweed was then president, and "May it Please the Court" made a terrific hit. The Association still survives.

to look at the property across the street. It was there that
Shelley's case had arisen, and as he told us this, I suspected
that he had gone to England just to sit there and gaze at this
property. But he was somewhat perplexed because the proprietor
of the pub had never heard of Shelley or of his case, and didn't
care a bit about either one.

Later, after we started practicing, I asked Professor Abbott
to help us on a case we were handling in Boston. He was excited
about it because he thought it afforded an opportunity to get
a clear-cut decision in this country on the rule in Shelley's case.
We represented the attractive widow of the even more attractive
but deceased son of a famous New England family. He had
been married three times before marrying our client. Each wife
had been divorced and given a generous slice of the family
fortune, to become effective after the husband's death. But it
was always the same slice. He also gave it to our client by will.
Each of the parties had Boston counsel, as did the trustee of
the estate and various other claimants. We retained a firm there
which had a couple of partners who were friends of mine from
Williams. Hearings before a master were held the last week in
the month throughout the winter and spring. But one afternoon
each week, everything stopped for the Lawyers' Bowling Tour-
nament. Every firm in Boston had a team, including three or
four firms taking part in our hearings. Naturally, I wasn't eligible to play, but I went along and became the official score-
keeper. I got to know many of the lawyers quite well. It was
very pleasant and quite different from practicing law in New
York. I think it still is!

Every time that I returned to New York I went to Professor
Abbott's apartment to report what had happened during the
week. Finally, after many weeks of trial, we agreed on a settlement. All the parties were satisfied and my client was delighted.
Eager to tell Abbott all about it, I rushed to his apartment when
I got back to New York. But he was horrified. He acted as if he
were mortally wounded, saying over and over again, "We'll
never know. We'll never know!" The court would never decide
our case. He wouldn't listen to me tell him how it was settled,
and he wouldn't talk about his fee. All he could think of was

that this rare opportunity to settle the law had been lost. I left, feeling like a heel. I had let him down.

While in law school, I served on a jury. My father thought we'd get more out of two weeks' jury service than we would learn in that time in law school so he arranged to have the Commissioner of Jurors call my brother, another student, and me as jurors in the City Court.

It was fascinating to see what actually happened in the court-room and to be one of the cogs in the process of the law. I've often thought of the negligence case we heard in which the foreman asked, as soon as we went into the jury room, "How much shall we give him?" When I suggested that we first con-sider whether it was the guy's fault, I was squelched with the rejoinder, "He was hoit, wasn't he?" My vote for one dollar reduced the verdict, but it was still for the plaintiff and not for the defendant. I sat on several cases and think I did indeed learn more out of these experiences than what I missed in class.

Moot courts were unofficial and voluntary when I was in law school. They held trials or appeals. Teams were chosen to try a case or argue an appeal against another team in the same court. They didn't then have contests against other moot courts. They were social affairs, and my brother Laurie had been made a member of Kent Moot Court. The next year I became a member.

After I was in our court for about a year, I suggested a class-mate for membership. He was turned down. I was disappointed, but thought nothing much about it because it wasn't too easy to get into a moot court and because, in this case, they told me he was turned down because he was a Columbia graduate. Columbia Law School liked to be quite superior to the college. Then I suggested another candidate and he was turned down too. I didn't see why. The second candidate was a Dartmouth graduate, not a Columbia man, and he was and is a fine person: Herbert A. Wolff, who later became my partner. A good friend told me the reason was the same in both cases: they were Jews. He thought I was an awful dope not to have figured it out, and told me so. I was furious, and my brother was just as mad when I told him. We raised hell with several of our closest friends in the court. They agreed with us and said that they had voted to admit both the candidates, but they had been licked. So that was that, they thought, and what was there to get excited about? But we were, and resigned, and were good and mad at some of our friends for not resigning with us.

I realize now that this was the first time that I had encountered an anti-Semitic incident; although I had gone through Horace Mann and Williams, nothing like this had ever happened. I had, of course, known about prejudice, but now it suddenly hit me that a man couldn't get into something just because he was a Jew. I had been aware that Laurie and I were the only Jews in the moot court, but it had never occurred to me that there was anything out-of-the-way about this. I hadn't been asked to join a fraternity at Williams, but Jews were in fraternities there, and that hadn't bothered me. I liked the non-fraternity crowd I was with, and I had decided that I didn't want to join and would not have if I had been asked. Fraternities were not such a big part of college life then, and quite a few of those who were asked didn't join—and, indeed, my closest friend in college was sorry that he had ever joined.

Maybe it had nothing to do with this incident—or maybe the Dean had heard about it and it did have a lot to do with it— but I was chosen for a new position in the law school then. Frederic B. Colver, a Princeton graduate, and I were made moot-court advisers. The purpose was to give every man in law school the opportunity of joining a moot court. That is the way it works today, I understand.

I guess that I must have been an awful pest for the Dean. Later on he was disturbed because I didn't accept membership on the *Columbia Law Review*. I didn't like the idea of having students publish a legal journal of importance, and I didn't think that these students should be excused from answering questions in the classroom just because they were on the *Law Review*. If it was that good, I thought, all the students in the class should be allowed to do *Law Review* work. I still think so. The Dean called up my father, whom he knew, and came to our house for dinner to discuss my refusal with him. After dinner, they went upstairs to my father's study on the top floor of our house. When Dean Stone left, I asked what had happened. All Father would say was, "I told him it was up to you."

An article recently appeared in the Columbia Law School *News* which criticized the *Law Review* because it singled out a few students as a small clique which remained aloof and "unsullied by contact with the rest of the student body." With my partner Herb Wolff, who had also turned down the *Law Review*, we wrote a letter to the *News* saying that in our day we had disapproved of *Law Review* students proudly answering "unprepared" when called upon by a professor who had momentarily forgotten their superior and exempt status. We continued:

There are many qualifications that go to make a good lawyer and some of these, of necessity, cannot be used as criteria for selecting *Law Review* members. They are too intangible. Franklin D. Roosevelt did not make the *Review*. Nor did Thomas E. Dewey. In our own class, the non-Reviewers included Arthur T. Vanderbilt, New Jersey's distinguished Chief Justice, Theodore Kiendl, one of New York's finest trial lawyers, John P. Hartigan, an able Federal Judge, as well as many other outstanding lawyers. Of course, it is also true that some of those who were on the *Review* have completely recovered from their youthful deification and have become leaders at the Bar.

We sent a copy to Chief Justice Vanderbilt, who wrote back:

I got my morning chuckle from the copy of your letter to the Columbia Law School News. Who could complain of being classified in the company to which you and Herb Wolff have assigned me?

Another classmate, Judge Hartigan, wrote us:

I was very glad to receive your letter, together with the very interesting enclosure with which I agree 99 and $^{44}/_{100}$%. If you had omitted my name, I would say that I agree 100%.

Other distinguished classmates who did not make the *Review* included William F. Gibbs, the famous naval designer and Judge Joseph F. Crater, the missing jurist.

I was a problem for the Dean in another area too: my classmate, Tom McEntegart and I passed our bar examination at the end of our second year. I didn't blame the Dean for not being overjoyed about it. We weren't supposed to take the examination until after graduation, and this intercepted forward pass let us become members of the bar before we graduated. Furthermore we had passed the examination not because we knew any law, but because Tom and I had discovered how to answer the questions without actually trying. It was simple. A long question with complicated facts meant that an essential fact had been omitted. A short statement with many objections meant all the essential facts had been given. We explained our method to Stone. Here's how it worked.

The question on the examination paper would be something like this: Does the following complaint state a good cause of action? The plaintiff alleges that on the 1st day of April, 1967, he was proceeding southerly on Seventh Avenue, in the Borough of Manhattan, City, County and State of New York, in his 1963 Rambler automobile, Rumsey model, bearing New York license plate C-8259, which expired on December 31, 1967, to a point 27 feet and 7 inches north of the intersection of Seventh Avenue and 43rd Street, when said Rambler was struck by a 1962 Chevrolet automobile, Crummy model, bearing New York license plate D-8360, which expired on December 31, 1967 . . . etc., etc., etc.

You can stop right there. It does not state a good cause of action. It says too much—gives too many details. All that stuff about the license plates is hogwash. The complaint is just no good, and you'll get 50 per cent credit for saying so. You then have to say why and maybe you can guess that, since you already know the complaint has missed some allegation that is essential. Anything you guess right is just gravy.

The other type of question went like this: A complaint alleges that on May 1st, 1967, John Smith made his promissory note in which he agreed to pay Joe Doakes $1,000 with 4 per cent interest in six months at the Chase Manhattan Bank but failed to do so. John Smith answers that Joe Doakes said it could be renewed if not then paid; as a second defense, that Joe Doakes promised he would use the $1,000 to make a donation to the Red Cross; as a partial defense, that Jane Doakes, Joe's wife, owed $500 to the National City Bank, which the plaintiff had paid for him; as a third defense, the note was not witnessed, etc.

The complaint is good. There are too many defenses. They are no good—you could probably guess some reasons why. Again, whatever you guess right is all gravy.

Stone tested our theory out for himself and found that we were right. He was mad as the devil. While we were sitting with him, he phoned John Kirkland Clark, chairman of the State Board of Examiners, and told him all about it. After that year, the form of the bar-examination questions was changed, and no one was permitted to take the bar examinations unless he had a degree from a qualified law school. From then on, a student had to know some law in order to pass.

Again, Stone didn't know what to do with us. Obviously we had passed without knowing the law. But was that any reason for saying we had flunked? Anyway, he decided to do nothing about it. Maybe he couldn't.

I'm glad to say that the Dean wasn't sore at me, and I got my degree with the class, in June, 1913. In March, he wrote to me expressing appreciation for the moot-court work that Fred Colver and I had done. Tom and I were admitted to the bar in November, 1912.

And now I was a lawyer.

II

CLERKING

I was lucky and didn't ever have to apply for a job. My father did it for me. He felt the lawyer he would like to see me work for was Benjamin N. Cardozo, who was not well known then, but Father thought him an outstanding lawyer. But Cardozo said no. He thought that I would learn much more with Edgar J. Nathan, of the firm of Cardozo & Nathan. Both Nathan and the other founder of the firm, Michael H. Cardozo, Sr., were Benjamin Cardozo's cousins. It was not just modesty on Cardozo's part that made him want me to go with them. His advice was sound. I got the job with Cardozo & Nathan, and learned a lot there, including how a law office works. Mr. Nathan, whom Cardozo so admired, was head of a firm which was counsel to a wide variety of clients, including banks and insurance companies.

Mr. Nathan was the senior partner, and my ideal of what a lawyer should be. He was a fine lawyer, with a wonderful personality—wise and understanding, calm, clear, and forceful. When the managing attorney's office had the jitters about today's calendar, a few words from Mr. Nathan would calm everybody and solve everything. He must have been wonderful with a client. His warm personality was immediately pleasing. It was impossible to imagine that he could do anything wrong, or be wrong. Here was a man you could rely on, and you knew that what he was telling you was right. His fine features, his neat dark moustache, and his well-fitting clothes all combined to strengthen this feeling.

I think that I learned more from Brison Howie, the managing attorney, than my brother learned from Franklin D. Roosevelt, who was the managing attorney at Carter, Ledyard & Milburn, where for a time Laurie shared the managing attorney's big desk with F.D.R. Laurie liked him and enjoyed working with him. However, I got the impression that there the managing job was then handled in a somewhat cavalier fashion, which was far from true at Cardozo & Nathan.

First, there was the problem of answering calendar calls. It was a real problem. Every day someone had to be in each court where we had a case. And that was usually several. Today, we and almost every other law office engage a representative from a court answering service which is in the business of appearing in court and saying "One week by consent," or "January 27th," or some other legal brilliancy that does not require Harvard Law School training. In those days, we had no answering service and it was my job to do that. I was scared in court. Even scared in answering, "One week by consent." After more than fifty years, I still am. But I experienced the thrill of victory in its elementary and primitive form in getting the adjournment.

Another part of the work was recording in the office docket what happened each day in each case. We had to enter there just what had gone on in court, what papers were served or received, and so forth. But the hardest job in the managing clerk's office, I felt, was preparing pleadings and other papers. The pleadings are the complaint and answer. The complaint states what the facts are on which our client bases his claim. The answer gives the grounds relied on for saying that our client does not owe anything to the other fellow. These papers are then signed by the lawyer or the client, served on the other side, and usually filed in court. Some of them are very simple, but others are extremely difficult to draw up and require much skill. The office of Cardozo & Nathan was an excellent place to learn this. Michael H. Cardozo, Jr., the son of the founder of the firm, was not only a skilled draftsman but a very able lawyer and teacher, and he required nothing less than perfection, both as to content and appearance of the document.

I also had good practical training from Ernest A. Cardozo, another partner, who was the brother of Michael. In one instance, a client was being sued for $25 as damages to the backyard of his neighbor's house on West Eighty-seventh Street. It was quite a battle and feelings ran high. The suing neighbor was a distinguished doctor who later became a good friend and client of ours, but he was not an easy person to deal with. After a few weeks, in which there were several conversations with our client but none with the other side, I was told that the case had been disposed of. When I asked what had happened, Ernest Cardozo, who was in charge of the case, told me, with a half-suppressed smile, that the firm had paid the $25. Our client need not know this, but he was being billed $25 for professional services rendered—and that was the end of it. He was delighted, the doctor was happy, and Cardozo & Nathan avoided heaps of work.

The American Exchange National Bank, one of Cardozo & Nathan's clients, was on the ground floor of our building at 128 Broadway and the firm was always being called upon to answer questions from the bank. One of the bank's officers, Mr. E. A. Bennett, asked if I could spend a few days at the bank to familiarize myself with banking processes. Like any other brand-new lawyer, I really knew nothing whatever about how a bank worked, except that it would cash your check if you had money on deposit, and what some appellate courts had held in cases I read at law school. Mr. Bennett turned me over to a man in one of the cages, and for several days I sat by his side as he worked. Letters of credit, drafts, acceptances, all these mysterious terms began to take on meaning for me as I watched him work. When Mr. Bennett's training program was over, I really think that I knew what he wanted to teach me.

Cardozo & Nathan was small enough for me to see how

things worked, but large enough to have all types of legal work, and the firm was active in litigation. I began to realize how important it was actually to understand what the precise facts were in any situation that I was working on. One easy way was to get a look at the place where the situation arose. For example, if it was an accident case, obviously you should immediately see the place where it occurred, take photographs, make measurements, and otherwise find out and record as accurately as you could all the circumstances surrounding the situation. In a business transaction I discovered that it was just as important to be familiar with the actual setup in which the transaction took place and to see where the parties worked. I am still surprised to find how many lawyers have never been to their client's place of business, although they may have represented him for years.

One of the cases I worked on arose after a fire destroyed a building across the street from us and excavations were begun for the new Equitable Building, which was to occupy the entire square block. These building operations resulted in the cracking of walls and other damage to our building and other buildings on the north side of Cedar Street, east up to Nassau, where the National Bank of Commerce was located. Our bank and the other property owners thought that they could collect for these damages. I had the job of helping to prepare for trial, looking up the law, finding out the differences between "adjoining" and "adjacent," "contiguous" and "contingent." I went down into the excavations and saw the underground stream that is still flowing beneath the Equitable Building. Mr. Nathan was to try the case for the plaintiffs. Charles Evans Hughes was the chief counsel for the defendants. Being involved in preparing for trial was exciting, but the case was finally dropped. The feeling was, I believe, that it wasn't a good idea for banks and others to sue insurance companies in the Wall Street area. No one wanted to get too precise about the *inter se* property rights. Anyway, I was learning that of all the lawsuits that are started, only a very few ever come on for trial.

Mr. Nathan was an outstanding fire insurance lawyer. He had been retained to defend the insurance companies that were being sued to recover losses arising out of the Triangle Waist Company factory fire. This was the famous fire on the east side of Washington Square that took the lives of 146 girls in 1911. The owners, Harris & Blanck, had been acquitted of criminal charges after a sensational trial in which they were defended by Max D. Steuer, the outstanding trial lawyer of that period.

Steuer was also the lawyer for Harris & Blanck in the civil cases in which they sued the insurance companies for damages sustained on their insurance policies. Besides pleading that the damage claims were padded, the fire insurance companies claimed arson—meaning that Harris & Blanck had themselves started the fire. The whole situation was tense, one might say highly inflammable. An able accountant, McKenna, had gone over the books of the companies and given Mr. Nathan his report. We had prepared a stipulation agreeing that this report could go in evidence at the trial. I was sent over to Mr. Steuer's office to get it signed. I did so and gave it back to Mr. Nathan. Maybe because I came back too soon, or maybe for some other reason, he sent for me and asked just what had happened. I told him that I had brought the paper to Mr. Steuer, he read it, thought for a moment, sort of smiled, and then signed it and gave it to me. A little later, Mr. Nathan sent for me again and asked me to read the stipulation very carefully and see if I didn't think that it could be claimed at the trial that we had stipulated that the books were "true and correct" instead of saying that the McKenna report contained true and correct copies of these book figures. I agreed, and he sent me back to Mr. Steuer to ask him to sign another stipulation in place of the one he had just signed. This was not an easy task, and Steuer was not as pleasant as he had been on the first visit. Very reproachfully, he told me to assure Mr. Nathan that he was not the type of person who would take advantage of the wording of a stipulation, even though *he* had not prepared it. This case, like the Equitable Building one, never went on. It was settled just before trial.

My brother meanwhile had begun to practice law. He wanted to start a new firm, with me, Herbert A. Wolff, who had been clerking at Stroock & Stroock, and Morris L. Ernst as the partners. We had known Herb at law school and thought he would make the ideal partner, as indeed turned out to be the case.

Morris Ernst had gone to Horace Mann and was in Laurie's class at Williams and on the debating team with me. He fitted in well with the plans Laurie had for the new firm, even including the fact that he was in the furniture business and had never worked in a law office. Again Laurie's judgment proved sound. Morris was the partner we needed. Because I was completely absorbed in my job at Cardozo & Nathan, and because I had absolute confidence in my brother's judgment as well as his ability to carry out successfully anything that he undertook, I relied on him. He made the necessary arrangements, including borrowing what money he thought was required.

The idea that four young lawyers could start a new law firm probably seemed crazy. We didn't have a single prospective paying client in sight. No one in his right senses would have advised doing what we did. So on May 15, 1915, we opened the doors of the new firm of Greenbaum, Wolff & Ernst.

III

OUR OWN FIRM

IN THE early morning of July 16, 1912, the day he was going to testify before the grand jury, the gambler Herman Rosenthal was shot and killed in front of the Metropole Hotel on West Forty-third Street. The good people of New York were really shocked, for they had been told that Rosenthal was to testify that Police Lieutenant Charles Becker was on his payroll. Four gunmen with the picturesque names of Lefty Louis, Gyp the Blood, Dago Frank and Whitey Lewis were indicted for murder in the first degree with Lieutenant Becker. They were all tried, convicted, and electrocuted. The district attorney, Charles S. Whitman, was later elected Governor. It all followed a classic movie plot.

This trial marked the beginning of my attendance at sensational trials, including the Hall-Mills case, the Bruno Hauptmann trial for the kidnaping and murder of the Lindbergh baby in New Jersey, the Snyder-Gray case, and, later, the Alger Hiss trials in New York. My companion at all of these appearances was my friend Arthur Sulzberger, who later became publisher of the New York *Times* by "marrying the Boss's daughter," as he put it. We both learned a lot from going to these trials. We saw and heard what actually took place in the courtroom—how the witnesses really looked, what the judge said, and how the lawyers conducted themselves. Today, very few people—even few lawyers—see what really goes on in the courtroom. True, they know all about television trials, but, believe it or not, even Perry Mason and his entertaining crew are no substitute for the reality.

The trial of Lieutenant Becker was held in the old Court of General Sessions in New York. John W. Goff was the presiding judge, a tough, white-haired man who never smiled. He seemed completely devoid of any sense of humor, and whatever share he once may have had of the milk of human kindness had run dry. His voice was harsh when you could hear it, but it was usually inaudible. The Judge drove the defendant hard, keeping the trial going late in the evening, day after day, although the defendant's attorney, former Judge John McIntyre, constantly protested. When the trial came to an end, Judge Goff charged the jury. After giving a full summary of the People's case, he told the jury, in a proper tone of voice (according to the stenographer's notes), that should they believe the defendant, they should find him not *guilty*, but, on the other hand, if they *did not believe the defendant,* they should find him *guilty,* and if they should believe the *District Attorney's witnesses* they should find the defendant *guilty.* All that the jury and the others in the courtroom heard were the emphasized words, stressing "guilty . . . guilty . . . guilty . . . guilty." The jury dutifully found the defendant guilty.*

But the Becker conviction was appealed. When the Court of Appeals got hold of it, a new trial was ordered. The Court said that when he charged the jury, Judge Goff had "outlined in much detail and most effectively the claims of the prosecution and the

---

* Much later I had an undefended divorce case before Judge Goff in the State Supreme Court. At one point he said something that I couldn't hear. I asked the Clerk, who told me that he had said that the witnesses must speak louder. A little while later the Judge said something that sounded like "s-s-s," and then walked out of the courtroom. Again I asked the Clerk, who told me that he had said, "Dismissed." I requested the court stenographer to please remain for a few moments, and then I asked my witness a couple more questions. The minutes were written up, and the next week I submitted them to the Judge with my proposed judgment. He signed it and the divorce was granted.

evidence which had been produced to support these claims," but
that he left it to the jury, "to evolve from their own unaided
memories the recollection of any arguments or evidence in behalf of the defendant." The Court also pointed out numerous in-
stances where haste had "become the essence of the trial," and
that defendant's lawyers, although physically and mentally ex-
hausted, were "harshly admonished to get along," and told that
"time is too precious." * The Court felt that this did not give a
fair trial, and reversed. At the new trial, Becker was properly
and legally convicted and duly went to the electric chair in
accordance with the laws of the State of New York, following the
four gunmen, who had been properly convicted† and dispatched
between the two Becker trials.

The Rosenthal murder had quite an effect on the Jewish community, which until then had taken much pride in the absence
of any Jews from the underworld and had vigorously denied
that Jews were connected with gangs. The shocked community
determined to do something about this state of affairs, and "the
Kehillah" (Jewish community), under the leadership of Dr.
Judah L. Magnes, an outstanding rabbi, began to work in cooperation with the police to try to wipe out crime among Jews
on the East Side.‡ Harry W. Newburger was engaged as their
attorney, and my brother Laurie became his part-time assistant.
They had a law office on the second floor of Two Rector Street
—which to all intents and purposes they shared with the rum-
bling old Sixth Avenue El—and it was in these quarters, at $90 a
month, that our new firm set up shop.

Our staff consisted of a telephone operator, file clerk, stenographer, and a secretary for the four new partners. Her name was
Ethel Hirshman—and she's still with us. Day after day we were

---

* *People* v. *Becker*, 210 N.Y. 274, 295–307.

† *People* v. *Seidenshner*, 210 N.Y. 341.

‡ Dr. Magnes was a delightful person—sensitive, handsome, and charming.
He later went to Jerusalem, where he was the founder of the Hebrew
University. He opposed the creation of a Jewish state and was heart-
broken when the United Nations voted for its establishment. He died
soon after.

kept busy. All kinds of small matters drifted into the office, and besides the usual run of office work, such as leases, wills, new partnerships and corporations, we had court work, and plenty of it. Mr. Nathan had been a trial lawyer as well as an office lawyer, and I took it for granted that every lawyer tried cases. So from the start I was constantly going to court. Most of the cases were in the Municipal Court, which could hear cases up to $1,000.

When we started to practice, nearly all of our cases were tried in one of three courthouses in City Hall Park. One was the old Tweed Courthouse just north of City Hall, which housed the Supreme Court. Just to the east of that was the City Court. Sprawling to the south was the old Post Office Building in which the Federal Court sat. The latter two are now gone, but the Tweed Courthouse still stands and is used for a variety of miscellaneous city offices.

The old City Court was a three-story, square structure built in the early nineteenth century. It was there that I had served as a juror while I was in law school, and sup-pros were returnable to that court. These are supplementary proceedings, which are steps to collect a judgment that the defendant has not paid. In such an instance, you may obtain an order directing the defendant to come to court and be examined as to his funds. Maybe you will uncover some money then, but probably you will not. If the defendant doesn't appear, the Clerk calls his name and certifies his default. Then you may seek to punish him for contempt. Such a proceeding was recently brought against Adam Clayton Powell, but today the matter is ordinarily handled in the lawyer's office and not in court. The Clerk's office in the old days was at the top of a flight of iron stairs to the right of the front entrance. I spent a good deal of time there, trying, usually without success, to get a judgment debtor to pay up.

In its heyday, when it held the Supreme Court, the old Tweed Courthouse was a very busy place. The County Clerk's offices were downstairs, and on the south side of the building were the offices of the Calendar Clerk. Upstairs were the courtrooms —the scenes of many celebrated trials and many not so famous but equally crucial to their participants. Across the street at 51

Chambers Street, above the Emigrant Industrial Savings Bank, the justices, including my father, had their chambers. Later on, all of this was moved up to the present Supreme Court Building on Foley Square, which has now become quite antiquated. Incidentally, my father was chairman of the Board of Justices, which planned for the new courthouse. The site the Board had chosen was not Foley Square but the south side of Washington Square, since that spot would be easily accessible from uptown offices as well as downtown offices. But the whole plan was wrecked when the Board committed the unforgivable sin of allowing the plan to become public before the "right" people had an opportunity to acquire options on the property that would have been condemned.

The old Post Office Building housing the Federal Court extended over the lower part of what is now City Hall Park. During the first months of World War I, I worked there as a dollar-a-year assistant to the Honorable John C. Knox, then assistant United States attorney, long before he became a judge. After taking care of things at my own office, I used to go to his and work with him late afternoons and evenings, going over applications of enemy aliens to work in certain areas.

The new firm of Greenbaum, Wolff & Ernst had an unpaid and invaluable consultant—my father. Nearly every night after dinner Father went up to his room on the top floor of our home. That was his law library, and the books went all the way up to the ceiling. When I was a boy, they rather bored me, but by the time I was in law school, I was fascinated by them and was allowed to use the library. I kept this privilege after we started practicing law, and talked over some of our cases with Father there. Naturally this was a tremendous help to us, and it must have made a deep impression on me because I still sometimes dream about that room. My father's secretary often came there in the evenings and they worked on opinions together. It was stimulating for me to hear them talk about the cases they were working on. Incidentally, these also included cases for other judges, who constantly used my father to help them arrive at their decisions. Without boasting, I think I can truthfully say that my father was one of the outstanding judges of his day. It was wonderful for me to have the opportunity to work with him and play some part in his life.

It was about this time that the Governor told my father he wanted to designate him to be a judge of the Court of Appeals. This is the highest court in New York State and naturally I was most eager for him to accept this great honor. But he did not take the job. His reason was that he just could not afford it. The salary was considerably lower ($13,700) than the salary of a Supreme Court justice ($17,500), and he would have had to live up in Albany, where the court is, and still keep our house in New York for the family. The decreased salary would just not pay for that.

The Governor then was Martin Glynn, and when Father declined to take the judgeship, the Governor asked him to recommend someone else. Father suggested Benjamin N. Cardozo, who had just been elected to the New York Supreme Court. Although the Governor did not know Cardozo, he authorized my father to approach him. I remember well the night that Cardozo was at the house; my father urged him to take the job, telling him he was just the person needed for that bench, that he had the ability to do it, and that he would make a fine judge. Then Father added that no Jew had ever been on the Court of Appeals and that he hoped Cardozo would be the first. Cardozo, who was unmarried and lived with his sister, had reasons for not accepting, but money was not one of them. Cardozo felt that he did not have the qualifications or experience: he had served as a judge only for a very short time; he would be frightfully embarrassed with his new associates on the highest court, as well as with the members of the Supreme Court, where he was then sitting. However, at my father's insistence, he agreed to think it over and give his answer the next week. When he came back, he told us that Father's arguments had persuaded him. As I recall, his words were something like this: "All right, Judge, because you want me to, I'll do it. I'll try to be a good judge and a good Jew, and I'll live at the North Pole and cut my pay in two." My father then told me to get the Governor on the phone, and he gave the Governor Cardozo's acceptance. I did not fully realize at the time what a historic event in American

jurisprudence I was witnessing. Judge Irving Lehman, who succeeded Cardozo as Chief Judge of the Court of Appeals, after-
wards wrote, "Ten years later, Governor Glynn told me that he
was prouder of that designation than of any other act of his
career."

When he was on the Court of Appeals, Judge Cardozo had
an office in the Bar Building in New York City, right next to
the Bar Association on West Forty-fourth Street. I remember
once, in the late spring, a client of ours had been convicted of
a bucket-shop * fraud and would be in prison all summer unless
the Court of Appeals would let him out on a certificate of reasonable doubt until court met in the fall. I asked the Judge
whether he would be willing to hear us argue this, and he said
he would and that we should come the following afternoon.
Next day we, meaning me and the district attorney who was to
oppose me, met there. At the beginning of the argument I asked
about how long we could have, since it would help me to know
this before I began presenting my argument. He looked at me
with great surprise and said, "Isn't this the case you asked me
about yesterday?" When I told him it was, he said that naturally
I could have as much time as I wanted, because if he decided
against me the man would be in jail all summer. I don't know
why this was so astonishing to me, but it was. Maybe any judge
would have done the same, but it was the first time in my
experience.

One morning shortly after that, I was going downtown to
work on the Sixth Avenue El when someone sat down next to
me. I looked up and was surprised to see that it was Cardozo.
I must have been looking very dejected, for he at once asked
me what was the matter. I told him that the afternoon before I
had been licked in a case that I had been trying for days and
that I hadn't yet recovered. He asked me if I thought I should
have won, if I thought the verdict was all wrong, if there were

---

* "A dishonest brokerage house that does not execute orders placed by
customers on margin and anticipates profit from market fluctuations ad-
verse to the customer's interests. . . ." *Webster's Seventh New Collegiate
Dictionary.*

any mistakes that I thought I had made, if I thought that the practice of the law was stupid, and whether I was sorry that I had ever become a lawyer. I answered yes to all of these questions, feeling, however, rather resentful and not at all liking the way he seemed to be gloating. Indeed, he seemed to be smiling through it all. He said that this was the way he always felt when he lost, and that lawyers were bound to lose cases, and that unless I felt the way I did, I would never be any good. While he was talking, I began to feel better, and by the time I said goodbye to him, I think I was almost all right again.

New matters came to us from unexpected sources. Alfred Jaretzki, Jr., was a boyhood friend of ours and was going to Harvard Law School as I was finishing at Columbia. His father was then senior partner of Sullivan & Cromwell, and Alfred went with that firm, where he is now a senior partner. Shortly after we had started our firm, Mr. Jaretzki, Alfred's father, sent for me and told me about a client of theirs, the Youreveta Home and Foreign Trading Company, which he had incorporated for Russian clients. The company was involved in quite a bit of litigation, consisting mostly of small claims arising out of its export and import business, and he wanted to know if we would like to handle it. I was very glad to do so and the work proved extremely interesting. The company had been organized before the Russian Revolution; those connected with it were, of course, anti-Communist, and many of them had had their property confiscated by the Bolsheviks. Some of these people became our personal clients and won our admiration and respect, including Moses Fainberg, the secretary of the company, who was a young Russian lawyer, educated in England. Property of the Youreveta Company in Siberia had been confiscated by troops operating under General Gregory Semenoff, who played a brief but sensational role in the drama of postwar Siberia. He came to this country en route to Russia,* where he was said to be scheduled to head up a military drive against the Soviets. The Youreveta Company, which was then in bankruptcy, believed that it had

---

* See George F. Kennan, *Russia Leaves the War* (Vol. I of *Soviet-American Relations, 1917–1920*).

a claim against Semenoff for seizing its property in Siberia. We
were retained to start action against him when he arrived here.
We got an order for his civil arrest in this suit, and when he got
off the train at Pennsylvania Station, the Sheriff greeted him
with the order of arrest, which created quite a stir. His lawyers
persuaded the Sheriff to go to Semenoff's hotel (the Waldorf-
Astoria, then at Thirty-fourth Street and Fifth Avenue) while
bail was being arranged. Those in his bedroom included quite
a crowd of reporters, who sat on the bed and interviewed him
while helping each other to his cigars and liquor. A round of
court battles followed, resulting in the affirmance of our order
of arrest,* the beginning of Congressional hearings on the matter, and the end of the General's projected Russian adventure.
But no damages for our client were ever collected.

In one of our early cases I opposed Max D. Steuer, whom
I had met in the Harris & Blanck case when I was with Cardozo
& Nathan. I got an awful shellacking from him. Steuer's name,
almost a household word in those days, is virtually unknown
today. Among trial lawyers he stood in a class by himself. There
were very good trial lawyers around and some excellent ones,
but in my opinion Steuer topped them all. He was not a very
impressive-looking man. He had no striking feature, except perhaps his eyes, which were startlingly sharp. He was not tall, not
handsome, nor was he a great orator. His outstanding characteristic in the courtroom was his unobtrusiveness. He talked in
a very low voice, almost a whisper, which had the effect of
making everyone listen attentively to hear every word he was
saying. This was not only his style in a trial court but also on
an appeal, where he was equally effective. He had an uncanny
ability to determine in advance the strength and weaknesses of
the case, and then the rare gift of being able to emphasize his
side's strength and play down its weaknesses. He brought his
papers to court not in an elegant leather briefcase but in an
ordinary red manila envelope. I unconsciously copied this, and
still do.

I don't remember being specially scared when I went on trial
against him. Maybe this was because, as I said before, I was

---

* *Boyle* v. *Semenoff*, 201 App. Div. 426.

just always scared in court. In this early case against him, we represented a woman who had made a separation agreement under which her husband agreed to give her $100 a week. He paid it for a couple of years, and then she was divorced and later went to a mental institution. When she came out, she was penniless and he had plenty of money. But the ex-husband wouldn't allow her anything, and she had to sue for arrears.

Before the trial I had carefully gone into the question of where the parties were living when the separation agreement was signed. She told me they had separated long before the agreement. I explained to her why this was important. A separation agreement made when the husband and wife are living together is against public policy because it encourages breaking up the marriage. At the trial we proved everything, even the interest on each installment, which my partner Herb Wolff had computed to the date of trial, and on the witness stand he proved it to the penny. But Steuer's cross-examination of our client finished us. Here is how it went:

Q.—I want to put my questions just as simply as I can.
A.—Yes, sir.
Q.—And if they confuse you at all, you will be good enough to say so, won't you?
A.—I will.
Q.—Yes. Now, don't you recall that, up to the 20th of April, you continued to keep house and live right there at 110 West 105th Street?
A.—I recall it now.
Q.—And having recalled that, that you and your husband continued to live there in 1898, up to the 10th of May, at 110 West 105th Street, just see if I can aid your recollection that it was from there that you then, having disposed of the furniture, went to board at 14 West 96th Street, at Mrs. Belmont's. Do you recall it now?
A.—That may be right.
Q.—Yes.
A.—But only for a very short time.
Q.—Well, I am going to get to the time. I just want to aid your recollection the best that I can. Take your time about it.
A.—Yes.
Q.—In making any answer, answer it always in your own way, and not because I have asked the question.
A.—All right; thank you.

After a few more questions she was saying that she guessed she was living with her husband when they signed that separation agreement. I knew as soon as the words were out of her mouth that we were licked. During the lunch hour, the client told me what a wonderful gentleman Mr. Steuer was. I gulped and said nothing.

What I admired most about Steuer was not his ability to cross-examine, but his penetrating analysis of the situation and his brilliant but simple way of making the jury see the facts as he presented them. As just indicated, he played down nearly everything, particularly his opponent's strongest point. When I say nearly everything, I mean nearly everything except the one or two points that he wanted to bring out. The result was that the jury—or the judge—saw the facts as he wished them to.

At a dinner party in my home one night, this was amusingly illustrated by a friend of mine who had just completed his jury duty. He was enjoying the satisfaction that one gets from having performed this duty and was telling us how Steuer had appeared before him three times and that he was really no good. He praised the opposing lawyers and said Steuer couldn't make a good speech, that he spoke so quietly it was difficult to hear what he said. I asked my friend about the first case. He explained what a brilliant job the other lawyer had done and that it was far superior to Steuer's. In answer to my question as to how the case came out, he said the other fellow really had no case at all, so naturally there was nothing to it, and in spite of Steuer's deficiencies his client had won. Then he told us about the next two cases, with the brilliant lawyers opposing Steuer, and how again Steuer had really done nothing, but since these other cases were weak, Steuer's clients won them too. I don't think my friend realized that Steuer had won all these cases, nor why. Steuer was as dumb as the famous fox.

A lawyer cousin of mine had given up a successful law practice to go into an importing business. After several good years the business went broke and my cousin wanted to get into law again. Steuer had interviewed him and seemed interested. Steuer knew he was my cousin and called me up to ask if I could find out confidentially whether my cousin had made $40,000 a year,

as he said, before he gave up the law. I said that I'd try. I
found out that he had indeed averaged over this sum for three
years—a great deal of money in those days. I told Steuer, and
within a week my cousin informed me that Steuer had thanked
him but regretted that he couldn't use him. Thinking that Steuer
had misunderstood me, I called him back. He told me he understood me all right, but didn't want anyone around his office who
had given up the law after making $40,000 a year just to make
more money in some business. He said that when he found out
that he could make $5 a week in the law, there wasn't enough
money in the Mint to make him take any other job.

During all this period, tremendous things were happening in
the world. While I was still at Cardozo & Nathan, in August of
1914, the war had started. I remember well that weekend of
August 1st, which I had spent at Easthampton with my family,
and coming back on Sunday on the overnight boat that then ran
from Sag Harbor to New York at the foot of Wall Street. None
of us could talk about anything except the war. Although everyone, including my father, had said there would be no war, the
impossible had happened. The war in Europe had begun. We
got used to it and life went on. But in 1915 the *Lusitania* was
sunk, and by the end of 1916 it seemed clear that America would
soon be in. On April 6, 1917, we entered the war. Like most of
the others of my generation, I wanted to get into the Army.
The Citizens Training Camp was opened at Plattsburg, New
York. In three months it trained civilians to become officers.
They were commissioned as second lieutenants and were known
as "ninety-day wonders." Many of my friends joined but when
I tried, I was turned down. When we were kids my brother and
I had found out that we were both color blind. Someone gave
us some red golf balls up at Lake Placid. I hit one down the
middle of the fairway. Laurie did the same. We couldn't find
them. The guys we were playing with thought we were kidding,
and they showed us the balls in the middle of the fairway. In
college, during a physics lecture on color blindness, the professor held up two skeins of thread in front of the class and said
that some people thought they were the same color. (To me
they were.) The rest of the class howled laughing—and so did I.

The color blindness had never bothered me, but when I tried to get into the Army, I discovered it was a real obstacle. At my examination down at Governors Island, I did fine until we got to the color-blindness test. The officer pointed to the flag outside on the pole and asked me what color the stripe at the bottom was. That was a cinch, and I told him. He then asked me what color the grass was. Everybody knows that, and I told him. We had now done red and green, and only brown was left. He asked me the color of the ice wagon. I instantly told him it was brown and thought I had passed. He then took me into a little room where there was a table with 1,000 skeins on it— all exactly the same color. He told me to pick out twenty like the ice wagon, twenty like the grass, and twenty like the stripe on the flag. That really stumped me. When he came back after about twenty minutes, all he did was smile and say, "Thank you."

In the meantime, I had been training weekends with Boyce's Tigers, a volunteer group which operated from Governors Island making overnight trips, including one to West Point. Obviously this wasn't going to get me in the Army. Now that I couldn't get in via Plattsburg, I decided to do it promptly via my local draft board, which was at P.S. 6, where I had gone to school as a kid. To be drafted, no color-blindness test was required, and if anyone asked to be called ahead of his turn, the draft board was more than willing to oblige. The chairman of my draft board was Stanley M. Isaacs, who had worked with my father at the Educational Alliance, and later became New York's only Republican councilman.* He was a fine citizen and performed his difficult draft-board duties with much skill and imagination, and he and the other board members soon arranged to have me called up.

I tried to clean up my work at the office. One of the cases was a will contest. Our client was the sister of a woman who

---

* Years later his wife, Edith, wrote a book about him called *Love Affair with a City*. In it she quotes a letter that Stanley wrote to me when I was Secretary Patterson's executive officer in World War II. Stanley volunteered to enlist in the Army, but this patriotic offer had to be declined because of his age. This was too bad because he would have made an outstanding contribution to the Army had he been eligible.

had died, leaving her entire estate—I guess about $1,000,000—
to a spiritualist medium. Our client was quite a miser and
dressed like a tramp. She always made dates to come to the
office around ten o'clock in the morning, because that was the
time of day she figured that she could pick up most newspapers
on her subway ride to the office. Although she was far from
broke, she would sell these newspapers for junk, and this paid
her subway fare down. (The fare was only a nickel then.)

Before the testatrix died, the medium had gotten to know
her better and better each day and had gradually coaxed her
savings from her bit by bit. Finally, the medium got the will
itself made in his favor as the beneficiary. There was practically
nothing left for the family. The case looked pretty good, and we
had assembled a lot of evidence to show that the medium had
exerted undue influence to get himself named in the will.

Since I would soon be in the Army and couldn't try the case
as we had planned, we needed to find someone else for it—but
who? We thought that Steuer was about the best man for the job
in New York, and my father confidentially had agreed. Since the
fee was on a contingency (that is, our compensation depended
wholly on our winning the case), we didn't know if he would
take it, but decided to ask him. After considering, Steuer
agreed, doubtless because he thought that my father had recommended it. We explained the facts to him at considerable length.
He didn't make a single note, but when we were through he
asked me to send him a short summary that he could go over with
me before I went into the Army. I wrote it out and sent it over to
him. Shortly after that, he phoned me and asked if a date that
I had given as April in my summary shouldn't have been
August. I looked it up and found that he was right. I knew that
he had a wonderful memory, but since he had made no notes
at all, I couldn't think for the life of me how he knew that the
April date was wrong. When I next saw him, he told me. He
had been much impressed by the sequence of events. In my
verbal explanation one particular event had happened *after*
another. This sequence was important to the case, and he hoped
that the stenographer had just made an error in the written
summary. He guessed that August was probably the correct

date just because it began with an A. After I was in the Army, Steuer tried the case. My brother later told me that Steuer had done his usual beautiful job—showing step by step how the medium had worked, how the poor lady was made to transfer her bank accounts, and gradually proving that undue influence had been exercised. We won, and Steuer well earned his fee.

IV

IN THE ARMY

IN September of 1917 I was shipped to Camp Upton at Yaphank on Long Island, where I was assigned to H Company, 305th Infantry, in the Seventy-seventh Division. Camp Upton is now Brookhaven, the atomic-energy installation, a very different place from what it was in 1917. When the camp was opened in 1917, it was one of our first National Army camps, and received all the drafted men from New York and surrounding areas. Since I was one of the early arrivals, pulling up stumps was among our jobs, and it is literally true to say we helped to build the camp.

After being an enlisted man for only a few weeks, I began to realize that something wonderful was happening to me. At first I couldn't figure out what it was, but as the weeks went by it dawned on me: I didn't have to decide anything—maybe that was the reason I was feeling so good. From reveille when the bugle told me "You gotta get up! You gotta get up!" until taps sounded telling me to go to sleep, everything was decided for me. Instead of resenting this, I settled back and thoroughly enjoyed it.

After completing my basic training, I was selected from Company H for officers' training camp. That was a big day for me, but soon I was down in the dumps; once again I was turned down for color blindness. I stayed with my company, and was assigned to the Division Judge Advocate's Office. This included work with war risk insurance under Colonel Marion W. Howze. There I attained the grade of regimental sergeant major, the highest noncommissioned-officer rank, and that was something. It seemed higher to me then than being a brigadier general was to seem later.

War risk insurance was so important to the Army that the War Department authorized transferring a captain and a lieutenant to be in charge of this work. The Seventy-seventh Division wired back, naming me and Howland S. Davis, another enlisted man, who had been a member of the New York Stock Exchange. Washington had not meant two *new* commissions, but that's what the Division did, and we were two very lucky guys.

Soon after I was commissioned to do this insurance job, Colonel Howze ordered me to set up a separate "Insurance Office" with others in charge. After it got started I had no more to do with insurance. As a captain in the Adjutant General's Department, I did judge advocate's work, and later the Colonel had me transferred to the Judge Advocate General's Department. It was much later that I really got to know the Colonel, and I'm very glad to say that we are still warm friends.

We had over 40,000 troops there at one time. Aside from the regular court-martial work that this population provided for the camp, there was a multitude of other legal problems connected with the building and operating of a new post. The commanding general was Major General J. Franklin Bell, who had been Chief of Staff under President Theodore Roosevelt.

The law again became an important part of my life and I was busy on court-martial work. I learned a great deal by watching and listening to the Colonel. In less than seven minutes flat after the first general court-martial order that the Colonel told me to prepare was circulated, every officer named in that order phoned the Colonel—and I had my first lesson in Army protocol. The commanding general who has jurisdiction issues the court-martial order. In it he names the officers who will sit on a court-martial. The order is prepared by the judge advocate, with the officers on the court listed according to their rank. This means that the highest ranking officers, say, the colonels, appear first, and their names are listed in order by the date on which they attained their rank. Majors, captains and lieutenants are then listed in like manner. But I had carefully arranged all the names alphabetically instead of by grade and rank. The Colonel showed me how to get out the new order. My bull was a good quick way to learn that everything in the Army goes according to rank—and that if Colonel Aaron's name appears before Colonel Zacharina, it isn't just because it comes earlier in the alphabet! I never made that bull again.

When the Division was nearly ready to be sent overseas, General Bell was ordered to Washington for a physical examination. He ranked General Pershing (not because his name began with a B), who was then also a major general and slated to command the American Expeditionary Force. If General Bell had gone overseas with the Division at that time, as the higher ranking officer he would have commanded the A.E.F. But the War Department didn't want him to be in command, and for that and other reasons, he was ordered to Washington. While he was there, orders came for the Division to move overseas. These orders were more than speedily carried out, and almost the first unit to leave was Division Headquarters under a brigadier general, who automatically became the Division's commanding officer.

Colonel Howze had anticipated that some difficulties would arise about court-martial jurisdiction when the Division left for overseas. He had previously called the Judge Advocate General in Washington and asked who would have jurisdiction in Camp Upton when the Division left and who would handle pending cases. No reply was received. He needled them, but it was not until the night that Division Headquarters was leaving for overseas that the orders came. They gave court-martial jurisdiction to the commanding officer of the camp and designated me as the camp judge advocate. It was quite a shock to me to be left behind. My bedding roll was yanked off the truck, and there I was.

During the excitement I was ordered to sign a receipt for

Camp Upton. In the Army everything is charged to somebody, and Camp Upton had been charged to the Division quartermaster, who was now going overseas with the Division. Next morning after I came to my senses, it dawned on me that I was now responsible for everything—including the kitchen stoves, the barracks, the stables, the horses, the ordnance, the warehouses with the uniforms, food, the flagpoles, and the reveille cannon on the hill. I had the presence of mind to make out another receipt for all this and order a junior officer to sign it. That got me off the hook, and my accountability-responsibility ledger was balanced. The junior officer, in turn, soon got the newly appointed camp quartermaster to sign.

One of the special trains on the Long Island Rail Road taking the Division to its Port of Embarkation was wrecked the next night. Several men were killed and a few from the 306th Infantry were injured. I did all I could as a lawyer for the men and their families. As almost the only remaining officer from Division Headquarters, I was also busy helping to regulate the troop movement of the Division. I was on duty at Headquarters from the time the Division left until I fell asleep at my desk at about 4 A.M. several mornings later. When a colonel found me asleep, instead of court-martialing me he ordered me to bed, where I slept for over twelve hours.

Now the Division was gone and things were quite different. General Bell, the Colonel who had ordered me to bed, and I were almost the only ones of the former Division officers who were still around. The new responsibility of being camp judge advocate was a heavy one, but I was surprised to find that I had no difficulty in meeting it, although I was then not yet twenty-eight. The training I had had under Colonel Howze and under General Bell was a tremendous help to me and of enormous benefit later on, in World War II. As camp judge advocate I was a member of the commanding general's staff; I represented him and was his judge advocate. This was particularly brought home to me on one occasion by the General. When I had been an assistant to the Division judge advocate, we got weekly reports from all the regiments on their special and summary court-martial cases. I kept records of them, and charted them in a pre-IBM sort of way. This indicated instantly how each regiment compared with the others as to number of cases, severity of sentences, frequency of offense and other items. Once I had shown the General that the record of the 306th Infantry was a bit out of gear. He told me to take this up with its commanding officer, Colonel Vidmer, and report back to him. I did, and then told the General, "I went down to see Colonel Vidmer and . . ." but the General interrupted and shouted at me, "You did *what?*" I repeated what I had said, and got the damnedest lacing I'd ever received. It went something like this: "So you went down to see him! You wanted to pay him a social call! I presume you thought he'd pay some attention to you, a brand-new little major!" Then he changed his tone, and explained to me that the position of the commanding general and the members of his staff demanded that I should never go to see, but always send for, a regimental commander, or anyone except another staff officer, because the General himself was speaking through me. From then on I never forgot when I represented a commanding officer that anyone of a lower rank than his came to me and I didn't go to him. That wasn't conceit; it was simply Army protocol and the way things were done.

After the Division left, it was discovered that wholesale thefts had been going on among civilian employees. Overcoats, blankets, and many other articles were being taken from the camp. General Bell felt very strongly that discipline required that the Army itself should try these cases and should not turn them over to civil authorities. The question was, however, could the Army try civilian employees at Camp Upton as "serving with the Armies of the United States in the field"? We had Article 63 of the Articles of War as our legal authority to support our jurisdictional claim, but needed some cases to put us on firmer ground. New York Supreme Court Justice Joseph Morschauser had volunteered to help us with our legal work during the summer, and the General had accepted his offer. He had been with us regularly, but when he was needed most the Judge just wasn't around. We couldn't wait and went ahead arresting a lot of civilian workers the next day. It was a Sunday, and I went along while we picked up one of the citizens, a minister, after he finished conducting services at his local church.

The Judge still didn't show up. The day after the arrests he walked into my office, and in reply to my frantic inquiry as to where he had been, he told me that he had visited several federal and state court judges. He had explained to them the law of courts-martial and had told them about the Army's jurisdiction over civilians "in the field" under the Articles of War, pointing out that a Port of Embarkation or, for that matter, the staging area at Camp Upton, was "in the field" in time of war. With the groundwork laid by Judge Morschauser, a few days later when writs of habeas corpus were applied for in the civil courts on behalf of the men we arrested, they were all denied. Nor was any point made that we did not have a search warrant when we picked up evidence in the preacher's house while he was conducting services in the church next door.

Several officers, including a high-ranking quartermaster, were court-martialed for their part in these thefts. One of a judge advocate's duties is to examine the record of a trial and then submit it to the general in command with his comments, including action which he recommends the general take. After I examined the records, I sent them up to General Bell's office, together with a proposed order of approval that I had prepared. He usually went over them carefully at night in his office. One night he sent for me and asked many searching questions about one particular case. He had been a judge advocate himself and knew what he was talking about. When I had answered all that he had asked, he signed the paper and said, "The bravest man I ever knew." He then gave me the signed record and motioned me to leave him alone. I did so, and left him sitting there looking straight ahead. Later I learned that this officer had served with him in the Philippines and was with him when the General won his Medal of Honor.

Morschauser was also a great help to us in another matter. Many of our soldiers at Camp Upton were not citizens; some had just not applied and others were not eligible. The Army wanted its soldiers to be citizens. Besides being an important

morale factor, citizenship would eliminate troublesome problems that might arise if an alien was captured in the uniform
of the American Army. Congress had just enacted a law which
eliminated a lot of waiting time between the date an applicant
filed a petition and the granting of his citizenship. The old
waiting period was five years. The new law shortened this,
but did not automatically grant citizenship. But the Judge
nearly did so. He persuaded the Governor to appoint an
Extraordinary Term of the Supreme Court to sit at Camp
Upton, designating the Judge himself to preside. The Suffolk
County Clerk from Riverhead moved his staff over, and we
started to process all the eligible soldiers in camp who were
not citizens. We did a land-office business. The opening day
of the court was quite a show, with many dignitaries present,
and the New York *Times* devoted part of its Sunday rotogravure
section to the occasion. The court continued to sit day after
day until all our naturalization business was completed.

In October I was finally shipped overseas. I went as a
casual with nine other judge advocates who had been commissioned directly from civilian life. We sailed on the *Mount
Vernon*, formerly the North German Lloyd Line's *Kronprin-
zessin Cäcilie*, which when the war started in 1917 had been
interned at Bar Harbor, Maine, for attempting to bring gold
back to Germany. We were in a convoy of over twenty ships
escorted by several naval vessels. One afternoon during a
band concert on the rear deck, with the soldiers lolling around
and the band playing "There Are Smiles That Make Us
Happy," suddenly the water broke on the port side near the
stern and a periscope appeared. Our escort vessel sighted and
sank a submarine. Anyway, that was the official version—but
I, who was among those lolling and had a pretty good view,
thought it was merely a whale making a sudden and frightened appearance. It was all over so quickly that I wasn't
quite sure just what had happened—nor were the soldiers
who wrote home about the thrilling event. According to their
letters: we had been struck by a torpedo; our ship had been
sunk; only a few were rescued, including, of course, the
writer; we were picked up by a lifeboat; we landed on an

island and there were rescued; and so on and so forth.
As an officer, I was one of the censors and can testify that
none of these reports was allowed to be sent. These yarns,
however, made me realize how difficult it is to be sure of
history. Certainly no doubt could be cast years later on the
firsthand account in a soldier's letter telling of his experience
on a troop ship that was hit by a submarine. I wonder just
how really accurate are the reports we read about the Civil
War, documented by authentic letters from soldiers.

On the trip I was designated as summary court officer and
was busy every day court-martialing soldiers because they had
lost money in a crap game to personnel of the United States
Navy. This was regarded as a serious offense by the commanding
officer of the Eighth Infantry, whose troops were on board, and
I had the unpopular task of fining each man who was found
guilty. This was usually one-third of his pay for a month. Near
the end of the trip, the weather got very rough and the Eighth
Infantry was delighted by the fact that their court-martial officer
was sick as a dog, dead to the world in his upper berth, and
the court-martial cases were adjourned for a couple of days.

When we arrived at Brest, we were put into the large U.S.
camp there—a vast expanse of mud, laced with duckboard paths.
Soon after our landing, the Armistice was declared. At the stroke
of 11 A.M. on November 11th, whistles, bells, and everything
else shrieked, rang, and howled. Uproarious impromptu parades
wound all around the town, and the noise kept up for hours.

Our contingent of ten judge advocates was shipped around
France. From Brest through Le Mans and Paris, we ended up
at Tours, where we were given a course in R.R. & C. (Rents,
Requisitions and Claims), and then we went to Chaumont,
headquarters of the A.E.F., where we were to get our assignments. Each of us was interviewed by General Walter Bethel,
judge advocate of the A.E.F. and a member of General Pershing's
staff. When my turn came, an old guy carrying two baskets
loaded with papers was just coming out of General Bethel's
office. I bumped into him and his papers spilled all over the
floor. Naturally I was terribly embarrassed. As he bent down to
pick up the papers, I saw that he had two stars on his shoulders,

and I nearly passed out. I found out this was General Edward Kreger, who was the Judge Advocate General's representative with the A.E.F. I helped pick up the papers and he went out. After this slapstick entrance, I had a pleasant and agreeable conversation with General Bethel, who wanted to know how soon I could be ready to go with him if I were chosen to be assistant to the Division judge advocate of the Fourth Infantry on its march up into Germany. I said I was ready then. He looked up in surprise and told me that I should be around at his office with whatever I wanted to bring along in two hours, when he was starting up into Germany in the car following General Pershing's. I was there. On the way I found out that the Judge Advocate General's representative was not on the friendliest terms with General Bethel's office, that General Bethel had just given him some papers that he had signed at about 3 A.M. that morning, that General Kreger had come in apparently to scold General Bethel for not having these papers ready because General Kreger had known that General Bethel had been at a very late party that night. Anyway, bumping into the General and spilling his papers all over the floor was the thing that apparently got me the assignment to go with the Army of Occupation. I didn't mind it at all.

It was a wonderful, exciting trip up through France and Luxembourg. All the little villages along the way were decorated and agog with excitement at the new world which lay ahead, and riding in the car just behind General Pershing was quite an experience. General Bethel told me that a problem had just been solved about entering Luxembourg, which had been neutral throughout the war. It was felt that having our Army march through to get to Germany would be too reminiscent of the Germans going through Belgium at the beginning of the war. A disagreeable memorandum about "violating neutrality" had been submitted to General Pershing. But a practical non-lawyer found the solution: General Pershing's most attractive aide was to present the General's respects to the Grand Duchess of Luxembourg and ask her if the General could pay her a visit for a few days and bring with him some of his colleagues. Permission was granted. The next night the General spent in

Luxembourg, and over 200,000 of his American colleagues came
along.

A few days later General Bethel left me in Trier, and I found
where the Fourth Division was and got a ride to it on a truck
at the railhead. During this trip I had become a good friend
of the General's. Later, after I was with the Fourth Division,
he came to visit and joined our poker games whenever he
spent the night with us while he was on inspection trips. He
was an extremely alert and efficient lawyer, and a fine officer.

While still on the march into Germany, one night all the
field officers in the Division were summoned to a meeting by
the commanding general. He read an order from GHQ telling
us that he had been made responsible "for the control and
management of civil affairs in occupied territory." The GHQ
order also authorized convening of "military commissions for the
trial of inhabitants offending against the laws of war or the
military government."

The order, he said, must be enforced. Sitting on the floor, I
was only half listening, but suddenly woke up when he said
that the Division would issue a similar order tomorrow and
each of those present would get a copy. As the assistant Division
judge advocate I realized that I had been put to work and
would be the one to draft the order. I knew nothing about the
law of occupying armies, but remembered there was a chapter
about it in Davis' book on military law—but where could I get
hold of that? Then I suddenly remembered that I had a copy
in my bedding roll. I dug it out and drafted the order. When
I gave it to the General in the morning, he said it was just
what he wanted. I realized that he knew just about as much
as I did about this subject—namely, nothing—but the order was
issued. In World War II it took the military-government boys
months to study this at their school down at Charlottesville.
They learned to occupy by the book. In a somewhat simpler
situation, we learned it overnight.

The Armistice provided for the lines of withdrawal of German
forces and the advance of Allied troops. Each day, as the
German troops were demobilized, horses and other equipment
were to be turned over to the local *Bürgermeister,* who was to

make delivery to the *Landrat,* who was the local German governor. The *Landrat* was required to deliver this matériel to the Allied commander who was taking over the area. We thought that the Germans were short-changing us all along the line on this deal (the first of many such problems that were to continue with the Germans for years thereafter). It was decided that the *Landrat* of Cochem should be tried for his violation of the Armistice. A military commission, with much high brass, was convened for this purpose. The *Landrat* had civilian counsel imported from Berlin, and I was designated as the trial judge advocate. The proceeding was under the jurisdiction of the Fourth Corps, and the trial was held in the famous castle of Cochem, on the top of a hill overlooking the Moselle River. Needless to say, the *Landrat* was found guilty and sentenced to pay a large fine. Later on I often used to see His Royal Nibs riding around town in an elegant little carriage drawn by high-stepping horses. While he gave me a dirty look, I wondered from what American outfit those horses had been swiped.

The Fourth Division occupied a large area south of the Rhine and west of the Moselle River. One day on a visit to the Seventy-seventh Field Artillery * in the area, its adjutant was talking to me about some problems affecting soldiers with fine combat records who had nothing to do while sitting around in Germany. For instance, the Division commander used to breeze through this town of Kaisersesch, which housed the local headquarters of the Seventy-seventh Field Artillery. When a soldier, not seeing the stars on the General's limousine, failed to salute, the General stopped the car and took the soldier's name. Charges were sent to the soldier's outfit, to be followed by a summary court-martial, and usually he was fined one-third of his pay for a month. The Adjutant asked me what could be done about this. I told him that nothing whatever could be done, but casually mentioned Court-Martial Article 22, which empowers even a summary court-martial to "compel witnesses to appear and testify." A few days later the General sent for me and showed me a request for him to appear and testify

---

* John J. McCloy was a junior officer in this outfit then.

as a witness at a summary court-martial to be held at seven-
thirty the following morning in Kaisersesch about twenty-five
miles from Division Headquarters at Bad Betrich. The charge
was failure to salute the General's car, and I was told to take
care of this. I replied by calling attention to the Court-Martial
Manual and said that it had been complied with and there
seemed to me nothing I could do. Soon thereafter I was told
to withdraw the charges. There were no more non-saluting
cases that I heard of after that.

When the Division Headquarters was still at Bad Betrich
along the Moselle River, I was sent for by the General's office.
The Chief of Staff told me that six soldiers in Battery F,
Sixteenth Field Artillery, were under arrest for rape. I was
ordered to go there immediately to make a thorough investigation and report.

When I arrived at the little town of Bongard, where Battery
F had its headquarters, there was an ominous note of quiet.
Soldiers snapped to attention when my car drove up, which
was at once recognized as coming from Division Headquarters.
Everything was spic and span. The Battery officers, commanded
by a handsome and snappy-looking captain, stepped forward
and saluted. He told me two rooms were at my disposal and
that four enlisted men had been assigned to me for such duties
as I wanted to give them, and "would the Major please state
if there was anything else required." The Captain looked
somewhat familiar to me. Who was this guy? I knew him, but
just couldn't place him.

I told the Captain I first wanted to interview the *Pfarrer*
(the priest) and the *Bürgermeister* (the mayor). These witnesses told me that the scene had occurred the other night
in a little house in a lonely spot across the brook. A girl lived
there with her father. Soldiers used to visit her regularly, and
a few nights before six of them had gotten tight and smashed up
the place. A touch of cross-examination revealed that the girl
wasn't exactly virginal and had been in this business for quite
a while. Then I sent for the father. My first question was,
"How much do you want?" His scared expression changed
into a big smile, and he dug a piece of paper from his pocket.

He had everything listed—a table, four chairs, two bottles of *Schnaps,* three windows, and what-have-you—all added up to an exact total, to the *Pfennig.* I told him he was nuts, in German, and he promptly reduced the amount by 50 per cent. When he gathered that he might collect half of this bargain price, his paternal instinct softened. It looked as if the great international incident might be adjudicated by a trial involving less than death.

Then it suddenly dawned on me. That captain had gone to Williams. It was Gordon H. ("Bummy") Michler, class of 1915, who had bought my motorcycle from me in senior year. I've asked him to tell what happened. He writes:

I would like to emphasize the dignified bearing of Major (Ed to you) Greenbaum on this occasion, in keeping with the best traditions of Divisional Headquarters, which unquestionably made a deep impression upon the local yokelry and the rude soldiery of Battery F, 16th Field Artillery.

After he had interviewed the witnesses, we had to come to grips with the subject at hand and the good Major's face revealed a somewhat pained and startled expression when he asked, "But do you realize, Captain, the seriousness of the charges you are bringing against these men? Under the Articles of War which govern our present existence, rape is a capital offense punishable by death. These men will be hung."

I cheerfully assured the Major that that was the best possible solution, judging from my wartime experience with this same Battery F, an outfit of swashbucklers who, like the Foreign Legion, were the best soldiers in the world in the front lines and the worst headache in the world under peacetime conditions at the rear. Not only would the solution offered remove six of the boys from getting into any further trouble, but their example might have a quieting influence on the balance of these desperadoes. On the contrary, a weak solution would undoubtedly lay the groundwork for rape rampant up and down the Rhine Valley, with the inevitable consequence of a substantial segment of the future German population bearing the brand of Battery F, 16 F.A.

Gordon Michler then adds:

Out of it all the Major worked a solution whereby the conduct of the charges was left in his less bloodthirsty hands, while the impression still prevailed in Battery F that the boys were bumped off one way or another and the rest of them better be good.

The Captain concludes his letter with a footnote about the caisson which carried the body of President Kennedy and later the body of General MacArthur at their funerals in Washington:

This caisson was drawn by six greys of Grey Horse Battery F, 16th F.A., whose history went back to a night shortly after the Armistice, when I was sent for by General (then Colonel) Troy Middleton, to tell me that the Advance Guard of the Army of Occupation then forming to march into Germany would be comprised of one composite regiment of Infantry, one Battalion of Engineers, and only one Battery of Field Artillery, Battery F, who had apparently made the grade on their war record. The smart grey-horse battery with which we led the Advance Guard into Germany became known after the War as Grey Horse Battery F, 16th F.A., stationed at Washington, D.C.

We had one court-martial case that gave us quite a headache, and involved an officer that we had to get back from the United States for trial. He was a lieutenant from the Fourth Engineers, an outfit that had been recruited in California. Shortly after the Armistice, letters and newspapers came from home telling the soldiers in that outfit how the Lieutenant had been welcomed with a big parade through an Arch of Triumph erected for him as the first one home from the Fighting Fourth. The celebration was so great that it left the men feeling that there would be no enthusiasm left for the rest of the regiment when they came home.

The facts were these: the Lieutenant had been in charge of a detail sent to repair a bridge over the Vesle River in August. Gas had come over and soon the Lieutenant was gone, and a sergeant had to take over the command. Several men were lost, but the outfit heard nothing about the Lieutenant after that until the news from home began to arrive. Feeling against him in the company ran very high. His papers were sent for, and from them it was possible to trace his course from the Vesle River to his discharge in California. These reports confirmed the suspicion in the company that he was guilty of deserting his command while under fire. It was determined that he should be brought back to Germany for trial. When he returned to the regiment, Colonel Raymond A. Wheeler,* the commander of the regiment, reported to Division Headquarters that he could not be responsible for what would happen to the prisoner if he were kept in the company. We ordered the prisoner to be brought to Division Headquarters, where he was held pending trial. At the court-martial I was the trial judge advocate and Captain Arthur R. Robinson of the Fifty-eighth Infantry was defense counsel. The Lieutenant's defense was that everybody in his home town knew that charges had been brought against him after the triumphant celebration, they knew what the charges were, and that he had been arrested and returned to Germany for trial. He urged that this was sufficient punishment and nothing would be gained by a guilty verdict. He stressed the fact that there was an "accessory penalty" under Article of War 44 that after conviction for cowardice, it was scandalous for any officer to associate with him. This, in effect, was a confession of guilt and a plea for mercy, and the Court responded by finding him "not guilty." No verdict of a general court-martial is effective until it is approved by the commanding general. Understandably the General felt that this verdict was wrong, and took the unusual course of sending the case back for further consideration, pointing out that the defendant had virtually pleaded "guilty" and admitted the facts brought out by the prosecution, and therefore it was the Court's duty to bring in its verdict in accordance with the evidence, and the commanding general could exercise clemency if that were proper. On reconsideration the Court adhered to its verdict and the Lieutenant was discharged.

Before the verdict was even published, we received requests from several soldiers in other outfits who were awaiting court-martial, asking that Captain Robinson be designated as their counsel. I don't know and never found out how they knew of the verdict. This mysterious grapevine, which is well known to exist in civilian prisons, was just as effective in the Fourth

---

* Colonel Wheeler subsequently became the Chief of Engineers and was the Army officer later detailed by the United Nations to act for it in clearing the Suez Canal.

Division, which occupied a large area in remote places throughout the Moselle Valley. After Captain Robinson got home, he was elected United States Senator from Indiana and later became the Republican leader in the Senate. Not only the soldiers of our Division but also the citizens of Indiana realized what an able man he was.

A Fourth Division soldier was reported to have died not "in line of duty" at a hospital in Coblenz. His record had been an excellent one, and his captain requested that Division HQ investigate. The case was assigned to me. The soldier had been sent to a hospital with an acute intestinal pain. When he arrived, he was kept waiting for a long time, and apparently because he could no longer stand the pain, he wandered out of the hospital, which was close to an old castle with a moat around it. Some Air Corps soldiers later found him in the dry moat surrounding the *Schloss*. He was carried to the hospital and soon died of the injuries he received from his fall into the moat. This gave rise to the report that his death was not in the line of duty.

The castle was occupied by an Air Corps squadron and I sent word to the commanding officer that I wanted to see him there at about three o'clock in the afternoon, and said that I also wanted to talk to other members of the squadron. When I arrived, I found myself in a very tense atmosphere. The commanding officer was an extremely nervous young captain who was very, very solemn. He was in his late twenties and appeared a bit older than anyone else in the outfit, who all seemed to be in their early twenties. I, myself, was twenty-eight at the time and was quite conscious of age. As soon as I told the Captain that I wanted to inquire about a soldier who had been found in the moat a few nights before, his expression suddenly changed. He nearly smiled, and the young officers on his staff relaxed at once. They readily answered all my questions, and took me to the place in the moat where the soldier had fallen. They sent for the men who, hearing his moans, had discovered the soldier and brought him back to the hospital. It wasn't long before I got a complete report of exactly what happened and had the material on which I could base my report. Fortunately I could establish that death was "in line of duty."

Then I accepted the Captain's invitation for a drink. In a pleasant atmosphere, I soon asked him what they had thought I wanted to see them about. After telling me nothing at first, one of the officers who was a law student in real life asked me if a judge advocate had the duty to report to his commanding officer everything he heard, even if it wasn't connected with what he was investigating and wasn't under his jurisdiction. This was a tough question. But I was getting curious, and didn't know the answer, so I said, "That depends." Then they told me. A few nights before, they had, as they said, "bombed Germany." When they heard that a judge advocate was coming to interview the Captain and that the rest of them should also be available, they naturally thought . . . Then they found it was only about the Fourth Division soldier . . . Anyway, they wanted to ask me a lot of questions. Had I heard about the bombing incident? Did I think they'd be found out? What would happen if they were? Should they do anything about it? Should they just shut up? And so forth and so forth. They were all talking at once, but gradually I got the complete story, which went something like this!

Their squadron had arrived in Europe after the Armistice and had been shipped up to this post in Germany right away. They had all been disappointed that they had no opportunity for combat flying. Indeed, they were not given any flying assignments at all and were just sitting around there. The only fun they had was to fly under the span of a bridge that crossed the Rhine in Coblenz. I had watched this myself several times, and although I rather enjoyed it, I could see that it was an unnecessarily hazardous pastime. Anyway, they had had a party a few evenings before and someone had suggested that it might be fun if they took a little flight into unoccupied Germany—strictly *verboten* territory—just north of us. They did so and dropped a few practice dummy bombs. There was no danger, but it was fun. Nobody could get hurt. They did the whole thing and were back in an hour or so. But the next morning they began wondering. Maybe it hadn't been such a smart thing to do. Lots of Germans must have known about it, and maybe questions would be raised. Maybe there would be an investigation. Maybe they'd be in trouble. Anyway, when the message came that a judge advocate was coming to interview the Captain, they were real scared, to put it mildly.

When they told me the story, I was a bit puzzled as to what should have been my answer to that law student's question and sort of wished that I had not let them tell me this tale. I didn't want these new-found clients. I told them not to volunteer any information to anyone else, gave them my telephone number at the Fourth Division HQ, and said to phone me if any questions were asked of them. I left wondering what I would do if anything did come up. Fortunately, nothing ever did, although I was more than a little worried when the Captain phoned me several days later. But he just wanted to pay us a visit at Fourth Division HQ and take me for a sociable ride.

These were just some of the many legal problems that arose in the Army of Occupation. It was truly the first time that any situation of this kind had been encountered by the United States Army, which had never before occupied an enemy country on such a scale. During this period, my local title among the Germans was Inferior Provost Court, which was like being a summary court officer, with jurisdiction for the trial and punishment of civilians for all minor crimes. Our headquarters, first at Bad Betrich on the Moselle, were later at Niederbreisig on the Rhine. We did our work with civilians through the *Bürgermeister,* and looking back on it all now, it seems remarkable how easy it was, considering the magnitude of the task and the fact that none of us had any prior training. But I do remember, years ago, reading in Jerome K. Jerome's *Three Men in a Boat* that all that was needed to govern the Germans was a typewriter and a bulletin board.

When the Division eventually returned home, I had further evidence of how much the Army needed its lawyers. After landing in Hoboken, several thousand of us got shipped to Camp Upton for discharge. I was their senior officer and soon got discharge papers for everyone—except me! Instead of getting that discharge, they gave me orders to go to Camp Dix in New Jersey to serve as the camp judge advocate. This was a big disappointment to me because the war had been over for a long time. Hoping that I could arrange something to get me out of the Army, I reported to Dix via Washington, D.C. I succeeded in getting an interview with the Judge Advocate General, Enoch H. Crowder. He had my record before him and spoke to me very wisely and understandingly, and ended up by offering me another job. He had just been designated to go to Cuba and draw up its Constitution, and he asked me to go with him as his assistant. Being too eager to get out right away, I refused, and even when he told me to think it over, I said no. My orders to go to Camp Dix remained. I went there and served. Later, I wondered if I had made the right decision—maybe not.

After a few months more, I was discharged and was back again at our own law offices.

V

BACK AT THE OFFICE

It was more than a year after the Armistice before I got out of uniform and back to work at Two Rector Street. Each month that I had been away, my partners had made a deposit in my bank account. They did this in spite of my protest that I should not share the profits while I was in the Army. In 1940 we had the same argument, and during the years of World War II that I was in the Army, I was paid a monthly salary by the firm. This is the only financial disagreement I ever had with my partners. I know how lucky I am and appreciate how they have treated me during the more than fifty years that we have been together.

My brother was married before the war, and during the fall of 1920, I married Dorothea R. Schwarcz, an artist, whose father had been lost on the *Lusitania*. She was then a painter and later became a sculptor. She spends all day in her studio and gives at least as much time to her work as I do to mine. This fact, which has contributed to her success, has made me doubly aware of the meaning of work and has given us both a better perception of life. Later on, when our older son, David, became a doctor, and the younger one, Daniel, an engineer, this awareness was increased. For reasons I am unable to explain, I believe that having a wife who is a sculptor and sons who are in different professions has broadened my own understanding and thereby helped me in my profession.

The firm had been doing well in my absence, and our work had increased. We were counsel for the National Jewelers Board of Trade, which was an association organized primarily for credit purposes, but having broad activities, including a collection service and an adjustment bureau. Their offices were on Maiden Lane, which was then the jewelry center of the city, and we soon moved our own offices to Seven Dey Street, which was closer to Maiden Lane.

Many of the jewelers became our clients too. One day one of them came to the office in great distress. A lawsuit for about $10,000 had just been started against him by another jeweler, and he said he didn't owe him a nickel. The suit was based on a series of notes, each for about $1,000, which had been made by the other jeweler and endorsed by our client so that his friend could get the money from the bank. The notes were all paid at the bank and returned to the borrower. Later he got in a scrap with our client and started the lawsuit. I explained that on the face of it, our client had signed the notes and presumably received the money. The other fellow could prove his case just by introducing the notes in evidence and then we'd have to prove that we never got anything. "How could we do this?" I asked. Our guy said it was ridiculous, that he just did it as an accommodation to help his friend, and everybody knew that the bank merely wanted another signature as a guarantee, and that this was done every day. I told him that was true, but when the other fellow introduced the note, we would still have the burden of proof to show it was paid. He was good and mad, and left the office with great disgust for the law. The next day he came back. He brought with him a suitcase packed with notes, which he threw down on my desk. I asked what they were, and he told me they were some of the notes the plaintiff had signed for him and he wanted me to sue on them, adding that he could probably find a lot more at his place. But I reminded him, "Yesterday you told me that you didn't owe him anything and he didn't owe you anything." "Let *him* have some burden of proof," he said. I phoned the lawyer on the other side, got him to the office, told him just what I've written here, and showed him the notes. That ended the lawsuit.

We had one case that stirred the jewelry trade. A jeweler, who was really an accountant, obtained large quantities of jewelry on memorandum. That is, he got the jewelry to show to others, with no obligation to pay for it until he sold it. But instead of selling the jewelry, he pawned it. He used the borrowed money to pay the jewelers. He kited checks one against another, in various banks. It was a royal to-do. He had separate accounts in five or six banks. If he got, say, $5,000 from a pawn-shop on one of the pieces of jewelry he had on memorandum, it would go into Bank A. He would draw three or four checks against this, which he would deposit to his own credit in other banks, hoping that he would obtain other money from hocking other jewelry to pay his loans. He must have known that this Ponzi-like process * would catch up with him. And it did when he had over a million dollars' worth of jewelry on memorandum.

We had much difficulty in locating the jewelry; finally we did get a large part of it back, but a lot was still missing and we tried to find it. The jeweler-accountant had been indicted and was out on bail. We hired a well-known detective agency to follow him, but this was not an easy job. Day after day we would get reports about him, but the detectives always lost him somewhere or other. To make sure that they could pick up his trail again, on various days we would have him sent for in court. The report after he left court would go something like this: "Subject left Part VI Court of General Sessions at 10:41; took the north elevator downstairs; on Franklin Street got in taxi bearing license number OL-3825; went down Broadway and got out at 120 Broadway; paid taxi driver and then went into telephone booth. Here we lost the subject. Time, $16.00; Expenses, $1.85." Newman Levy, who was with us at this time, told this at a small dinner party one night. The next day the head of the detective agency came around to see me. He had

---

* In 1919 Charles Ponzi bilked the public out of nearly $10,000,000 through a scheme involving financial manipulations of International Postal Reply coupons.

heard about it from a friend who had been there, and said that although he was a great admirer of Newman Levy and enjoyed his writings, he thought he was very unfair to make up a story like this. I assured him that it had not been made up, and went to the safe and got out the report of three days before that is quoted above. He was much embarrassed and explained his difficulty in getting competent men.

Later Newman wrote a book called *My Double Life,* describing his "adventures in law and letters." He tells why he liked working with what he called our "gay firm"—"gay" apparently because, as he says on page 167:

We were definitely not Pillars of the Bar; we were just first-rate lawyers. And there was a delightful variety to the practice. While Laurie Greenbaum might be organizing a bank in Mamaroneck or taking care of a summons for speeding in the traffic court, Morris would be battling to legalize birth control, Eddie Greenbaum as trustee in bankruptcy for Ivar Kreuger might be laboring to straighten out the fabulous affairs of the Match King, and Herbert Wolff would be closing the title to an apartment house, or spending days in court without compensation to rescue one of his Hudson Guild boys who had gone astray.

One case I worked on after I got back was not so gay. Alan Wolfe, who had served in the Fourth Division with me, got much interested in this case. He came to the office to get me to work with him to try to save another Fourth Division man. He brought along Walter V. Flynn, the president of the Division Association, who was a lawyer and then the secretary of Supreme Court Justice Irwin Untermyer. The man, who had served in the Fourth Engineers, had been convicted of first-degree murder and was to be executed in the state prison in Trenton, New Jersey, early the next week. He had shot a girl in the woods near Tuxedo, New York. While he was driving her back to their home in New Jersey, she died. He was in a panic. He spent the night at home with the body in the car, and instead of reporting to the police as he had planned, he drove off the following morning with the body still in the car. He kept driving for days and then dumped the girl's body in a ditch somewhere down south. It was found there, and he was arrested and brought back to New Jersey for trial. The tabloid front pages played the whole thing up as "the Ghost Murder." He was soon

tried and convicted, and his appeal ended in a unanimous affirmance of his conviction.

While in the Army, he had been a good soldier with a fine
combat record and had never before been in trouble. His commanding officer, General Jay Morrow, brother of Dwight W.
Morrow, and many of his former comrades made strong statements for him, showing that his character was totally inconsistent
with the crime. The prosecution showed no motive. The defendant's story was that he had been shooting squirrels and that
it was all a terrible accident.

Obviously he had killed the girl. He had been tried and convicted, and this had been unanimously affirmed by the highest
court in the state. He was to be executed in a few days. What
could be done? The boy's mother was, of course, frantic, and
she was backed up by his former comrades, who insisted that
he was not guilty of murder, although no one disputed that he
had killed the girl. Had he promptly told the police what he
subsequently said, he probably would not have been tried for
murder. But by dragging the girl's body around for days in the
car and then dumping it in a ditch, he had created a picture of
guilt that could not be easily forgotten.

In spite of the lateness of the hour, we decided to see what
we could do. It is not easy to get an execution delayed, particularly in New Jersey, but the Governor did grant our request
and gave us a few days to have a hearing before him. We made
the point that there was no motive for the crime and that the
death was accidental. We called as a witness the former head
of the New York Homicide Squad, who demonstrated before
the Governor that the place of the entry of the bullet and other
evidence at the trial was wholly consistent with the defendant's
testimony. However, the Governor denied our plea for clemency.

Our last chance was to go to the federal court. There had to
be a question of law to permit the court to intervene. It was
undisputed that the shot was fired in the State of New York
and death occurred in the State of New Jersey. In its opinion,
the New Jersey Appeal Court had mentioned this fact rather
casually. No point had been made of this either at the trial or
on the appeal, and the State's jurisdiction had never been chal-
lenged.

It is a basic principle of law that a trial cannot be held in a jurisdiction where the crime did not take place. Obviously no crime took place in New Jersey. I discussed this with Professor Herman Oliphant, of the Johns Hopkins Institute of Law, with whom I was then doing some work. We hastily prepared a memorandum of law on this point in which Oliphant said that this was a fundamental question of human right, adding that "this question involves more than this man. Does any man, and hence do all men, have a constitutional right to be tried where the act is done? That this is a right secured by the common law, an abundance of cases shows. Is that right among those protected from destruction by the Constitution of the United States?"

We prepared a writ of habeas corpus and presented it to the federal judge sitting in Newark. When we went into his chambers with the prosecuting attorney to ask the judge to sign the writ, he was reading the evening paper's latest report about the Ghost Murder. Not knowing on what matter we had come to see him, he regaled us at length with the gory details of the ride down south and then asked us if we had heard that some gangster lawyers from New York were now representing the killer. I replied that I had been in the same outfit with the defendant during the war and was now representing him. Then I got up and said goodbye. The judge asked me what I had come to see him about, and I told him, to ask for a writ of habeas corpus in that case, but since he had made it clear that his mind was made up, I would prefer to present the writ to another judge. In spite of my objections, he insisted on signing the writ, making it returnable before him at ten o'clock the next morning.

A little later I was having supper in a nearby club in Newark when I was surprised to be called to the telephone. It was the judge. He told me that he had looked up the law and wanted to change the time for arguing the writ from the next morning to that evening, and that I should come right away to his home to argue it. I replied that I respectfully declined to do so as I believed he had no power to change the time. He then asked me if I knew where the prosecutor was because he wanted to speak to him. I said that he was having supper with me and put him on the phone. The judge told him that he should immediately inform the Governor to instruct the warden to go on with the execution that night as originally scheduled because the judge had decided to deny the writ. But the prosecutor replied that he would not so inform the Governor, and that if the Governor asked him his opinion, he would advise him that the Governor had no power to change the time of execution since he had already put it off for a later time. That meant there would be no execution that night. I didn't have such a good night, but my worrying did not include the question as to what the judge was going to do to my writ in the morning.

It didn't take the judge long to deny the writ the next morning. He scarcely listened to any argument. We at once filed an appeal to the Circuit Court of Appeals and soon argued the matter before the circuit judge. He gave us ample opportunity, clearly understood what we were arguing, and after considering the question, he denied our application, saying, "At this late date and with the question of law most doubtful, and with the Court's affirming the decision, I do not feel justified in interfering with the processes of the State Courts and therefore must deny the application."

We renewed our plea to the Governor by quoting this and urged that "New Jersey should not execute a man when the highest United States Judge in the State feels that the legality of his conviction is 'most doubtful.'" However, we got no further time, and the execution took place that night. It was a long night for all of us.

I still have the letter that the soldier's mother wrote to me thanking us for what we had done and telling us that her son's last act was to request her to tell each of us "that your efforts were not futile, because it gave me courage and the understanding that you had faith in my word that the shooting was purely accidental and you stuck to the 'motto of the Fourth Ivy Leaves' * and no man could have had finer friends. Thank you."

---

* Because the Fourth Division was written "IV," it became known as the "Ivy" Division; the motto of the Division is "Loyal and Steadfast," which is supposed to be characteristic of the ivy plant, the insignia of the Division. The Ivy Division is now fighting in Vietnam.

This narration of the case should not close without a tribute to Abe J. David, the prosecutor of Union County, who while fully protecting the State of New Jersey exhibited the highest ideals of his profession and in a tense situation treated his adversaries with the utmost fairness and courtesy. I believe that he welcomed the fact that the federal court was given the opportunity of passing on the points that we made. It is interesting to speculate whether the federal courts today would uphold a murder conviction obtained by a state where death occurred but no blow was struck in that state.

A sequel to the Sacco-Vanzetti case also occupied a good deal of my time. It arose out of a suit for libel brought against *The Nation*.

The Sacco and Vanzetti case was important to all lawyers in those days. When the two men were executed, on August 22, 1927, I was in Williamstown, Massachusetts, and remember well how terrible and sunk I felt. Desperate last-minute moves had put off the execution several times. But that night the end came, and they were both hanged for the murder that had happened seven years before.

In the December 7, 1927, issue of *The Nation* an article had appeared accusing Colonel Calvin H. Goddard, a ballistics expert for the prosecution in the Sacco-Vanzetti case, of a major error in a subsequent case in which he had said that the fatal bullet and test bullets had been fired from the same pistol. But later it was established that the pistol had not left the factory until after the murder was committed. This article threw doubt on Goddard's testimony in the Sacco-Vanzetti case. Goddard sued for libel, with Charles Evans Hughes's firm as his counsel. This enabled him to say, "I'm suing them for libel," whenever he was confronted with *The Nation* article.

We were the lawyers for *The Nation* and were retained to defend. As part of the investigation, I visited Felix Frankfurter, who was then a professor at Harvard Law School. He had worked hard on the case and had written an important article ably defending Sacco and Vanzetti. He felt that our case presented the opportunity he had been waiting for of vindicating Sacco and Vanzetti in a courtroom. We were glad to be able to serve in such a case, and *The Nation* said, in its issue of April 18, 1928, "Since Mr. Goddard has chosen to bring the case to court, we shall have the opportunity to present the facts in full and to have them passed upon judicially." I made several trips to Cambridge, where Frankfurter was most helpful and got me in touch with Sacco and Vanzetti's counsel among others. Finally our case was about to come up for trial, and I arranged to go to Boston for a final visit. But just before I left, Charles E. Hughes, Jr., telephoned to say that his client was prepared to drop the case if we would publish a retraction of some statements in the article. Naturally I felt pleased, but told him I would have to consider carefully what he wanted us to say.

When I told Frankfurter what had happened, he said that he assumed that we, of course, wouldn't allow the plaintiff to withdraw the case because this would give us no chance of trying this issue out in court. I told him we couldn't stop the plaintiff from dropping his case, and that my job as a lawyer was to defeat the plaintiff's claim and protect my client from having a judgment against him. I pointed out what, of course, he well knew, that if Goddard won the case, he would get a substantial judgment, maybe $50,000 or $100,000, and that Oswald Garrison Villard, the publisher of *The Nation,* had the money and would have to pay. Frankfurter called me a "fake liberal" and said that otherwise I would insist on going on with the case. Naturally I resented this and pointed out again that the plaintiff could drop the case whether we objected or not. He persisted in repeating that I was a "fake liberal." After I got back to New York, the case was dropped. *The Nation* made no retraction, and in its issue of June 25, 1930, merely reported "that suit has voluntarily been withdrawn."

Maybe Goddard could have licked us on a trial and shown that the bullet from Sacco's pistol was the murder bullet. Today that is confidently asserted.* If this were so, why did Goddard drop his case? He could have collected any money that a jury

---

* See, for example, *Protest—Sacco-Vanzetti and the Intellectuals,* by David Felix, who says that the defendants were clearly guilty and that the intellectuals who defended them were starry-eyed.

might have awarded him. Moreover, the judgment would have been very useful to him in vindicating him of the charges in *The Nation* article. Or maybe his lawyers had advised him that he would probably lose the case and should drop it. I don't know. I wonder.

Whether Sacco and Vanzetti were guilty or innocent, their case was certainly a great education and experience for those of us who lived through it and followed it. It made a tremendous impression on me. I still have in my library the six printed volumes containing the evidence, exhibits, briefs and opinions in the case. Two of the things that impressed me then and still do are these: Why did it take seven years before the case was disposed of? Why weren't the appeal courts interested in whether Sacco and Vanzetti were guilty or innocent? They weren't, and from a strictly legal viewpoint, they were right. That is not the concern of an appeal court. Indeed, one of the criticisms against Judge Webster Thayer, who tried the case, was his statement that the Massachusetts Supreme Judicial Court had "approved" his judgment when he should have said it had "affirmed" it. Nor did other appeals, motions for habeas corpus, certiorari, stays and other relief consider the question of guilt or innocence.

In an appeal that I once argued before the Appellate Division in New York for an East Side tailor in a criminal case, I said something about the innocence of my client and was reprimanded by the Court with this statement: "You are raising the question as to whether this man is guilty or innocent. We have nothing to do with that. We are not interested in his guilt or innocence." (I wish I had a stenographic record of that statement, but I am pretty sure that is substantially what was said.) The ground of an appeal usually is that some rule of law was violated, not whether the defendant is guilty or innocent.

In Sacco and Vanzetti's case the appeal was denied because, as Charles P. Curtis ironically phrased it, "if the trial court has followed the rules, (a) the decision must be just, (b) probably is just, and (c) we have no right to question it." He added that the appeal court gave no common-sense explanation of its decision because it "was unable to communicate with laymen," and failed to define its task.

Maybe the nearest thing to a guilty or innocent judgment
was the report of President A. Lawrence Lowell of Harvard,
President Samuel W. Stratton of M.I.T. and Judge Robert Grant,
the committee of three appointed by Governor A. T. Fuller
which advised him not to interfere with the court order. In
discussing the case with Al Smith once, he told me I was unfair
to criticize this report because they were honest men and made
what they believed was an honest report. He added, "What did
you expect? If the Governor had appointed Lillian Wald,
Norman Thomas and me, what do you think we would have
done?"

Another, quite different matter which consumed a great deal
of our time during this period involved guaranteed mortgages.
After the 1929 crash, the bottom had fallen out of the country's
credit. A very popular investment in those days had been a
guaranteed mortgage. It worked this way: an apartment house
would be erected at a cost of, say, $2,000,000, with $1,500,000 borrowed on a first mortgage. That mortgage would then be broken
up in parts; certificates would be sold for $10,000 or $5,000,
$1,000 or $500. They were guaranteed by mortgage companies
such as the Title Guarantee and Trust Company and the Lawyers
Mortgage Company. Then when the crash came, no one wanted
to buy those certificates any longer. Claims against the mortgage
were worthless. This, in turn, resulted in claims against the
mortgage companies, and we became counsel for the State
Superintendent of Insurance, who had to take this over. Our
job was to work out this situation for the benefit of the
creditors, the holders of these certificates, as well as fulfilling
the Superintendent's job of handling the companies' own affairs
—that is, for creditors other than the mortgage certificate holders.

It was a long and arduous job, entailing a great deal of work
on the part of my brother and my other partners. It also meant
that we had to employ about fifty additional lawyers, putting
a staff in each one of the companies as well as in our own office.
The work involved lots of litigation, going all the way to the
United States Supreme Court.* In good times a loan on real
property would be secured by the mortgage on the property

---

* *Abrams* v. *Van Schaick*, 293 U.S. 188.

and the guarantor was seldom called on to pay anything. If, for some special reasons, the mortgage was not paying its interest or the principal, the guaranty was useful. But if *all* the property was unable to pay and *all* the certificate holders called on the guaranteed mortgage companies at the same time, these companies couldn't possibly meet their obligations and would have to throw in the sponge. That's what had happened, and that was the situation that had to be met. The claims ran into hundreds of millions of dollars. The problems were finally solved, but the guaranteed mortgage business no longer exists.

For the first time I had a bit of experience somewhat similar to that of the British barrister—that is, I tried a couple of cases without the advance work that the American lawyer usually puts in. Generally, of course, we have the case for months and months before trial, but in these two cases, I was called in at the last moment. One was a will contest before Surrogate James A. Foley. The case had come to us through a Williams classmate of my brother's from Pittsfield, Massachusetts. He was a lawyer, and the case had been well prepared by him and my brother. But Laurie was taken ill on a Saturday, and the following Monday I began to try the case. It is hard to get a jury to knock out a will, but this jury did it. The other side then moved to set the verdict aside. After long deliberation, Judge Foley decided in our favor, although he did not like a will to be overturned and always did everything he could to uphold a will. When Foley was elected surrogate, it was generally thought that he would be an out-and-out Tammany judge, because he and his family had always been straight organization politicians. Yet I believe he was the best trial judge I ever appeared before. He was able, fair, courteous, and strict. He was the complete master of his courtroom.

Another case I tried on a last-minute basis was also my brother's. It was an interesting situation, involving a claim against an insurance company on a term policy of $125,000 on the life of an officer of a corporation.* The policy expired at midnight. The man who was insured left Detroit by train

---

* *Hirshman* v. *Equitable Life Assurance Society of the United States*, 249 App. Div. 729.

in Lower Berth 8, and the porter was to call him at six o'clock
the next morning. The porter testified that he called the man
and he didn't get up. He called again—the man didn't move.
He had died during the night. The question was, Did he die
before or after midnight? If before midnight, he was insured,
and if after midnight, he was not insured. As you can imagine,
it was difficult to prove just when death had occurred. The
case became known, not only around the office but around my
home, as "The Man in Lower 8." The witnesses, including his
wife, the conductor, the porter, hospital attendants, the medical
examiner, and others, testified about his sleeping and urinary
habits, some saying he was dried up, others calling him a walking
Niagara Falls. Lawyers and other people around the courthouse
used to drop in to listen to the testimony. The jury was tied up
for a long time and finally disagreed. For weeks after this,
whenever I was in court, I was greeted by lawyers, many of
whom I didn't know, in the elevators or elsewhere with the
question, "Did he die before or after midnight?"

Nine of the jury were for my client and three for the defendant.
This meant that the case had to be tried all over again. I
wanted it put down for a prompt retrial. The judge asked if
he could do anything to help settle it, and I told him that I
felt the jury's verdict was sound. He looked surprised, and
I said that I thought three-quarters should be the amount of the
settlement. After beefing around a lot, it was finally settled for
that.

One cannot, of course, generalize from just two cases, but I
gained the impression from trying them under these circumstances that the barrister does not feel handicapped by un-
familiarity with the case if the case has been thoroughly
prepared. I also felt there was the possibility of an advantage
from not knowing the client and other witnesses too well. This
is certainly what barristers and more experienced trial lawyers
in this country think, and it differed from the view that I
previously held.

I do not want to give the impression that most of our practice
was in court. It was not. But we did have a good deal of court
work, and we have accumulated "Cases and Points" running

to sixty-two volumes. "Cases and Points" are the bound volumes
of printed records and briefs of cases that have gone to court
and been appealed. They represent only a fraction of the court
work, of course, since only cases that are appealed are printed
in "Cases and Points," and most cases are not appealed. But
this collection does give an interesting indication of some of the
court work that has gone through our office.

Several of our cases had to do with matters of so-called
international law—meaning only that they arose in foreign lands,
one in Russia, for instance, and another in Sweden (and
incidentally John Foster Dulles was involved in both).

We represented some Polish clients who had life insurance,
written abroad, with the New York Life Insurance Company.
The company repudiated the policies after Russia had appropriated its property in Russia. Interesting and important legal
questions arose. Was this repudiation justified? If not, what was
the rate of exchange from rubles to dollars? Our clients sued
in the New York Supreme Court. My father, who had just retired
from the bench and, at our urging, was then with the firm as
counsel, gave us his opinion that our position was sound and
that the company was liable. He advised that we should try to
settle at the rate of exchange at the time of the confiscation
(about twenty-four cents a ruble) and not hold out for the full
rate of the ruble (about fifty-one cents). We finally succeeded
in working out such a settlement with the company, which was
represented by John Foster Dulles, of the firm of Sullivan &
Cromwell. After the settlement, I made two trips to Warsaw,
with a power of attorney that enabled me to pay these claims
from a letter of credit opened in my favor by the New York Life
Insurance Company. I was a Santa Claus in Poland, and felt
that we were rendering a real service by enabling these people
to get their money without awaiting the outcome of a protracted
lawsuit.

The case presented one of the most difficult problems that a
lawyer comes up against: whether to settle and how strongly to
urge a client to settle. The decision, of course, is the client's
and not the lawyer's. But a good lawyer-client relationship
necessarily presumes that the client will rely heavily on the

lawyer's advice. There is no simple rule telling the lawyer what he should do. Each case is different. One of the things influencing me in these Russian cases was our clients' urgent need for money in Poland at that time. What one hundred dollars in American money would mean to them there was tremendous. Many of the insureds were dead and their next of kin were in financial straits. My power of attorney enabled me to make the payments without Polish court authority. And, of course, my father's opinion that even if we should win the trial we probably would not get the normal rate of exchange was another important factor in our decision to settle. Later on, after a victory in the lower court in a similar case, the Court of Appeals reversed and dismissed the complaints.* After much work over a long period, the clients got nothing—and the lawyers got less.

The next case of an international nature was one from Sweden: the Kreuger & Toll bankruptcy.

On the wall in my office is a bond of the Kingdom of Italy for £500,000 with interest at 6 per cent, payable semiannually at Barclays Bank Limited in London. It is guaranteed as to principal and interest by the Kingdom of Italy and is signed by A. Mosconi, Minister of Finance. The bond is a fake and the signature was forged by Ivar Kreuger.

But I like to keep it as a souvenir of Kreuger & Toll. It was given to me as the American trustee of that company by its Swedish liquidators. After returning to Sweden from a visit here, they sent it to me with another Italian bond which I was to give to John Foster Dulles, who was counsel for the bondholders' committee. The two bonds came in a tongue-in-cheek letter, saying that they thought the American estate should share more fully in the Kreuger assets. The American assets in the estate were then only about $84,000, against which claims of more than $300,000,000 had been filed by over 16,000 creditors. Prospects for a big dividend were slim.

Ivar Kreuger, the fabulous match king, had shot himself on Saturday, March 12, 1932, in Paris. The news of his death was a shock to the financial world. London, Paris, New York, and

---

* *Sliosberg* v. *New York Life Insurance Company*, 244 N.Y. 482.

other capitals were stunned. But to the people of Sweden the blow was staggering. After an emergency meeting of the Cabinet at the Palace in Stockholm on Saturday, Parliament was called into session and at one o'clock Sunday morning, it passed a moratorium. Flags were at half-mast throughout the country. The Stock Exchange was closed for several days to let the country get its breath.

My connection with the case started soon after that. Foster Dulles told me that I had been suggested as trustee in the American bankruptcy proceedings that had been started and that my name was acceptable to counsel for the various parties, and asked me whether there was any reason why I could not serve. I knew of none and was soon appointed by the United States District Court. Thus began a fascinating experience.

The story of Ivar Kreuger is quite a tale. It has often been written—from William Stoneman's *The Life and Death of Ivar Kreuger* to Robert Shaplen's recent account, *Kreuger—Genius and Swindler*. "The biggest thief in the long history of larceny—a man who could think of embezzlement in terms of hundreds of millions," said John Kenneth Galbraith in his introduction to the Shaplen book, which is an expanded version of the three-part profile that appeared in *The New Yorker* magazine. It is not my purpose to tell the whole story again here, but since the present generation knows practically nothing about Kreuger, I am afraid that I will have to relate some of this detail.

Kreuger was a fabulous person. The economist John Maynard Keynes characterized him as "maybe the greatest financial intelligence of his time," and said that through his company, Kreuger & Toll, in the 1920's he created "a canal between the countries with abundance of capital and those in bitter need of it." Shaplen calls Kreuger the greatest swindler of modern times, and notes that his object lesson "was largely responsible for the subsequent reform in accountancy and company direction both here and in Sweden."

Kreuger was born in Sweden and came to the United States as a young engineer. While living here, he worked on the construction of the Flatiron Building among others in New York, as well as on such jobs as the stadium at Syracuse University.

He learned a good deal about American finance and the power of monopolies. Upon returning to Sweden, he established his own construction company in Stockholm with an engineer partner named Toll, and the new firm of Kreuger & Toll played an important part in modernizing the city of Stockholm.

The construction business proved too limited a field for Kreuger, with his awareness of the possibilities of monopolies and international business. He well understood the importance of volume and knew that the Gillette Company did not make its profits from the sale of razors but from the continued sale of blades. In seeking a product with this characteristic, he naturally thought of matches. The product required constant replacing. Matches destroyed themselves. They did so more rapidly and more completely than safety razor blades or anything else. From his early boyhood Kreuger knew the match business. His father and grandfather had been in it. And so were many neighbors in the community where he was born. But they had had only a small business. Recently, some of them had joined forces to form the Swedish Match Company, pulling together the match-making industries of Sweden. But Kreuger's plans went far beyond that. He was thinking of acquiring match-manufacturing concerns in many countries.

Kreuger's idea was that Kreuger & Toll would lend money to different countries, in return for which the foreign country would give his company a monopoly, and on every match sold in that country a royalty would be paid. It was an era of expansion, and countries needed capital. There was no World Bank, and direct borrowings from investors in foreign countries had reached a peak. By taking advantage of this need for money, Kreuger hoped to develop an international monopoly.

To get the money to lend to foreign countries he obtained large sums of money from many investors in the United States and abroad. He actually succeeded in controlling three-quarters of the world's match business. His knowledge of finance and business and his remarkably fertile imagination enabled him to create what he needed most—confidence. The confidence that was shown in him by important people in Sweden earned him the confidence of the King of Sweden. This, in turn, inspired the confidence of Lee Higginson and Company in the United States, and gave him the status he needed to carry on his gigantic business. In 1929, Kreuger & Toll was the most widely distributed security in the world; its common shares were selling at 730 per cent of par and its convertible debentures were at 863 per cent of par.

To reach this pinnacle, Kreuger had created the International Match Company and about 250 other companies. He manipulated them in devious ways so that their transactions with each other were permeated with fraud. He had many associates and employees in these companies, but no one of them knew about anything more than his own particular limited area. Kreuger knew every tainted detail. He conducted this huge enterprise as a one-man business. Unknown to those who dealt with him, this massive structure became his mechanism for practicing deceit on a scale that had never before been conceived. The business pyramided and grew until it suddenly collapsed.

Just before Christmas in 1931, Kreuger arrived in New York and stayed at his penthouse apartment on the southeast corner of Seventy-fourth Street and Park Avenue. Among those who were eager to see him was President Hoover. The President was heartened by his optimism, and in summing up his own views to reporters after his visit, Kreuger said, "I don't feel there is any reason for the American people to feel so nervous over the situation in Europe." He added reassuringly, "As a matter of fact, I do not think that the European people take to heart their problems as much as you do in America. European problems will be solved, and there is no reason why the American people should become hysterical about them." But he soon had cause to be nervous himself. He had received bad news. The International Telegraph and Telephone Company had decided to call off a deal to purchase his Ericsson Telephone stock—the figures didn't seem to be as represented. The Swedish banks were disturbed and wanted Kreuger to return for discussions. He needed cash badly and was desperate as to where he could get it. During the hectic Washington's Birthday weekend, he phoned from his Park Avenue apartment to Paris, Berlin, Warsaw, Amsterdam, and often to Stockholm. The calls were made at all hours of the day and night. They were shown on the Telephone Company records that we subpoenaed, but they did

not reveal the conversations. Although we don't know what was
said, we do know that Kreuger was unable to raise the money.
He was ill and running a fever. His associates in Stockholm
repeated that the banks were pressing there. He finally arranged for further credit, but he had to meet with his Swedish
creditors. With Donald Durant of Lee Higginson, Kreuger
sailed on the *Ile de France* and met some of his Swedish associates in Paris on Friday, March 11. Before going back to
Stockholm, they arranged to meet him the next morning. When
he did not appear, they went to his apartment. There they
found his body lying on the bed. He had shot himself.

It was hard to believe that the great man Kreuger was dead.
But it was even harder to understand that his business was
imperiled. And the incredible fact soon began to dawn—the
business was crooked. Gradually, individual investors began to
think, "Instead of making huge profits, maybe I'm going to lose
what I put up." The country's hero, trusted by all, was gone.
What had become of the money?

Kreuger & Toll was a Swedish business. Its assets were mainly
in Sweden and the estate was to be administered there. Swedish
liquidators were appointed. Price, Waterhouse and Company
was engaged to audit the books and undertook a world-wide
investigation. They produced a series of more than 125 reports
on a huge variety of subjects. The Kreuger & Toll ownership
of International Match Company and the Swedish Match Company made it necessary to examine the affairs of these companies, as well as those of banks, financial enterprises, and other
operations in Sweden, Poland, Spain, Liechtenstein, Germany,
France, South America, United States and elsewhere around the
world. But the books could not be reconciled. Bonds of the
Italian government were found to be forgeries by Kreuger.
Claims against subsidiaries were merely book entries; assets supposed to have great value were nonexistent. A gigantic fraud
had been perpetrated.

The job of the American trustee was to collect all assets that
could be found in this country and distribute them among the
creditors. The assets were few, but the claims were many. My
first task was to select counsel. I chose George Roberts, as an
outstanding lawyer with sound judgment and a member of Win-

throp, Stimson, Putnam & Roberts, whose senior partner, Henry
L. Stimson, had just returned to the firm after serving as Secretary of State and was well known in Sweden. The claims were
processed in an office that we set up at 140 Nassau Street, right
next door to the office of Referee Harold P. Stevenson. When
the bankruptcy started (which was to take about five years),
the only assets on hand were a small bank account, some office
furniture, and one stock certificate representing 60,000 shares
of the Ohio Match Company.

The manner of life of the man who controlled this sprawling,
world-wide structure naturally was of great interest to the men
attempting to unravel his affairs. Kreuger was a lone operator—
and as such, he had to have a remarkable ability to be everywhere at once in order to take care of his empire. Each of his
houses and offices—in Stockholm, New York, Paris and Berlin—
was a completely staffed, working establishment and was kept
ready for him at all times. In New York he had a small but
elegant office suite in the Lee Higginson Building on Broad
Street. The furniture, which included a handsome desk and other
fine pieces, was auctioned off by the Parke-Bernet Galleries in
New York after his death and provided mementoes to auction-
goers, some of whom perhaps were unhappy creditors. He
never married, but had women companions in numerous places,
and there are many stories about his relations with them. His
love of flowers was real and intense. On the terrace of his Park
Avenue penthouse he had an extravagant garden, which was
taken care of for him by Kay, the florist on Seventy-fourth Street
and Lexington Avenue, who lost one of his best customers when
Kreuger killed himself. This love for flowers was one of his
earliest passions. When his young Swedish roommate got married at the time that Kreuger was working on the construction
of the Flatiron Building on Twenty-third Street, Kreuger's
gift of flowers was huge—out of all proportion to his salary—and
on every wedding anniversary a similar gift was made. On his
trips to New York, he always managed to visit the bride and
groom, who lived in a small suburban home. Subsequent contacts with greatness did not draw him away from his early
friendships. Even though the rest of the world saw him as a
master swindler, these friends remained loyal to him and to his

memory. They resolutely defended his complete integrity. But he had no warm friends or defenders among the men of big business with whom he associated.

The personal magnetism of the man and his enormous success made it possible for him to borrow money in an unorthodox manner. When he was on the crest of the wave he borrowed $4,000,000 in New York without any collateral. He gave a statement to the Guaranty Trust Company, which made the loan with three other banks. But the statement was a bit unusual. It included assets described as X, Y, Z. Kreuger explained confidentially that these items represented money due from three foreign countries—Spain, Italy, and another. But this was so secret that he couldn't write it on the paper. The fact that this story was wholly fictitious seemed to give added weight to the statement and testified to the mysterious atmosphere that Kreuger succeeded in building up about himself and his activities. Actually, the statement was dictated to his New York secretary. He redid it several times. To make it look more plausible and palatable, he increased some items and reduced others. No auditor certified as to its correctness, and no certification was requested.

But there was one person who had suspicions. He was an accountant with Ernst & Ernst, who were doing work for Lee Higginson and Company, and told Donald Durant about his doubts. Durant was provoked. To him, Kreuger was the greatest financier ever known and he didn't like this question. But the accountant persisted, and Durant agreed that he might talk directly to Kreuger. He did so. He pointed out that the Kreuger & Toll statement showed large deposits of *Reich* bonds held on deposit in the Kreuger Bank in Berlin. He asked whether Kreuger didn't agree with him that it would be better to have these bonds on deposit in some other German bank. Kreuger listened politely and thanked him profusely for the suggestion, which he said was a good one and added that he himself should have thought of it. A few days later, Kreuger gave Durant the original of a cable from Berlin, signed "Deutsche Bank," stating that it had received from the Kreuger Bank a large quantity of *Reich* bonds which the Deutsche Bank was holding for Kreuger

& Toll's account. Durant showed the cable to the accountant and chided him as to his finicky overcautiousness. But the fact was that the Deutsche Bank did not hold these *Reich* bonds or any other bonds for Kreuger & Toll's account, and it was later discovered that the cable had been sent by a coat-check girl in a Berlin night club. After the accountant had talked to Kreuger, he had telephoned her and told her to write down exactly what he would tell her and that she should send it in a cable to him. His dictation included the signature of the Deutsche Bank. She was a good friend and gladly did so.

The administration of the estate was an international affair, and I worked in close cooperation with the Swedish liquidators. An international committee, consisting of Norman H. Davis from the United States, Hugh Kindersley of England and Jakob Wallenberg of Sweden, was created to help solve the inter-company problems.

For example, who was the owner of the 60,000 shares of Ohio Match Company stock? The certificate for this stock, representing a half-ownership in the company, was among the papers of Kreuger & Toll at the time of the bankruptcy, and I had it in my safe-deposit box from the time I became trustee. We found canceled vouchers showing that Kreuger & Toll had paid for it. Mr. Roberts, as my lawyer, took the position that if, for instance, he wanted to prove that he owned the suit he was wearing, he would show that he paid for it by providing his canceled check to Brooks Brothers; that he had worn the suit for several years; and that no one else had claimed otherwise. By the same token, he said, all the complicated claims and cross-claims of the other Kreuger companies did not disprove this. Norman Davis, as arbitrator, agreed. This case and many others would have gone on for years in courts in this country and elsewhere had there been no over-all settlement machinery. Creating it was a constructive piece of work done by John Foster Dulles and other lawyers, including another former Secretary of State, Bainbridge Colby, who was counsel for another Kreuger & Toll bondholders' committee.

The American bankruptcy proceedings eventually solved its mass of problems, including suits against American banks arising out of the pledge of 350,000 shares of Diamond Match Company stock, suits against Lee Higginson and Company and former directors of the bankrupt, claims against the estate of Ivar Kreuger, and numerous other matters. An outstandingly important issue in the settlement was resolved by a court decision that the so-called American certificates issued by Lee Higginson Trust Company, which were widely sold in the American market, were stock and not bonds.* The decision was naturally a bitter blow to the thousands of American stockholders, including many churches, colleges, widows, fiduciaries, and others, particularly in New England, who got nothing for the millions they had invested. Typical of the entire Kreuger picture, the investors had bought these American certificates without any real knowledge of what they were buying—without even knowing whether the certificates were stocks or bonds. They received nothing on their investment, and the bondholders got the bulk of the estate, amounting to 43 per cent of the face amount of their claim. This was not bad compared with other bankruptcies of this period. The Kreuger & Toll papers are now deposited in the library of Princeton University, where they may be studied by scholars.

Even after the full story of the great fraud began to come out, the tremendous confidence Kreuger had generated continued to have its effect. During the examination of one of the Lee Higginson partners, he stated that certain action taken by his firm had been based on official instructions that were given to them. Even though he could not produce this authority, he was absolutely positive that the firm had it and insisted that it was in existence. In the late afternoon, the matter was put over until the next day. When I arrived in my office early the next morning, I was surprised to find the Lee Higginson partner waiting for me. He was unshaven, his suit unpressed, and he looked as though he hadn't slept all night. He hadn't. But his face was covered with

---

* This matter was originally argued before Judge Robert P. Patterson. After argument, however, he disqualified himself because he had discovered that a trust of which he was trustee owned several shares of the stock of Marine Midland Bank, the trustee of the Kreuger securities, although the decision would not have made five cents' difference in the value of the Marine Midland stock.

smiles. He was triumphant. He held out a paper that he wanted me to see immediately. There it was, signed by Ivar Kreuger! I doubt whether he realized that he had produced nothing—no statement signed by an accountant or other responsible person. Nothing but another document signed by Kreuger. I didn't want to spoil his glee. I gave him a receipt for it, put it in the safe, and urged him to go home and get some sleep. He thought he had vindicated his firm. He had found the paper which Ivar Kreuger himself had signed.

One naturally asks, Could a fraud like this be perpetrated again? Probably not, as far as the issue of securities is concerned. But could credit be obtained on statements such as Kreuger furnished, with descriptions of assets like X, Y, and Z? I think the answer very likely is yes. Credit is based on confidence. Consider what happened in the Insull case, in McKesson & Robbins, and, more recently, in the Billie Sol Estes case and in the Anthony De-Angelis case in New Jersey. In commenting on the DeAngelis twenty-year sentence for his manipulation of the warehouse receipts for vegetable oil, the New York *Times* said, on August 18, 1965, that he "was accused of engineering the biggest commercial fraud since the early 1930's when Ivar Kreuger bilked a galaxy of international bankers for an estimated $500,000,000." But after the DeAngelis case, the Atlantic Acceptance Corporation of Canada also bilked a new assortment of outstanding bankers and prominent investors, including the United States Steel Pension Fund, Moody's, Morgan Guaranty Trust Company, First National City Bank of New York, Ford Foundation, Chesapeake & Ohio Railroad, Princeton University, and the University of Pennsylvania. The New York *Times* reported this on November 14, 1965, adding that this operation "followed the pattern of Ivar Kreuger, the Swedish match king, whose empire came crashing down in the early 1930's." It continued: "Canadians are mindful of the Kreuger parallels and of the elastic standards" that have encouraged this operation.

Can you phone abroad today and have a girl friend send you a cable which she could sign in the name of a well-known bank? My information is that you still can. But I wouldn't advise your doing it.

VI

THE TREASURY DEPARTMENT

HENRY MORGENTHAU, SR., and my father had been close friends, and Henry, Jr., and I were friends since our childhood. After we grew up, he became a farmer, growing apples at Fishkill Farms, near Franklin D. Roosevelt's place at Hyde Park. He acquired and became the publisher of *American Agriculturist,* one of the two leading farm journals of the East. In it Henry conducted a weekly column answering questions and giving advice to his farmer-readers about projects submitted to them by all sorts of city slickers and other enterprising characters. He gave very courageous and useful answers, often disregarding the caution urged by his lawyer. Lawsuits for libel resulted now and again, and as his lawyer, it became my job to defend them.*
In this way, I got to know Henry well both in and out of the office.

He and his wife were very close to Roosevelt and Mrs. Roosevelt as neighbors and friends. While F.D.R. was Governor, Henry had been his Conservation Commissioner. A couple of days before Roosevelt's first inauguration as President, Henry

---

* See, for example, *Varvaro* v. *American Agriculturist, Inc.,* 222 App. Div. 213.

phoned, asking me to lunch at the Commodore Hotel. There he told me that it wasn't until the day before that Roosevelt had informed him what he wanted him to do in the new Administration in Washington. It was to tackle the job of financing farmers and creating a new loan organization (later to become the Farm Credit Administration). Henry had some very concrete problems he wanted to talk to me about. I was able to help him with some of them, but then he came to his last one—and that was to get him legal counsel. He took a piece of paper out of his pocket. On it he had written the kind of man that Roosevelt had told him he should get. He wanted a lawyer who was born on a farm in the Middle West and had been brought up there. He had to be well and favorably known in the East, particularly in New York. He had to be outstandingly able, with great force of character, and a true liberal. Furthermore, he must come to Washington the following day and start his new job right away. I told him there wasn't any such person. But in typical Morgenthau fashion, he persisted, repeating that Roosevelt had told him he had to get this fabulous character, and he gave me his Washington phone number where I should phone him tomorrow. I again told him that I was sure I couldn't do it, but promised to try anyway. He said goodbye and that he expected to hear from me tomorrow.

Thinking his request fantastic and unattainable, I really forgot all about it. At least, I thought I had forgotten all about it. But suddenly that night, I woke up with the answer! No psychiatrist has ever explained to me the magic of that unconscious thinking which often solves this sort of problem for me. It was instantly clear who Henry meant. Obviously it was Herman Oliphant. He filled all of Roosevelt's specifications except the last one. He didn't know Henry and, I guessed, had never even heard of him, and I was sure he wouldn't go to Washington. But anyway, I had promised, so I would try. This was particularly hard for me because I was dependent on Oliphant. He was doing a job with me that would be wrecked if he left. He was the director of the Survey of Litigation in New York under the auspices of the Institute of Law of Johns Hopkins University. We had organized this work and got it going after a lot of difficulty, and the last thing I wanted was to have him go.

The first time I had met Oliphant was some years before, down in Baltimore, at the home of the Institute of Law. The Institute had just been started, and its purpose was to study the administration of justice. It is hard to believe now, but as far as I know no previous attempt had ever been made to see how the law worked. Plenty of study had been given to various points of law, but none as to what actually happens in court or whether what the law really intends was being carried out. It was assumed that if the Constitution or a statute says that something should be done, it is done. Although it is common knowledge that this is not so, it was nobody's job to do anything about it. For example, the Constitution says, as does the Magna Carta, that speedy trial shall be denied to nobody, but we know that there is often a long delay before a case is tried. In civil cases it has become usual for years to go by before a trial can be held, and after the trial, there is often grave doubt as to whether the judgment of the court will be carried out. The public has discovered that in many—indeed most—of the cases it reads about, the "law" seems somehow divorced from reality and quite different from "justice."

The Johns Hopkins Institute was to look into this situation. Although most people were completely unconcerned about it, the project had always intrigued me, and I decided to go talk to them about some ideas I had. I went there cold, without knowing anybody. Herman Oliphant and his three colleagues, who constituted the faculty and the staff, were very polite to me and allowed me to tell them what I had been thinking about—which was to conduct a study of actual cases tried in New York to find out where the weaknesses in the process were. How long did it take, for instance, and how much did it cost to get them disposed of? Oliphant listened to me a long time that first day, and he and his associates were interested in this idea I had. They later agreed to undertake the work, and Oliphant was assigned to direct it. Eventually the study got under way, and was going well. Naturally, I didn't want to ask Oliphant to see Morgenthau—but I had made the promise to Henry.

I phoned him the next morning, Saturday. Oliphant came over and I explained to him as well as I could what the job was to be. He asked a lot of questions, including many about Henry. As I had expected, he had never met or heard of Henry, and said he was not interested. But as a favor to me, I finally got him to agree at least to go to Washington and meet Morgenthau. He went the next day, and Morgenthau's complete honesty, followed by Roosevelt's bubbling enthusiasm, won him over. Here was a farmer boy, a crusader, hearing of an opportunity that suggested infinite possibilities to his imaginative, creative legal mind. He joined the new Administration, and as one of its most brilliant minds, he made major contributions to many of the New Deal's most important accomplishments. In his quiet, effective way, keeping out of the limelight and the newspapers, virtually unknown to the public, he became Counsel to the Treasury Department and one of the New Deal's main props until his death in January, 1939.

I saw Herman Oliphant frequently over the years, and he never failed to delight me. He was a sparkling person with a delicious sense of humor that was communicated through his bright blue eyes. He had a vital interest in everything about him. He generated excitement in those to whom he talked. You couldn't just start talking and then drop the subject. If it was about a legal matter, it was like going to law school again. The task was first to find out what the law was, try to agree as to what it should be, and then decide how to change it. Whether he was working at the Johns Hopkins Institute of Law, or at the Treasury, or anywhere else, there was always this wonderful process going on. Something could be done about it.

As an example of how contagious his enthusiasm was, one summer I was going to Europe to spend time in Switzerland, with a visit to London. He said that was just wonderful because Johns Hopkins Institute wanted a job done on how the Masters Courts in London worked. I thought he was crazy to ask me to do it, but I ended up not only making the study, but writing a book, with an English barrister, called *The King's Bench Masters,* the only other book I ever wrote. I worked on other projects, too, with "Oliphant's Law School," including originating new laws and trying cases to establish new law concerning liquor, tax suits, and procedure. In one case we not only got a new law passed by the state legislature in Albany, but we later had it repealed when we found out that it didn't really work. I don't know anyone but Oliphant who ever managed that.

When he was at Johns Hopkins, he lived near the Pimlico Race Track. His wife, Jo, not only bred saluki dogs, but early in the morning she timed the horses at the race track. Believe it or not, she made money on both of these intellectual pursuits, and this gave Herman the keenest possible enjoyment. When Prohibition prevented him from getting the liquor that he wanted, he brewed it in their cellar, explaining how perfectly legal this was—and demonstrating how perfectly vile it tasted. He objected to my disapproval of his product and complained to my wife that I really was not interested in learning how to make good liquor. When our well ran dry, up at Martha's Vineyard one summer, he sent me detailed instructions on how to dig a foolproof shallow well and was disgusted with me when he found out later that I had lost his instructions. One summer vacation he spent at La-push, a tiny Coast Guard station in the State of Washington near the northwest tip of the United States. Later I visited there and saw the small Indian village that Oliphant had described, with its huge ancient canoes that were still in use. Another summer he was on a Coast Guard ship that patrolled for icebergs up in the Arctic sea lanes, and he later went gold mining in a remote camp out west. A third summer he worked with the sculptor Gutzon Borglum, carving Washington, Jefferson, Lincoln and Roosevelt out of the mountain (the Mount Rushmore National Memorial in South Dakota).

There was much uncertainty in the Treasury before the Supreme Court's decision about the constitutionality of the legislation taking us off the gold standard. If the act were to be held invalid, there would be frightening financial problems. If part of the act were sustained and only part were knocked out, the problems would be less serious. As I recall it, Oliphant had figured that there were seven possible decisions. He had prepared proposed action papers, including drafts of speeches by the President, for each of six contingencies. The seventh one happened. The Supreme Court sustained the act. No other action was needed. I've often thought of this since when a lawyer is completely at a loss as to what he should do when a court decides the other way in his case that had only two alternatives. If Oliphant did not know how to carve the mountain, mend an antique Indian canoe, or brew his legal liquor, I'm sure that he could never have done such a superb job as Counsel of the Treasury Department.

From Inauguration Day in 1933 until I went into the Army in 1940, I think I must have gone down to Washington at least twice a month in response to calls from Oliphant and Morgenthau. It was not only *pro bono publico*, but what was worse, it cost my firm plenty in other directions. Because of some antique conflict-of-interest law, my partners and I had to disqualify ourselves from accepting many cases, in which substantial fees were involved, because of my connection with the Treasury Department. Many of the clients had no improper motive and did not have the slightest idea what we were talking about when we refused to handle their cases.

The work I did with Oliphant and Morgenthau embraced such subjects as helping to reorganize the Treasury Department and getting personnel to serve there, particularly tax consultants. One day Morgenthau asked me if he had what I would consider members of an All-America tax team working in the Treasury. I was quite surprised by the question and the form which it took. However, it was easy to give the answer, which was that I certainly didn't think any of his men would make an All-America team. He then asked me if I would give him names for an All-America team. I said it wasn't easy to do that, but I could give him names of persons who could be included on an All-America team. As a result of these conversations with him and my subsequent talks with Oliphant, Bernhard Knollenberg, Roswell Magill and Randolph Paul were all brought into the Treasury. I think most lawyers would agree that they qualified as All-America.

Other jobs included confidential discussions and work on tax cases, problems involving trade with Russia and its subsequent recognition, and many other subjects that were fascinating. Mostly I was needed in Washington for only a couple of days, but there were some problems that required my presence for long stretches at a time. One of these was in connection with the repeal of the Eighteenth Amendment. The Roosevelt Administration's plank for repeal was swiftly acted on. By February 20, 1933, Congress voted for the Twenty-first Amendment, repealing Prohibition, and promptly transmitted it to the states for their individual action. A thirsty country voted rapidly, much more rapidly than had been anticipated. By November it was evident that when Utah voted on December 5th it would be the thirty-sixth state to vote for the repeal amendment. And when that happened, it would be goodbye to the Eighteenth. This speedy action followed the pattern that the country had set when it had become dry in January, 1919. I was then in the Army of Occupation in Germany, and my father wrote me,

During the past two weeks more than three-fourths of the state legislatures have approved of the amendment prohibiting the sale of alcoholic liquors. In other words, after January, 1920, the United States of America will be bone-dry. People generally are astounded at the result. So confident were most people that such amendment would not be ratified by the Constitutional requirement of the votes of three-fourths of the state legislatures that there were no public meetings nor widespread campaigns in the press or other publications conducted against the adoption of the amendment. So there will be precious little chance of sipping Berncasteler Doctor * or any other wines or liquors in free America after this year.

Suddenly the Administration found itself with repeal only a matter of weeks away. Some regulation would be badly needed. It was decided to do this through codes drafted by the National Recovery Administration (NRA) for each branch of the liquor industry. Up till then, the processing of codes had been moving very slowly, and no code had yet been approved. But in about three weeks, repeal would be a reality. Oliphant urged that the interdepartmental committee which had been created for the

---

* Berncasteler Doctor was our favorite drink in the Army of Occupation on the Moselle River.

purpose of approving these codes and which so far had been unable to accomplish anything be charged with the job of getting out the codes and setting up an appropriate agency to administer the industry by December 5th. This meant, literally, night and day meetings for the committee. As can well be imagined, there was a good deal of excitement and publicity in regard to this. It should be remembered that the country had been dry for years, and now it would be able to get all the hard liquor it wanted, plus beer and wine.

I was suddenly appointed chairman of the committee by the President. On the committee were representatives of State, Treasury, Justice, Agriculture, and Commerce. Each department had its own interest and to a large extent its own solution. And each industry—wine, beer, and distillers—had a huge lobbying organization, energetically contending that it could police its own industry and that it needed the very minimum of Government control. We had a constant series of separate meetings with each industry, including some that were held in the Commerce meeting hall with hundreds in attendance, and many round-the-clock meetings with our committee. Our own meetings became so quarrelsome that we got nowhere until I appointed a subcommittee of every member of the committee but one man. The subcommittee finally reached agreement on everything, and it was then approved by the full committee with only one lone dissenter.

I never realized that I had so many friends in the liquor business, or friends of friends, or that I knew so many lawyers for friends, or for friends of friends. They all suddenly wanted to invite me to dinner, or to a party, or see me, or phone me. After several nights of this, I worked out the plan of spending each night at a different hotel, club, or other spot, which I would select every afternoon. President Roosevelt was down in Warm Springs through all this, but I conferred with Oliphant and Morgenthau daily, who, in turn, spoke to the President, often while he was in the swimming pool. Occasionally I was included in that conversation and he said that he could always hear my hiccup. He also jokingly reminded me that we were going fifty-fifty on everything I got out of the job, and that he guessed he could easily retire on that.

Around this time, Marvin McIntyre at the White House approached me about setting up a Federal Alcohol Control Administration. He and Oliphant were both working to get me to be chairman of this new outfit. After he was persuaded that I wouldn't buy it, he conspired to get the right man to appoint. One day the President suggested Joseph H. Choate, Jr., the New York lawyer, who had been in his class at Harvard. I said that I thought this would be swell, and before I knew it, I was witnessing a unique exhibition of salesmanship. It began by McIntyre's phoning Choate and telling him that the President had asked him to come down to Washington to see him about something tomorrow morning. Next day the President was still in Warm Springs. I was at the White House with McIntyre. After scolding the President for having not yet finished his breakfast, McIntyre gave the President his instructions just as if McIntyre were the one in command. Choate arrived, and I don't think he had ever heard of the proposed new Alcohol Commission. McIntyre at once got the President on the phone for him, and they began talking about everything, while McIntyre listened on another wire. After quite a bit of conversation, which I, of course, couldn't hear, McIntyre cut in and brought the phone call to a close. We then talked more to Choate, and when he took the early afternoon train back to New York, the evening papers telling about his appointment must have made him realize what a busy morning he had had. He made a good Commissioner, and I got back to New York.

Another Morgenthau-Oliphant assignment that required a great deal of my time was the tax case of Charles E. Mitchell.

Charles E. Mitchell, chairman of the board of the National City Bank and National City Company, made $10,000 a day in 1929. But he paid no income tax on any of it. He didn't have to, he said, because he lost most of it on the sale of his City Bank stock to his wife, and he might have had to pay back the rest of it, and so it wasn't really income.

Four years later he told the Senate Banking and Currency Committee that the sale of stock to his wife was "really a sale of convenience to reduce his income." This statement was given wide publicity, and people began to ask questions: "How can a man make over $3,500,000 in a year and not pay any income tax on it? Why do I have to pay so much tax when I make only a small fraction of that?"

A grand jury was called, and these and other questions were put to Mitchell. After getting the answers, the grand jury indicted Mitchell for making a false income tax return. It charged that he should have paid a tax of over $725,000 on his 1929 income. (Taxes were much less in those days. At the current rate, the tax on his 1929 income would be about $2,640,000.) The trial began in May of 1933. Seven weeks later it ended with the jury's verdict of "not guilty."

Mitchell, Wall Street's greatest salesman, had New York's best trial lawyer, the famous Max D. Steuer. They made an impressive team. They got the verdict in spite of the able prosecution led by our most capable prosecutor, George Z. Medalie, and his assistant, Thomas E. Dewey, who was then unknown.

Most taxpayers seemed to disapprove of this verdict. One of them was President Franklin D. Roosevelt. Counsel to his Bureau of Internal Revenue advised him that because of the acquittal, Mitchell didn't have to pay the tax and penalty. But the President wouldn't accept this. He asked, "What will the garageman at Hyde Park say? He'll ask, 'Why should I pay my taxes if Mitchell pays nothing?'" The President insisted that the Government proceed to collect the tax and the 50 per cent penalty which the law provided when a taxpayer was guilty of fraud.

Here is where I came in. I was asked to handle the tax suit against Mitchell by my friend, Henry Morgenthau, Jr., who was then the Secretary of the Treasury, or, rather, by his counsel, Herman Oliphant. I hesitated before accepting. I knew that the job would be a tough one, requiring hundreds of hours of hard work with very meager financial compensation. I told them I would have to talk it over with my partners, and, if I took the job, would need to get the help of some lawyer who knew the facts and had assisted in the criminal prosecution. When I returned to New York that night, there was a message from George Z. Medalie, whom I had known for years. He strongly suggested that I take Tom Dewey as my assistant, adding that he was an able and alert young lawyer who knew the facts from

A to Z, and said that Dewey wanted to come to see me that very night. Although I was tired, Dewey came to my house, urged me to take the job, and said that he would work like a dog with me. After solving some "conflict of interest" problems, my partners agreed, and I started to work on the case immediately.

Five years later, in March of 1938, the United States Supreme Court decided that Mitchell had to pay the tax, as well as the 50 per cent fraud penalty.

What happened in these five years? Why does it take so long to get a final decision? What do lawyers do when they try a case like this? * The story is worth telling rather fully because it typifies a hard-fought case.

Well, the first thing one must do is to learn the facts and study the law. You must learn ALL the facts. Everything you can possibly find out. What will be the facts used at the trial? This is what will really determine whether you win or lose your case. You have to look at every piece of paper. You have to see every possible witness. You have to know everything before you know what you will really need at the trial. And beyond the facts of the case, you need to know a great deal about the other fellow. I had never seen Mitchell, for instance, and knew nothing about him except what I had read. I wanted to study him, to find out a little more about him.

Stockholders had brought a suit against Mitchell, claiming

---

* Our opponents, incidentally, were William Wallace and Leonard P. Moore, who later became a judge of the Circuit Court of Appeals. During the long litigations that followed, I grew to be a good friend of opposing counsel, and I still regard Judge Moore as a warm friend.

Making friends with other lawyers is one of the real privileges of our profession. I am told that the fact that we are cast in adversary roles helps prevent lawyers from having feuds with their rivals, as is often the case in other professions. My brother once wrote me about another lawyer who told him that he had learned to make friends with a lawyer who licks him, because such lawyer must be a "damn good one." "Some modest guy!" my brother wrote. Generally, I don't wait until the guy has licked me. But I've also learned not to have lunch with opposing counsel during a trial. Once when I did this, my client regarded it with suspicion when the jury came in with a verdict against him. To the client, everybody on the other side, and particularly the other lawyer, is an enemy.

damages for what they called mismanagement. I thought it would be helpful to see how he acted under examination and cross-examination, and I decided to sit in on the trial. I am very glad I did, because it taught me a lot about the man and gave me more facts about my own case. During recesses, I got to chatting with Mitchell in the hall. He told me that he had gone to Amherst and wanted to be a lawyer, but that he hadn't been able to afford it. He also told me how much he admired Steuer, and said that when he was on trial in the criminal case, he and Steuer clicked together perfectly, particularly when he was on the witness stand and Steuer was examining him. They usually tried to end the morning session with some telling point that would make a good headline for the afternoon papers, because nothing in the afternoon sessions would be in time for the afternoon papers. Right at the end of the day was another good spot to get something in evidence with a view to the morning headlines. One of the issues in the stockholders' trial was Mitchell's motive for negotiating for the purchase by the National City Bank of the stock of the Corn Exchange Bank. He wanted to make the point that although the National City was well known to large depositors here and abroad, it was not well known to small depositors. Here's how he put that point across: He said it was profitable for a bank to have large numbers of small depositors, but that it took years to build up such a business, requiring the opening of branches throughout the town. This demanded continual advertising and contacts with the public. Therefore it was much better to acquire an existing bank if one could be found. He was explaining all this in the quiet but convincing manner which had helped to make him Wall Street's greatest salesman. By this time everybody in the courtroom was listening attentively to every word he said. Then he began to ask himself some questions: What bank is there that has dozens of branches and is well known in every part of town? What bank has depositors from every walk of life? What bank's name is advertised everywhere, in newspapers, on the subways, on calendars that one sees in homes, in offices, even in courtrooms? And now he was looking straight at the Corn Exchange Bank calendar on the wall just over the Judge's head. At that moment, the clock was pointing to two minutes to one. It was time to adjourn—with every eye in the room looking at that calendar.

It wasn't such a wonderful story for the papers, but he did magnificently. You couldn't help admiring him or liking the man.

You not only have to know your own case, but you have to remember that the fellow on the other side knows a lot more about the case than you ever will. He lived through it long before it was a case, and in court he will tell only those facts he thinks will help him. He doesn't have to tell the other facts. He only has to answer the questions that the lawyers ask him. You can be sure that he won't tell everything he knows unless you ask him about everything.

In this case, there were hundreds of facts. At the criminal trial, they had had many witnesses and more exhibits. But there were literally thousands of other papers and documents that never became exhibits. It was very fortunate for me to have Tom Dewey's help. He had gone through all these papers before and during the criminal trial, he knew all the essential facts, and he was eager to help.

What were these facts?

In 1929 Mitchell had received $3,489,000 from the National City Bank. After the big crash, when he was going over figures at the end of the year to calculate his income tax, Mitchell decided that $666,666.67 of that—which was the amount he had received from the National City Company in July as his share of the Management Fund—wasn't income. Business wasn't so good in the second half of 1929 and maybe someday he would be asked to pay back what he had got from the Fund in the first half. That's why, he said, he didn't even mention it in his tax return. His next problem then was to reduce the rest of his income so that he would avoid paying any tax at all. He did so by deducting what he said was "a loss of that amount." This was accomplished by making a "sale" to his wife, Elizabeth, of 18,000 shares of National City Bank stock, enough to give him his needed loss, and documented it by writing her a letter "registering" the sale to her of the 18,000 shares. So his tax return showed no income, and he paid no tax.

Today, no such easy road is open. After the Mitchell case, Congress closed this loophole. Now, losses on sales cannot be offset against regular income. Such losses can be offset only against gains on sales, and even then losses on sales to members of the family are *verboten* for tax purposes, whether or not the loss is a legitimate one.

It was our job to establish that, even under the old law, Mitchell's sale to his wife was a fake and the $666,666.67 was taxable income. And, since this had all happened years before, unless we could prove that Mitchell's tax return had been fraudulent it would be too late to collect the tax, because the statute of limitations provided that after six years a return could not be questioned unless it was fraudulent. In other words, we had to show that in spite of the fact that Mitchell had been found "not guilty" of attempting to evade the tax, the deficiency we were attempting to collect was due to "fraud." Obviously, this required considerable study of the law and the upsetting of some past legal precedents, including one by the Supreme Court, which had already decided the other way * and according to the Treasury Counsel barred the suit. F.D.R. said we should have this decision overruled, but that wasn't so easy.

Several able Government agents were assigned to us, and all the papers from the criminal trial were made available. I learned as much as I could from these papers, but realized that Mitchell still knew very much more about the case than we did. It seemed to me that it was essential to find something new, something not disclosed at the criminal trial. I told Dewey that he must come up with something of that nature—maybe something that Mitchell had forgotten—to use when we cross-examined him. Dewey agreed in principle, but said there was nothing of that nature.

During that summer, my family was at Martha's Vineyard and Dewey's at Tuxedo. We lived at my house on East Seventy-fourth Street, where we worked evenings after we finished our regular day's work at our offices. From time to time, I needled Tom about getting that new bit of evidence. One night he

---

* *Coffey* v. *United States,* 116 U.S. 436.

produced it! In a paper, which later became Exhibit YYY,
Mitchell had sworn that in 1927 his wife's personal property was
worth not $30,000, as assessed, but only $5,000, that her jewelry
and all her other personal effects were only worth that amount.
I was delighted and excited. This could be just what we were
looking for. It was especially important because Mitchell was
contending that at that time his wife could well afford to buy
the bank stock from him at a price of $3,800,000, as she had a
great deal of property, including large quantities of jewelry.
Tom Dewey's find gave us a very useful weapon for the trial.

Our first court battle was to be in Washington before the Tax
Court—then called the Board of Tax Appeals. We worked hard
and long to get ready for it. Finally, we started, on April 30,
1934, before three judges: Ted C. Adams, W. C. Lansdon and
Ernest H. Van Fossan, the Board members assigned to this
hearing.

We had all the papers arranged in separate file cabinets,
which we brought into court so that we could lay our hands
on anything we needed almost immediately. The cards were
coded under headings like "Sale to Elizabeth," "Management
Fund," and gave us a quick key to what we needed. The papers
and filing cabinets were under the supervision of Dorothy L.
Shereff, who was then my very capable secretary, and several
times during the trial when Mitchell answered a question and
saw her walk over to the file cabinet, he would suddenly say,
"Wait a minute, I may want to correct that . . ." Tom and I
had agreed that I was to carry the ball principally on the sale
and he on the Management Fund, although we had both worked
on each of these subjects. But it was not until we were on the
train to Washington that we made the final decision as to trial
procedure. I would cross-examine Mitchell and Mrs. Mitchell,
and Tom would take most of the others. He was obviously disappointed not to cross-examine the Mitchells, but he was a good
soldier and made no complaint.

Mitchell was the first witness. He told his story plausibly and
well. When it came my turn to cross-examine him, Mrs. Mitchell's assets were the first thing I took up. He had said that in
1929 she was worth around $1,000,000, including personal prop-

erty of $150,000 and jewelry worth about $85,000. Then I showed him a piece of paper and asked, "In whose handwriting are the words 'Elizabeth R. Mitchell'?" He answered, "That is my handwriting." Exhibit YYY, in which Mitchell swore that in 1927 the value of his wife's jewelry was only $5,000 and that she had no other personal assets, was then put in evidence. We had scored our first point.

Mitchell had not seen, and probably had not thought of, that piece of paper since he had signed it seven years before. He hadn't known what was on it until after it went in evidence, and he wanted to get a look at it. In answer to a question I put, he told the court that he "certainly" did make a distinction between an actual sale and a sale to register a loss. I quickly jumped to another subject, and he asked for a brief recess. He told me later that his mind went completely blank and he needed time.

At the trial we were able to prove these facts: Realizing that he had a large income in December, 1929, Mitchell determined not to report the $666,666.67. He then figured that he had to take a loss of about $2,872,000 to wipe out the rest of his income. That's how he decided how many shares of stock he would "sell" to Elizabeth. So he signed a letter to her and the stock was "sold." Since the stock was then pledged by Mitchell for a loan at J. P. Morgan and Company, he was unable to deliver the stock to her. Not only didn't she get the stock, but she gave him no written note or other legal obligation.

In January of 1930, at the stockholders' meeting of the corporation, Mitchell was asked if he had sold any stock and he answered, "Not a single share." To meet the interest payments on the money his wife "owed" him, *he* gave *her* presents on all kinds of occasions, including his own birthday. With them she paid him "interest." And in March, 1932, when the stock was continuing to go down, Mitchell thought up a claim to make against the National City Company. He sent it on with a letter from a law firm giving its opinion that the National City Company was obligated to pick up Mitchell's stock at cost. He did not mention in this letter, nor did he tell his own counsel, that he had "sold" the shares to Mrs. Mitchell. Shortly after he presented the claim, and before it had been acted on, Mitchell "bought" the stock back from Mrs. Mitchell at $212 a share, although the market then was only $45 a share. At that time, he was broke and in the red to the tune of about $3,000,000. He then became the "owner" of the 18,000 shares, with a claim against his company for the original cost. The company got an opinion from the great John W. Davis himself, who said that he could see no basis for Mitchell's claim. The claim was no longer pressed.

We proved these and other facts about the "sale" to Elizabeth and that Mitchell had received the $666,666.67 from the Management Fund on July 1, 1929. At the company's board meeting on December 30, 1929, at which Mitchell presided, it was resolved that the amounts paid on the Management Fund in the first half of 1929 should be repaid only out of any amounts to which the parties "may be entitled" in any subsequent year. Mitchell never paid any of it back, although he did receive money from the Management Fund in future years, including $383,000 in 1930. The company never tried to get the 1929 money back and never even asked for it.

After we finished proving our case, we filed briefs. Long after, in August, 1935, the case was decided. We had won! The decision was given by the full Board of Tax Appeals, consisting of sixteen members. Judge Van Fossan was the only one of the Board members who originally heard the case who was still on the court. Since the hearing, Judge Adams had died and Judge Lansdon retired. Van Fossan held that the transaction was a sham, a mere pretense, conceived and carried out with a fraudulent purpose to avoid taxes. He decided that the Management Fund payment was taxable income "beyond question," and the action taken in December, 1929, by Mitchell was characterized as "the employment of deliberate artifice to give color to his fantastic action in not reporting the payment for taxation. They appear as mere gestures lacking in the sphere of reliability, that which distinguishes the genuine from the pretended." It was held that the omission of this item from income was fraudulent. Mitchell was ordered to pay a tax of $850,000 and a 50 per cent penalty. Van Fossan's opinion and that of the other judges consumed sixty-six printed pages. The opinions were far from unanimous and included a statement that the earlier Coffey case, decided by the Supreme Court, completely barred any action against Mitchell.

Mitchell was ready to continue the fight and decided to take it to the Circuit Court of Appeals. Tom Dewey had now become Special Prosecutor for the County of New York and could no longer work on the case. Robert H. Jackson was now Solicitor General, and he assigned Department of Justice aides to work with me on the appeal. Getting the brief together was not an easy job, but we finally argued the appeal in January of 1937 before Judges Augustus N. Hand, Thomas Swan, and Harrie B. Chase. At the beginning of my argument I referred to the fact that Mitchell had paid no income tax at all for 1929 although he made about as much in one day, including holidays, as any of the three judges made in an entire year. Judge Hand (properly, I guess) reprimanded me for this statement. However, I could see the judges on either side of Judge Hand doing some figuring on a piece of paper, showing it to Hand, and whispering to him.

It was in May that this court decided the case. The Court held that it was bound by the facts and that there was substantial evidence that the Management Fund was income and that the loss on the sale to the wife was not genuine. The omission of the first item and the deduction of the second were, according to the Court, fraudulent attempts to evade taxes. Mrs. Mitchell's purchase of the stock was described as "highly improbable, if not fantastic." As to the Management Fund payment, the Court said, "we can imagine no legal ground for saying that it was not taxable income." But, coming to the main legal question, the Court held that the acquittal necessarily meant that Mitchell was guilty of no fraud. The Supreme Court's decision in the Coffey case, the Court said, required it to treat the imposition of the 50 per cent fraud penalty as barred by the prior acquittal. So the Court eliminated the penalty of $356,350 and affirmed the judgment without the penalty.

Now both sides were in the middle. Here it was decided by a high court that Mitchell's fraud penalty couldn't be collected, but he had to pay the tax in spite of the acquittal. Would the Government appeal?

The Solicitor General at this time was Stanley Reed, who later became a United States Supreme Court Justice. He decided that it was important for the Government to appeal the case. Indeed, he had to, to uphold F.D.R. But you can't appeal to the United States Supreme Court unless the Court gives you permission. Our next step was to ask for that. So here was another job, preparing the papers for what is called a writ of certiorari. Our petition for this writ ended with the statement that "public policy demands that the Government should be free to proceed by criminal action without forfeiting its right to the collection of any additional tax which may be found to be due." At the same time, Mitchell asked for certiorari to review the question as to whether he had to pay any tax. The Supreme Court considered our arguments and decided to hear the Government's appeal, but refused to hear Mitchell's.

That was fine. Now we could get a final decision from the Supreme Court. But another round lay ahead. We had to get our brief ready for the Supreme Court. It's tough enough preparing a brief for any court, but the ones for the United States Supreme Court are much the hardest. These cases not only involve difficult questions, but important ones—questions which are to determine the law for the entire country. A newly appointed Supreme Court Justice recently told me of the deep sense of responsibility he felt when he realized how much regard the courts all over the world have for the opinions of the United States Supreme Court.

When the Government has a case before the Supreme Court, the counsel who is to argue the case has to wear a frock coat. I didn't have one. But I managed to borrow one from my brother-in-law, who never explained to me where he had gotten it! Government counsel also had to go through something like a dress rehearsal, in which members of the Department of Justice take the part of Supreme Court Justices and hear the arguments and question counsel. Thurman Arnold was one of the assistants who was of great help. He was asked to develop a point he had made and talk it out further the next day. But he had the same difficulty that I had had in sustaining the point, and we had to abandon it. I do not know if such rehearsals are still conducted, but it is a most valuable technique, and I'd like to see it done in private practice.

During this performance, no one took the part of Justice Hugo L. Black, who had just become a member of the Court. No one in the Department seemed to think that he would ask anything that wouldn't be easy to answer. But were they wrong! Very soon after I started arguing he began his questions, and they were by all means the toughest questions that anyone asked. Almost my entire time before the Court was taken up by the Court's questions and my answers. When my time was up, Chief Justice Charles E. Hughes, without any request from me, told me that because of this I could take as much additional time as I wanted. I deeply appreciated this unusual and gracious action, but only took a little while because I felt that I had succeeded in making my main points while answering the questions which the Court had asked.

Finally, in March, 1938, the Supreme Court decision came down.* We had won! The Court held that Mitchell not only had to pay his tax but the 50 per cent penalty as well. The opinion was written by Justice Louis D. Brandeis. He held that the acquittal was no bar to the fraud penalty. It was merely an adjudication that the proof on the criminal trial had not been sufficient to overcome all reasonable doubt of guilt. "It did not determine that Mitchell had not willfully attempted to evade the tax," he decided. He also said, "Nor was the proceeding banned under the doctrine of double jeopardy." The Court held that "the additional tax was not a criminal penalty," because in collecting its income tax, "the Government relies primarily upon the disclosure by the taxpayer of the relevant facts," and that "to insure full and honest disclosure, to discourage fraudulent attempts to evade tax, Congress imposes sanctions. The sanctions may be either criminal or civil, and in this case it was civil and not imposed as a penalty but to reimburse the Government for the heavy expenses needed to collect the tax

---

* *Helvering* v. *Mitchell,* 303 U.S. 391.

when misstatements have been made." Accordingly, the Court held that the Coffey decision did not apply.

All the Justices agreed except Justice James C. McReynolds. Justice Stanley F. Reed didn't participate because he had been connected with the case before he was a member of the Court, nor did Justice Benjamin N. Cardozo, maybe because he knew me.

And that was that! Long days and nights of work, weeks of investigation and brief writing, days of testimony, hours of arguments in all the courts were over.

The day after the Supreme Court decided the case, I got a letter from my client, the President of the United States, expressing appreciation for what he called my "contribution to the public service." He referred to the fact that Mitchell had been ordered to pay taxes of over $1,000,000, and added "but the amounts involved are not important. The Government's challenge of the practice to which Mr. Mitchell resorted in this case has served largely to end these practices." The highest court in the land had decided that whether or not a taxpayer made a lot of money or a little money, he still had to pay his tax.

VII

C.C.B. AND OTHER MATTERS

Soon after I started practicing law, my father told me that his friend "C.C.B." wanted to meet me. C.C.B. was Charles C. Burlingham, and he was an admiralty lawyer. I found that he knew everybody, at home and abroad, and he always wanted to meet all the new young lawyers. Soon he asked me to give him a list of names of lawyers to serve on a new committee that he was organizing. After several days' hard thinking, I called him up and started to give my names. They were something like these: John W. Davis, Charles Evans Hughes, Sol M. Stroock, Samuel Seabury, and—bang! He hung up. Several weeks later I saw him again. He told me that what he wanted from me were the names of lawyers that he'd never heard of, and that I should try again and give him a new list with a summary telling something about each person. That was the beginning of a relationship that developed into a warm friendship which lasted until his death at the age of over one hundred in 1959.

He was very handsome, and, although not a young man, he was youthful looking, with a small, grey, stylish moustache. There was a sprightly, bad-boy quality about him that was delightful and completely captivating. This devilish quality made it easy to understand how everybody (or nearly everybody) fell for him. When he came into a room, things were different. When he was at a meeting, it was fun. He could not tolerate stupidity or indifference. And, somehow, the dumb and dull didn't exist for him.

He led the Bar Association campaign in 1920 to support George W. Alger and Bernard S. Deutsch for the State Supreme Court against Aaron Steuer and Samuel H. Hofstadter, who had been nominated by both the Republican and Democratic parties. It was practically impossible to beat this odds-on Republican-Democratic combination, particularly in a Presidential year. But C.C.B. felt that it was necessary to fight what had been done—the sudden joint nomination of Hofstadter, the Republican state senator, who was the chairman of a legislative committee investigating New York City political activities, and Steuer, the son of a leading Democratic organization lawyer. I believe this was the only time the Bar Association ever put on a real fight in a political contest. Candidates were nominated on an Independent Judges ticket; the Bar Association building was used as campaign headquarters; and the Association raised a campaign fund, and rounded up lawyers and other citizens, men and women, to work on the judicial campaign. Although we couldn't win against two candidates who had the combined support of both the Democratic and Republican parties, the Association's Independent Judges Party scored more votes on the ballot than any other party, thus entitling it to first place on the ballot at the following election. Its votes exceeded those cast for Herbert Hoover for President. But to C.C.B.'s disgust, the lawyers did nothing to follow up, and there was no Independent Judges ticket on the ballot the next fall.

It was during this campaign that C.C.B. showed the vigor, enthusiasm, energy, and humor that drew me and other young lawyers to him. These qualities, along with his resourcefulness and skill, later made him the highly effective manager of La-Guardia's campaign for mayor. C.C.B. was the real leader of the Fusion movement and was truly the conscience of the city in many, many other matters. Virtually unknown to the public, he was the "First Citizen of New York" to the New York *Times* and the *Herald Tribune*.

Although he was president of the Bar Association and served in many other offices, he often did his most effective work unofficially. Once I was on a typical committee that Burlingham had appointed. He liked these *ad-hoc* committees best since they could act without waiting for approval by the Executive Committee of the Bar Association or without having to comply with by-laws. This particular committee was concerned with the operation of the jury system in the Supreme Court in New York County, and C.C.B. was our inspiration and help all the way through. In each trial part, a jury panel reported every morning, and the jury for that day's trial was impaneled in that courtroom. Each judge played to a full house. All the other jurors waited around. It seemed obvious to all of us that time was being wasted and that there should be one central part from which jurors could be selected for all courts and sent out to the other parts. After many meetings and long arguments, the Presiding Justice of the Appellate Division had finally agreed to try out our plan for next year. At Mr. Burlingham's persuasion, the Judge told us to send him an order to sign. Naturally, we were delighted, and I was given the task of drafting the order and sending it to him. I did so. He was then on his summer vacation, and a few days later I received the order back with a letter from him saying that several things were wrong with it. I was sunk and phoned C.C.B. As I was reading him the letter, he interrupted and asked me if it was in longhand. I didn't understand what he was getting at. Then he asked again. Was it typewritten or in longhand? When I told him longhand, he said, "That's fine," and it dawned on me that he was glad that the Judge had no copy of his letter. He told me to write a letter thanking the Judge and saying that I had spoken to C.C.B. about it and was changing the order. He then told me to make a couple of unimportant changes and return the redrafted order. I did so and soon received it back signed by the P.J. The central panel was put into effect for a one-year test, and as far as I know, it is still operating under that order.

This was just one of many things C.C.B. taught me. Know what you want. Get it done. There's no need to advertise it. It's much easier to do if someone else gets the credit.

Years later, while scheming with him on another plan, we

wanted to get the reaction of F.D.R., who was then President. C.C.B. wrote to him and was a bit mad at the President, whom he had known from boyhood, for not replying. When I was up at his house, he decided to call up the President; in a minute he was talking to the White House and then to the President. C.C.B. complained that he had not received an answer to his letter. I could, of course, hear only one side of the conversation, but gathered that the President said that he had replied. C.C.B. admitted that he had received a letter from the President, but it was on another subject and said nothing about our matter. Apparently the President told him that it was all in the same letter, which C.C.B. denied, adding that he never finished reading the letter because it was "silly." I heard laughing at the other end of the wire. C.C.B. promised that he would read the letter and get in touch with the President again. After finishing this official conversation, in which he was using the words "Mr. President" all the time, he completely changed his tone and started on another subject: "Now, Franklin, my boy, I want to tell you something." More laughter at the other end of the phone, followed by a full and frank critique by C.C.B. of some important Administration policy. The call ended by the President's inviting him down to the White House for a visit, and a time was arranged.

C.C.B. then dug F.D.R.'s letter out of a pile of correspondence on his desk. Sure enough, about six pages of the unread letter related to our subject. Who else would not even finish reading a long letter from the President of the United States in reply to his own because it started off on a subject that looked "silly"?

It was C.C.B. who besides getting me to work on projects that he had started encouraged me to start things on my own. He would come to meetings, lend his name to any efforts he deemed worth-while, help raise money, and generally give his thought and prestige to whatever he felt was important or valuable. He wrote innumerable notes to those who could help. His style was to enclose them in return envelopes that had come in his mail, which he would readdress to me and others. It was he who kept me going on many projects. Nothing fazed him, and he would not let anything faze me.

To me, Charles C. Burlingham embodied the highest values

in our profession, and I truly believe that it was my association with him over the years that inspired me to keep working on law reform, which I have done virtually all of my professional career. As a lawyer, I am proud to be a member of a profession dedicated to the administration of justice. Our courts are created for that purpose and truly strive to carry it out. Their work is done by a body of men—judges and lawyers—devoted to this task. Most of them give themselves wholeheartedly to it. Yet, the machinery of our law in almost every phase of its administration, including the manner in which its judges are chosen, lacks efficiency, operates clumsily, and cries out for improvement. I fully realize the seriousness of what I have just said and do not say it lightly. Later in this book, I shall speak more about this and attempt to support these statements.

In addition to the strictly legal work of the office, most good lawyers are busy on many outside activities. If they are lawyers in the true sense of the word, they are naturally much interested in many of the things that go on in their community. It is this interest in the world around them that originally led them to become lawyers, and it is their neighbors' awareness of the lawyers' sensitivity to community affairs that brings them to lawyers to talk about these matters and to get help when they have troubles of their own. My partners are good examples. My brother Laurie was active in the affairs of his community in Westchester County—in Democratic politics, social activities, and other public affairs. He was instrumental in founding the Quaker Ridge Golf Club and the Beach Point Club, and became president of both. For many years he was a member of the New York State Social Welfare Board and was appointed its chairman by both Governors Herbert H. Lehman and Thomas E. Dewey. My partner, Herbert A. Wolff, succeeded my brother as chairman of the Social Welfare Board, and during the war Herb also served on the Draft Appeal Board. He has been active in the Ethical Culture Society and has served as its president. He has done a great deal of legal work for this organization, including participating in cases before the United States Supreme Court relating to the question of whether belief in God is a requisite to being a notary public or to eligibility as a conscientious objector. Another partner, Morris L. Ernst, has given much of his time to public work, and besides being a member of many official boards and agencies, he has written widely on civil liberties, censorship, and kindred subjects. Similar work has been done by Leo Rosen, Harriet Pilpel and other partners, including William Wolff. Bill's recent death was a tremendous loss to all of us. He was a man of brilliant legal mind, with an enchanting, warm personality.

My own public service was, I suppose, stimulated by the example of my parents. My mother gave much time to community activities, and my father was involved in a variety of activities, including the founding of the Federation of Jewish Philanthropies of New York, and he was the first president of its predecessor, the Federation of Jewish Philanthropic Societies. He was also a founder and trustee of the New York Public Library, which was a consolidation of the Lenox, Astor and Tilden libraries along with many smaller libraries throughout the city, including the Aguilar Free Library, on East Fifty-eight Street, headed by my father. The huge building erected by the New York Public Library, from Fortieth to Forty-second Street on Fifth Avenue, and Bryant Park to the west took the place of the old reservoir, which used to occupy the area running over to Sixth Avenue (now the Avenue of the Americas).

My interest in public affairs was also aroused by Felix Warburg, a great friend of my father's, who lived just two blocks away from us. (His house, on the southeast corner of Fifth Avenue and Ninety-second Street, is now the Jewish Museum.) When I was in law school, he got together a small group of young men and women, including Arthur Sulzberger and David Heyman, for the purpose of getting us actively interested in philanthropic work in the city. We met at his home on Saturday afternoons and he told us what he, as one person, had done in the community life of New York City. He was a very real person, with a great sense of humor, and we were all very fond of him. He had five children of his own and must have liked young people. Although we knew that he was a very distinguished person, we were never ill at ease with him and it was fun being with him. He was very handsome and, with his elegant black moustache, gave the impression of being just what he was—an aristocratic member of the distinguished German banking family of

131 East Eightieth Street
(second house from right) around
the turn of the century

Laurie and Eddie Greenbaum,
January, 1894

Judge Samuel Greenbaum

March into Germany, November, 1918

PHOTO BY U.S. ARMY SIGNAL CORPS

Selina Greenbaum

131 East Eightieth Street
(second house from right) around
the turn of the century

Laurie and Eddie Greenbaum,
January, 1894

Judge Samuel Greenbaum

March into Germany, November, 1918

PHOTO BY U.S. ARMY SIGNAL CORPS

Lieutenant Colonel Charles C. Teare,
Fourth Division Judge Advocate,
and his assistant,
Major Edward Greenbaum,
in Germany during World War I

PHOTO BY U.S. ARMY SIGNAL CORPS

Dorothea Greenbaum, holding hammered-head sculpture "The Breeze," at Martha's Vineyard

NORTH AMERICAN AVIATION, INC., INGLEWOOD, CALIF.

North American Aviation strike in June, 1941, before Army take-over

North American Aviation strikers after Army take-over

NORTH AMERICAN AVIATION, INC., INGLEWOOD, CALIF.

Herman Oliphant

C.C. Burlingham

Undersecretary of War Robert P. Patterson, at Camp Lee in 1943

PHOTO BY U.S. ARMY SIGNAL CORPS

Undersecretary Patterson, General Charles de Gaulle, General Henry ("Hap") Arnold, at dinner given by Patterson in 1944 in honor of De Gaulle

Brigadier General Greenbaum and Thomas A. Knight greeting Undersecretary Patterson at Army Service Forces Conference in Dallas, 1944

General Mark Clark
and Edward Greenbaum,
outside Firenzuola
during the Italian cam-
paign, September, 1944

Brigadier General Greenbaum, Secretary of War Patterson,
Major General Leslie R. Groves, at Army-E awards ceremony
in Oak Ridge, Tennessee, soon after Hiroshima

PHOTO BY U.S. ARMY SIGNAL CORPS

Jack Madigan receiving a civilian award from Secretary Patterson for his contribution to the war effort

Dorothea and Edward Greenbaum, outside her studio in Princeton

Warburg and the son-in-law of Jacob H. Schiff, the head of Kuhn, Loeb and Company. Our meetings were very practical ones. Each week he invited a different person to tell us about the work of his organization. For instance, I remember one week Edward T. Devine told us about the Charity Organization Society (now the Community Service Society), and we followed it up with a visit there. The result was that with a little urging, Mr. Warburg soon had all of us working for some institution. He must have used similar means on his own children, because each one of them has done extremely useful work in a variety of organizations throughout the city.

I went to the Federation Settlement on East 105th Street and became director of one of the boys' clubs, although I wasn't much older than some of the boys. It was called the Tro Club, and I was active with this club for many years, including staying with the boys after they were told by the Settlement they were too old to be there. They then took a clubroom on their own, and I remained as their director. I learned a great deal about neighborhood and political activities from this experience, though it only occurred to me later on how significant it was that both the local Democratic leader and the Republican leader had arranged to be honorary members of the club.

I then got interested in Surprise Lake Camp, a boys' camp at Cold Spring-on-the-Hudson founded by the YMHA and the Educational Alliance. But the divided ownership and management had led to difficulties, resulting in the suggestion that the camp be run by an outside group. My father, as president of the Educational Alliance, and Mr. Warburg, representing the YMHA, picked Herbert H. Lehman, Henry Morgenthau, Jr., and me to run the camp. I was made chairman, and we soon found that we had a very big responsibility.

Our first piece of business was to change the name from Educational Alliance-YMHA Camp to Surprise Lake Camp. After considerable opposition from both boards of directors, this was done, and the removal of the hyphen soon made the camp a unified operation. It has remained so ever since, and with the cooperation and help of some of its former campers, including Eddie Cantor, the camp has become outstanding.

My activities with the camp led me into the Big Brothers, and from there to the Jewish Board of Guardians, which we consolidated from a group of miscellaneous organizations including Hawthorne School, Cedar Knolls School, and Lake View Home for unmarried mothers on Staten Island.

But the community activity which took most of my time was the Survey Committee of the American Jewish Committee. During the early thirties, most Jews in this country suffered tremendous emotional experiences. I certainly did. Even though we did not understand what was actually going on in Germany, we knew enough to be alarmed. I felt that I wanted to do something to prevent anything similar from happening here. But I did not know what.

One day Lewis Strauss, whom I had known for years, said he wanted to talk to me about all this. He told me that the American Jewish Committee, which my father had helped organize years before to uphold the rights of Jews, wanted to start an active group who would devote themselves to the task of combating anti-Semitism in this country. He said that if a young and active group would attack this problem, the A.J.C. would make the necessary money available. It was a challenge, a very real one. I thought hard about it and decided that I would be willing to work on such a group. But I did not know what we should do or how we should go about it. I felt that certain things were essential before we could formulate any plan. First, we should get others of our age—in their early forties—with the time and ability to put in who would agree to serve. We would resign from all other committees and give as much as half of our time to this work. We would meet whenever necessary, and break other dates for that purpose. We would take turns being chairman of the group for three months each. Lewis said he would join if I would be the first chairman. I agreed, and we went to work assembling a group of men and women of the highest caliber.*

We started at the offices of the A.J.C., deciding first to try

---

* See Nathan Schachner, *The Price of Liberty.* Carl J. Austrian, Alfred L. Bernheim, Harold Guinzburg, Lucile Heming, Newman Levy, James Marshall, Walter Mendelsohn, Richard C. Rothschild, Alan M. Stroock, David H. Sulzberger, and Ethel H. Wise were among the initial group. Most of the men were lawyers.

to find out all we could about our problem and then—and not until then—to tackle it. We determined to try to remain objective, realizing that there was a good deal of hysteria among Jews and Jewish groups working on this problem. The Anti-Defamation League and the American Jewish Congress were among these groups. They had a very great emotional urge to do something—it didn't matter what—but very little idea of what to do and even less of how to do it.

At the start we recognized that there were different types of anti-Semitism. First, there was what might be called "social" anti-Semitism, reflected in the restrictive policies of clubs and summer hotels. Then there was the "economic" type that attracted frustrated, out-of-work men, who were the easy prey of rabble-rousers seeking a scapegoat—alien, Catholic, or Jew. We felt that there was little we could do about these types, but the third dimension of anti-Semitism, then coming out of Hitler's Germany, was very much our concern. This was a new political anti-Semitism that was being used as the emotional spearhead for a world-wide Nazi program. It sought to make people aware of a mythical "Jewish menace" and to import into this country the paranoid idea that the issue was civilization versus the Jews. If one accepts this sort of thinking, Jews are classed as enemies of mankind and anti-Semites as its defenders. Although every intelligent person knows this to be false, in those days there was a great temptation for Jewish groups to answer all the charges thrown at them and thus play into Nazi hands by making this spurious issue the main concern. The real point was, of course, what all this implied, what the Nazis were really fighting—religion, the Bill of Rights, democracy itself.

It was our task, therefore, to stand shoulder to shoulder with all our fellow citizens in defense of the principles our country was founded to uphold. Instead of a defensive policy that would be both self-indulgent and weak, we determined to remember that most Americans were on our side; we would continue to be proud of our traditions, as Americans and as Jews, and we would do everything within our power to defend the American way of life, the rights of freedom of speech, freedom of religion, and all the other democratic tenets which the Nazis were attacking.

In 1938 the German-American Nazi Bund scheduled a mass meeting to be held on Washington's Birthday in Madison Square Garden. The leader of this group was a character named Fritz Kuhn. This meeting aroused a great deal of excitement; the Garden was picketed, and there was real feeling that the meeting should not be allowed, even among the board of directors of the Garden. General John Reed Kilpatrick, who was then president of Madison Square Garden, came to see me—not because I was chairman of this Survey Committee, but because I was a Jew and an old friend of his. The week before he had rented Madison Square Garden to the Communists, and he didn't see any reason why the Nazi group shouldn't have it, provided they broke no laws. I told him that I agreed with him, and that it was our feeling on the American Jewish Committee that if we truly believed in democracy and freedom of speech, that meant freedom of speech for the other fellow too. The Nazi meeting was held. At the end of the Garden hung a huge portrait of George Washington, surrounded by streamers, swastikas, and other insignia of the Nazi Bund. Fritz Kuhn stood beneath the portrait, and in his very harsh accent he talked about "the Chews." This speech was broadcast on a national radio network. Everyone had an opportunity to hear the man, and the next morning newspapers throughout the country reported the meeting, mostly with pictures on the front page. In my opinion, this wide coverage finished Fritz Kuhn and his Bund once and for all, just as effectively as TV exposure later annihilated Senator McCarthy.*

We tried, without much success, to persuade the other Jewish organizations to control their righteous indignation, even under the stimulus of vicious attack and, instead, to work with other

---

* At the end of the year, Kilpatrick was given *The Nation's* award for civil liberties. He never understood why he got it, and felt that he only did what any decent citizen would do. I wrote the *Times* about this when the General died in May, 1960. (This was the same Kilpatrick who played on our baseball team when we were kids and was later to become the famous All-America football player from Yale. In World War II he did an outstanding job as commanding general of the Port of Embarkation at Newport News, and I was with him there on V-E Day.)

American groups in opposing anti-Semitism as a threat not only to Jews but to Americans as a whole. But the Jewish War Veterans picketed the Fritz Kuhn Madison Square Garden meeting, and most other Jewish groups opposed it. Similarly, when Gerald L. K. Smith became active in this field, his meetings usually led to picketing and protests, which simply advertised him and his ideas. We preferred to ignore Smith, or to make fun of him when we could. When Smith's "Committee of One Million" met on Martha's Vineyard, my friend McAlister Coleman wrote in the *Vineyard Gazette:* "The Committee of One Million met last night. Only eleven could be present." That fairly well indicates how it was treated on the Vineyard. More people quoted these lines than anything that Gerald L. K. Smith said that night.

But it was not easy to impress other Jewish groups with this fundamental approach. To them, it sounded as if we wanted to hide the fact that we were Jews (that's a hard one to do, even if it made sense, which it doesn't), and our attitude gave very little opportunity for the emotional appeal of a picket line or a parade. We understood this and were willing to accept the fact that we would never have a large following, since our policy denied its adherents the emotional enjoyment necessarily attached to parades or mass meetings of Jews at Madison Square Garden. We felt, however, that the answer to the problem of anti-Semitism in the United States rested not with Jews but with non-Jews.

As part of our task, we also made it our business to do all we could to inform ourselves as fully as possible about everything that was happening among anti-democratic fronts and fifth columns, whether anti-Semitic, anti-Negro, anti-Catholic, or pro-Communist. This required a staff of highly qualified lawyers and professional help in the field of investigation, as well as the co-operation of the FBI and other governmental agencies. Thus we tried to bring the American people to an awareness of the true meaning of Nazism. We tried to show its totalitarian, anti-democratic nature, as well as its racist ideology. We sought and obtained the support of newspaper and magazine editors, columnists, broadcasters, church and women's organizations, labor unions, and veterans' groups.

Some idea of the magnitude of the effort may be gathered from the fact that, over a period of several years, an average of 400 radio stations a *day* carried ideas and material originating in our program, not to mention the countless magazine and newspaper exposés of Nazi methods and propaganda, together with the material supplied to dozens of old-line organizations that wished to join in the campaign to preserve American ideals and standards.

The results of the work as a whole, as with all campaigns of public education and information, are hard to appraise. Because one cannot turn back the clock and ascertain what would have happened with a different program, or no program at all, one cannot be sure of the effectiveness of what was done. We do know, however, that active anti-Semitism is no longer an urgent national problem today. We believe that the work of this Survey Committee, the first massive, unified campaign of public education on civil rights in this country, was well done and made a very real contribution to our democracy.

VIII

BACK IN THE ARMY

THE spring of 1940 was an unforgettable time for all of my generation. The war that had started in 1939 was changing from a "phony war" into something frightfully real. As everybody knows, the news from abroad was staggering. Suddenly, Hitler had taken Denmark, Holland, and Belgium. Nothing could stop him. Paris fell, and the complete destruction of the British troops was averted only by the miracle at Dunkirk. The invasion of England seemed next.

Driving up to Williamstown for our thirtieth class reunion, several of my classmates and I talked of nothing else. We asked ourselves what we could do to stop this drive if Hitler turned on us. How could German planes be kept from blitzkrieging our Eastern cities? How could we stop the Nazi tanks from taking over these beautiful green fields that we were driving through? How could we prevent them from taking that peaceful little village over there? What would become of our own Berkshire college town? While we had been thinking of other things for years, Hitler had mounted a vast war machine. Everything would go by default unless we could stop him. But how was that possible at this late date? The end of everything seemed near.

That summer brought the Battle of Britain and the story of
the heroism of those who fought it and of those who spent their
nights in the London Underground. These were the things that I
thought about while fishing in my old catboat in Martha's Vineyard. The only ray of hope was the new Prime Minister, Winston
Churchill, who talked to us about blood, sweat, toil and tears, and
told us, "We have before us many, many long months of struggle
and suffering."

I felt that the United States must get into the war eventually,
that we were utterly unprepared, and that it was high time for
everyone who could do anything to offer his services.

President Roosevelt then dramatically appointed Henry L.
Stimson as our Secretary of War and Robert P. Patterson as his
assistant. I wrote congratulating Patterson. He replied, referring
to me as an "old soldier" because I had been in the Seventy-
seventh Division with him. Not long after that I went to see
Patterson in Washington and told him that if he wanted me, I
would come. He said he did, and followed up my visit with a
letter saying he "needed me last week." My wife was working
in her studio downtown, and I phoned her to meet me at a drug-
store at Fortieth Street and Park Avenue. There I showed her
Patterson's letter. She knew how I had been feeling, read the
letter, gave me a kiss, and said she'd be ready to go whenever I
was. From that moment, a different life started for us both—but
first we had a soda—and within two weeks I was in the Army
again.

Patterson told me he wanted me in as an officer, not as a
civilian. As he put it, "You wouldn't go into the Justice Department except as a lawyer, would you?" This made it a bit tough,
but he was right. However, it was not so easy to get ordered to
active duty. I had been a Reserve officer in the Judge Advocate
General's Department, but they said they had no "vacancy" for
an active-duty officer. Patterson said he wanted me in uniform at
once, and he didn't care what branch of the service I was in.
After taking the same physical as a twenty-year-old boy, I was
finally commissioned a lieutenant colonel and ordered to active
duty in the Signal Corps. The only reason that I ended up in
the Signal Corps was that they had a vacancy—and I was color-
blind.

The day before I had agreed to report for duty, I was in Washington trying to help get the family settled and my younger son Dan entered in Landon, his new school. After leaving him there, I telephoned Patterson's office and was told to come down for lunch. I did so, and as my wife said, I didn't get home until more than five years later!

When he was appointed, Patterson was a judge of the United States Court of Appeals, the highest federal court in the country next to the Supreme Court. The Bar considered him an outstandingly able and vigorous lawyer, and he had been named to the court as a result of a suggestion made by a group of lawyers. As a judge, he increased the Bar's respect for him. But Patterson had another important asset for the job. He was a soldier—a doughboy—and he loved and respected the Army. The story is told that when Roosevelt appointed him Assistant Secretary of War, the Judge was on K.P. duty at a Citizens' Training Camp in Plattsburgh, New York. When told of his appointment, he said, "They could get lots better, but if they want me I'll go." Like many stories about Patterson, it was true. It was typical of him that in the summer of 1940, when Europe was falling apart, he was again training to be a soldier. He had served on the Mexican border and then with the Seventy-seventh Division throughout World War I. There he won the Distinguished Service Cross, and the respect and admiration of all those who served with him.

It was Grenville Clark, the law partner of Elihu Root, who had suggested to the President Stimson's appointment as Secretary of War. Stimson had previously held that position, and had also been Governor General of the Philippines and Secretary of State under Herbert Hoover, as well as serving as an artillery colonel in the Seventy-seventh Division. He had the experience, wisdom, and calm judgment needed to lead the Army through what lay ahead. But Clark knew it would be a grueling job for anyone, particularly for a man who was then seventy-three. He therefore suggested that Roosevelt also appoint Patterson as Assistant Secretary to take over much of the work that normally would be the Secretary's. On this condition Stimson had accepted, and his appointment was announced on June 20th and confirmed by the Senate on July 11th. But the President did

nothing about the Patterson appointment. Stimson got impatient
as the weeks went by and finally determined to take action.
What he did was the equivalent of telling the President he
would resign unless Patterson was promptly appointed. Mr.
Clark described it this way in a recent letter to me:

Although it had been firmly agreed that Patterson would be appointed, FDR procrastinated as to that by reason of his obligations
to Louis Johnson who was then Assistant Secretary and had expected
to be Secretary if Woodring went out. Finally after some weeks of
delay HLS got tired of it and asked me whether I agreed that something drastic must be done. When I did agree, he wrote in his handwriting on one sheet "I hereby appoint Robert P. Patterson Assistant
Secretary of War" with a space for the President's signature and on
another sheet attached to it "Mr. President, this appointment should
be signed today." Showing these to me, HLS asked my opinion as to
whether they were too strong medicine and when I said that I thought
them all right, he thought a while and then said, "What would you
think of my instructing the messenger who takes them to say that he
was told to wait for an answer?" I replied that this was equivalent
to his resigning if the appointment didn't come back that afternoon
but that I thought it was time to do it. Accordingly, the messenger
went with those instructions and about an hour later HLS asked me
to come to his room (at that time I had a room near his) and as I
came in merely held up the appointment with FDR's signature on it.*

As Assistant Secretary of War, Patterson was more than usually busy, since besides his own official duties, he was relieving
Stimson of many of the Secretary's normal tasks. Fortunately,
two other Assistant Secretaries were soon appointed: John J.
McCloy, another lawyer, was assigned to duty in Stimson's office,
and Robert A. Lovett, a banker who had also been a lawyer,
became Assistant Secretary for Air. Both had served in World
War I, McCloy overseas in the Seventy-seventh Field Artillery
of the Fourth Division, and Lovett as a flyer in the Air Corps.
These four men—incidentally, all Republicans—formed a team
that the country was very fortunate to have. They worked together night and day for five long years and supplied the firm
leadership needed for an Army that was to grow from 269,000
men in 1940 to more than 11,000,000 before the war was over.

---

* See Appendix, pp. 225–28, for the entire letter.

Patterson's statutory job was immediate and full-time. Congress had created the post of Assistant Secretary in 1861. Following World War I, Congress gave responsibility to the Assistant Secretary for "the supervision of the procurement of all military supplies and all other business of the War Department pertaining thereto." But the job went far beyond that and far beyond the War Department. For Congress also made it his task to assure "adequate provisions for the mobilization of material and industrial programs essential to wartime needs." When General Eisenhower was a major in the Assistant Secretary's Office in 1931, he had characterized this duty as "a task without parallel or precedent in any peacetime organization." This job, it should be noted, embraced the needs of the entire civilian population. For when war comes, civilian economy is vitally affected. You can't produce planes, ships, guns, ammunition, tanks, and other military requirements and still continue to manufacture the millions of automobiles and other goods that we normally use. Who is going to make the military matériel? Where? With what? To supply our military forces with their needs, the entire nation has to change its way of life. Many of the goods needed in wartime just don't exist; the Army has to make them, and in many cases it must even build the plants that will manufacture them. You can't follow the well-intentioned advice of one civilian working for the Army at the Volunteer Ordnance Works in Chattanooga who put this in the suggestion box: "If Uncle Sam needs this stuff so much, why doesn't he just go out and buy it?"

The task was gigantic, but it did not frighten Patterson, although neither he nor anyone else could have foreseen the ultimate size of the job ahead. Patterson well understood its importance, urgency, and magnitude. Here's how he described it: "We have a job to do that dwarfs anything ever before undertaken by this country. In the last World War our armies were equipped and armed by our Allies. This time it is the other way around. We must equip and arm our own Army and we must help in the equipping and arming of the armies of our Allies!"

During the period between wars, the Assistant Secretary's Office had been seeking to prepare for its statutory assignment. The Government had not taken this too seriously, and prac-

tically no money had been available to carry it out. The staff
that Patterson found when he took over was totally inadequate,
in both size and ability.

This was the fall of 1940. The War Department was in the
Munitions Building, on Constitution Avenue, which the Department had occupied "temporarily" since World War I. There was
no Pentagon. It hadn't even been thought of. There was no
need for it. Things were going along about the same as before,
except that, as *The New Yorker* magazine said, because of the
"emergency" it took a bit longer to get anything done. That was
about the only difference.

I received a letter from George Backer, a friend of Irving
Berlin's, saying that Berlin had offered to produce and direct
an "all-soldier show" as he had done in World War I. Patterson
and I well remembered *Yip, Yip, Yaphank* from when it had
been produced and shown at Camp Upton, and I spoke to
Colonel Pfeil (that was his real name) of the Adjutant General's Office about this. It took about a month to get the reply,
which informed me that "Mr. Berlin's offer of assistance is sincerely appreciated and will be made of record and reference
as the future needs of the War Department may warrant." The
Colonel pointed out that the "entertainment policy" of the War
Department was necessarily influenced by the short one-year
period then authorized by law for our military training. After
the one-year law was later amended, *This Is the Army* was born
and made as fine a record as *Yip, Yip, Yaphank* did in World
War I.

There was only a handful of personnel around. We ate in
"Ulcer Gulch"—the cafeteria in Munitions—and on nice days
had lunch outdoors in "Ptomaine Park." When I went to lunch
with Patterson, he would stand in line with his tray, waiting his
turn. When people began to realize that this energetic character
was the new Assistant Secretary, there were mixed reactions,
evidenced by raised eyebrows from some and friendly smiles
from many others. But he was entirely unaware of the surprise
and bewilderment, the disapproval and pleasure that he caused.

The first thing that Patterson assigned me to was tax amortization. And it wasn't a very specific assignment. Here's what it
was all about:

Plants and equipment were needed, and needed at once, to manufacture war matériel. Without them it was obviously impossible to do the job of procuring the military supplies that were needed. These facilities first had to be built. But who would build them? We needed more of everything. For example, Glenn Martin was making aircraft at its plant near Baltimore. But we needed many more planes than it could build under the existing setup, and Glenn Martin had to have a much bigger plant if it was to turn out more planes. But this would cost the company, say, $5,000,000. The company didn't want to put that into a new building and later find out that the Government's great production needs had stopped. Then Glenn Martin would have a new plant it couldn't use. So the thought was that the Government would induce Glenn Martin to build the plant by providing that if the company built and paid for it, 20 per cent of the cost could be deducted each year for five years on the company's income tax return. But to be entitled to this deduction, Glenn Martin would have to get a "Necessity Certificate," saying that the new plant was a facility essential to our defense. All right on the new plant, said Leon Henderson and others from the Defense Commission, but why should Glenn Martin be allowed to take a deduction for the cost of those new houses they wanted to build for the thousands of new workers that would be working at the new plant? In effect, the Government would be paying for the new plant and the housing that the company would then own. Take another case. We needed many tanks, but who had the facilities to make them? Baldwin Locomotive and American Locomotive were about the only people who had facilities that could be converted into tank plants. But they wanted to know what they could use these plants for in normal times.

The job was first to work out a tax-amortization formula that was acceptable to War, Navy, the Defense Commission, the Treasury Department and various other agencies, put it in a statute, get it passed by Congress and then signed by the President. All this was done and a law passed giving the deduction on certificates issued by the War or Navy departments with the concurrence of the Defense Commission. We then had to create the machinery for the Army to do this, and put it in

operation and get it moving, remembering that the job was to
create a huge production machine to supply and equip the
largest fighting force that the world has ever known. Like everything else we were doing, the plants were needed at once, and
the tax amortization had to start immediately. I helped organize
the tax unit and later was its acting chief. Before the work was
over, we issued certificates totaling over $5.5 billion. It was
quite a project.

The jobs of planning, producing, and procuring and purchas-
ing were performed by the supply services. These were the
Ordnance Department, Signal Corps, Quartermaster Corps,
Chemical Warfare Service, Medical Department, and the Corps
of Engineers. Later the Transportation Department was created.
There was then no separate Air Force. The Air Corps was just
another service. Even though Lovett was Assistant Secretary for
Air, its procurement and that of all other services were under
Patterson's direction. In 1940 and most of 1941, he personally
had to sign and approve every one of the purchase contracts
made by the Army. It was obviously essential for competent
lawyers to go over these contracts, and it was obviously impossible for Patterson to do this himself on each contract. He
urgently needed legal help; the contracts were pouring into his
office by the thousands.

The supply services didn't have their own lawyers. Legal
help was supplied by the Judge Advocate General's Department,
then headed by Major General Myron C. Cramer. Fortunately
he was a big man. He could see that it was essential that the
services have their own lawyers to advise them on these matters.
His wise acquiescence to such a plan, although not greeted with
enthusiasm in his department, made it possible to do the job
that had to be done. It was Patterson's office that had the job
of getting the lawyers to do the work.

But, first, it was necessary to give greater responsibility to the
services. Patterson succeeded in getting the power to delegate to
them the right to sign contracts up to $500,000 and later raised
this sum to $5,000,000. Now, the services had responsible con-
tracting officers, but there were few real, first-class legal assistants, who were indispensable for this work. Returning one day

from Wright Field in Dayton, Ohio, where Air Corps Procurement was centered, I did some thinking along these lines, and it looked to me like this: the legal work done by the judge advocates assigned to Wright Field seemed competent, and the officers there were technicians who knew the rules and the routine. They were probably doing a satisfactory job on the current business, but how could they be expected to handle the huge volume of work coming up? How would they meet the many new situations that were bound to arise? When I discussed this with my boss, Patterson, he told me to take it up with Lovett, the Assistant Secretary for Air. I did so and asked Lovett what he would have done in his banking firm if they were financing an outfit that did an annual business of $30 million that would increase to nearly $10 billion next year. He immediately saw the point and acted. George A. Brownell, a fine lawyer from New York, had just arrived in Washington to become Lovett's assistant. With Brownell's help a legal staff—made up of leading lawyers from all over the country, and headed by Donald C. Swatland—was created at Wright Field, and it became, I believe, one of the ablest group of lawyers ever assembled in this country. It was almost impossible to find a place to live in Dayton then. John P. Donohue, now a New York Supreme Court justice, was given the job of locating billets for the legal personnel. Through a local women's group, he was able to lease a mansion, furnish it, and feed the inmates. It was called "Casa Mañana" and provided a very pleasant and livable place in this overcrowded community, immeasurably increasing the productivity and happiness of its inhabitants.

The other services were to reach an annual expenditure of more than $33 billion for their equipment and supplies. Next to the Air Corps, the Ordnance Department was the largest service, with an annual expenditure of $8 billion. But getting lawyers for Ordnance was easier for us than for any other service, since Ordnance had a long and proud record and had done much preparing, including setting up nine district offices and eight arsenals throughout the country, so that its procurement was decentralized. These arsenals included Springfield and Charlestown in Massachusetts (established in the eighteenth century

and recently ordered closed), Picatinny in New Jersey, Waterford in New York, Frankfort in Pennsylvania, Hartford in Connecticut, and Rock Island on the Mississippi. Each had its own
job: small arms in Springfield, where the Garand rifle was developed, heavy artillery in Waterford, small-arms ammunition
in Frankfort, and other ammunition in Picatinny, and tanks in
Rock Island. Purchases were made through the district offices
located in key cities such as Detroit, Philadelphia, Chicago,
St. Louis, San Francisco, New York, Hartford, and Boston. Each
was under a skilled Regular-Army Ordnance officer, and each
was thoroughly familiar with the potential manufacturers in the
area. Ordnance, which called itself "the brains of the Army,"
knew what it was doing and what it wanted to do. Its legal
work in 1940 was being handled in the orthodox way under the
Judge Advocate General's Department. In charge was Captain
Irving A. Duffy, a most attractive and able young lawyer, who is
today a vice president of the Ford Motor Company. He was
Regular Army, a Columbia Law School graduate, and wore a J.A.
insignia on his uniform. Otherwise, he was as Ordnance as a
bazooka and very well liked by all. Duffy's office in Washington
and the civilian lawyers recruited in the districts were fully
able to handle the work.

But this was not true in most of the other services. They just
did not yet recognize the need for lawyers. The Medical Department was an example. The men in charge saw no need for
an outside lawyer, and resented the idea that the Department
couldn't handle its own problems. But after a short while, when
they realized that purchases were to rise by millions and millions of dollars each year and that the number of items were
snowballing, they began to recognize that outside help was
needed. Soon they wondered how they could have ever gotten
along without Tracy S. Voorhees. When I was looking for a
man for this job I found his letter to me, among many others
from friends, asking to be called to the service. In it, he had mentioned the fact that he was on the board of trustees of a Brooklyn
hospital. (The Surgeon General asked me why, if he had to
have a lawyer, must he have a fellow who would think he knew
all about medicine because he was a trustee of a hospital.)

Voorhees did an outstanding job and the Medical Department boasted of the many fine accomplishments here and abroad which were due to his ingenuity and perseverance. Conrad Snow, a Harvard Law School friend of Patterson's, with the help of Kenneth Johnson, who later became head of the New York School of Social Research at Columbia University, steered the Signal Corps through many difficult situations. We got Edward H. Foley, who had succeeded Oliphant as Counsel to the Treasury Department, to be lawyer for the Quartermaster. His able assistant, Charles L. Kades, went with him. Before going overseas for other duties, they did a fine job. Jacob K. Javits became counsel for Chemical Warfare and displayed the ability that he later showed as a United States Senator.

Staffing the services with lawyers was just one of Patterson's many legal responsibilities. And he always needed lawyers right in his own office. Warren S. Ege of Omaha and William L. Marbury of Baltimore, who were Harvard Law School friends of Patterson's, were the first of the many lawyers that Patterson had working for him. During the summer of 1940 they started the operation that enabled the Army to contract for and build thousands of war plants throughout the country.

Patterson's technique was to get the best people he could— not for a specific job, but to be on his team. Once they were there, they would do whatever was assigned to them. Julius H. Amberg of Grand Rapids, as well as Arthur E. Sutherland and Benjamin Kaplan, now professors at Harvard Law School, Marion H. Rushton of Alabama, Miles Knowles of Detroit, Sturgis Warner, just out of Harvard Law School, Franklin J. Hammond of Boston, and, later, Kenneth C. Royall of North Carolina were among the lawyers who contributed greatly to solving the many problems that constantly required a lawyer's help, both in the Patterson office and elsewhere in the Army at home and abroad.

While I was still involved with tax amortization and other assignments for Patterson, he decided that he wanted firsthand information as to what Ordnance was doing. So he told me he was transferring me there. I felt sunk! I asked, "What am I to do?" He said that he didn't know, but its work was tremendous

and he wanted to know more about it. I was to be on duty there
and find out all I could. This seemed to make me some sort of
spy or informer, and I soon found out that was exactly how
Ordnance regarded my assignment. I had not been asked for
by Ordnance. They were told by the Assistant Secretary that a
lieutenant colonel from his office with Signal Corps insignia was
to be assigned to them. So I went, and was put on duty in the
office of the chief of the district offices, Colonel A. B. Quinton, Jr., a very tough and able Ordnance officer. Ordnance had
just appropriated the brand-new Social Security Building down
in the southeast section of town, where Quinton's office occupied
a huge one-room portion of the ground floor. Quinton soon told
me he had no use for Reserve officers, even less for lawyers,
particularly those from New York, and none at all for those
who were wished on him, especially if they were to be informers.
After weeks of suffering under this ogre, somehow or other I
did manage to acquire a bit of knowledge of the vast kingdom
known as Ordnance. Quinton's office was an excellent place to
see what was going on.

Gradually I learned to know and admire Quinton. Instead of
regarding me as a spy, he came to think of me as a useful entrée
to the Assistant Secretary's Office. So did the others, including
Major General Charles M. Wesson, the Chief of Ordnance. One
day Quinton told me to report to the Chief's office. There I was
ordered, much to my pleasure, to take that awful Signal Corps
insignia off my collar and put on the Ordnance insignia, those
bursting bombs, because I had been transferred to Ordnance.
I had made the grade in spite of the fact (really because of the
fact) that throughout my tour at Ordnance, Patterson was constantly phoning me and sending for me. This included one
frightful day when Quinton had arranged to have me included
at a lunch meeting at the Chief's office. Just before lunch, Patterson phoned telling me to join him and Jim Forrestal for lunch
at his office in fifteen minutes, and he hung up. When I asked
Quinton what I should do, he slammed his fist on the desk and
said nothing. I went to Patterson's office.

Nor did my duty under Quinton preclude the Chief of Ordnance and his deputy, Major General Charles T. Harris, from
giving me other assignments, including working on the draft of

a statute which was to become the Lend-Lease Act. This, I believe, originated as a draft that General Harris gave to Quinton and me to force us to put something in writing. After numerous talks with us, voicing his objections to having the Chief of Ordnance continue to give the British large quantities of war matériel, which we had to call "surplus," General Harris drew up his draft. When we went over it, we gave him all sorts of criticism. He smiled and told us that's just what he wanted us to do. He had put it on paper to egg us on to prepare something which he could use to press for a law making someone other than the Chief of Ordnance responsible for giving Army matériel to the British.

We worked hard on this and finally drafted something that became the basis for discussion with Assistant Secretary McCloy. It was at his suggestion that we held informal talks on the draft at my home on Twenty-ninth Street with Ben Cohen of the President's Office, Ed Foley, and Oscar Cox from the Treasury Department. It was polished up, put in final form, introduced as H.R. 1776, and enacted as the lend-lease law.

Around this time, and before the bill was introduced, I drafted some material that we sent to Judge Samuel I. Rosenman at the White House for consideration by the President for a speech he was soon to make. He made it in December, 1940, and it became known as the "Arsenal of Democracy" speech. What we sent over told how the Ordnance Department and the Army were working with industry, and that America was becoming the "Arsenal of Democracy." These words had been used just before by Secretary Stimson in a speech to the American Federation of Labor in New Orleans, but they had gone practically unnoticed. In the draft we sent the President, we said that "American industrial genius, unmatched throughout the world in the solution of production problems, has been called upon to bring its resources and talents into action." We went on to say that "watchmakers, manufacturers of farm implements, cash registers, automobiles, sewing machines, lawn mowers and locomotives are now making fuses, bomb-packing crates, telescope mounts, shelves, pistols and tanks." On the night of his speech, I was delighted to hear him use this exact language.

Patterson also gave me other assignments, including sending

me to California on the first Army take-over of a war plant in
a labor dispute. That was in June of 1941—about six months
before Pearl Harbor. It was at the North American Aviation
plant, our only contractor making B-25 bombers, the ones that
General Doolittle later used to bomb Tokyo. Although we were
not yet at war, the pressure on all of us was intense, and this
was one of our most important plants. A strike had been called
which was said to be Communist-inspired. It involved a jurisdictional dispute within the union. If production was stopped
at this plant, it would be a crippling blow to our bomber program and might lead to strikes elsewhere. It was rumored that
the strike would not be permitted and that the Government
might even take over the plant rather than let production stop.
That's about all I knew about this situation then. I had been
enjoying a rare Sunday afternoon off from work when I was
sent for to come right down to the Munitions Building. There
I was told that I was to go right out to the North American
plant in Inglewood, California, be ready for the take-over of
the plant, and work with the Army in operating it. The Air Force
briefed me about the plant, and the Judge Advocate General's
Office informed me about the law in regard to take-overs, how
Presidents Lincoln and Wilson had taken over plants in previous
wars, about the need for firm action, and numerous other
things I should remember, including the Government's right to
enforce its contracts. Then "Judge" Patterson asked me, "You've
often been counsel for the receiver in bankruptcy, haven't you?"
When I answered "Yes," he said, "Well, this won't be anything
like that. Go out there, size up the situation, and do whatever
you think best." Assistant Secretary Robert Lovett told me that
I should telephone him as soon as I got there, on a special wire
that would be held open. That ended the briefing, except that
Assistant Secretary John J. McCloy added that the job would
be the same if production had stopped because of fire, flood,
or anything else. That became our motto in this and later cases.
We were only there to get production going. The labor problem
was not our direct concern.

Charles H. ("Dutch") Kindelberger, president of North
American, flew out with me. The poor guy was all in from days

and nights of negotiations, and I made him take the first sleeping pill he ever used. After we landed in Los Angeles next morning, we went directly to the plant. Huge crowds were milling around. As soon as I got in, I was steered to the direct line to the War Department and told that Assistant Secretary Lovett was on the Washington end and wanted me to tell him exactly what I saw. Lovett said that the President had just signed an executive order taking over the plant and that Secretary Stimson was ordered to carry out the order. The Secretary had just delegated Colonel Charles E. Branshaw, the Air Force procurement officer in the area, to be in charge and to run the plant. Lovett told me to put this on a notice right away, have it signed by Colonel Branshaw, make copies, and post them all around the plant. I did so. I still have one of them, mounted on a piece of cardboard about two and a half feet by three feet in my wife's studio in Princeton, where we live, and here is what it says:

In accordance with the directions of the President, the Secretary of War has this day directed me to take immediate possession of the Inglewood plant of North American Aviation, Inc.

Pursuant to these orders possession of the plant has been taken by the United States.

CHARLES E. BRANSHAW
Lt. Col. Air Corps

June 9, 1941.

Then I tried to report as a radio commentator would. Looking out the window, I saw troops slowly moving toward us, step by step. They were in columns of four, with loaded rifles and fixed bayonets. They marched forward, one, two, three, four—halt. Every twenty paces they halted to give the massed pickets sufficient time to move back. Slowly and calmly this process continued. Gradually the space became clear around the plant entrances. More and more troops came up. There were over 2,500 of them from the Fifteenth Infantry, which had been on maneuvers in the area, and the Third Coast Artillery. This was quite a contrast to what had happened on the preceding day, when the local authorities could not handle the situation and much disorder occurred, including the use of tear gas, which was thrown against the wind and badly messed up the police. When the entrances were clear, Colonel Branshaw opened the gates and over loud-speakers invited and requested employees to return to work. By noon more than 1,200 of the morning shift did so.

That afternoon tanks were set at key points, and the troops were stationed all around. The crowd was estimated at over 10,000, and there was a lot of milling and shouting. The situation was very tense and scary. Knowing that the rifles were loaded did not ease my mind any, but the skill and restraint of those in charge did. Gradually the tension gave way and calm took its place. By nightfall, campfires around the plant were burning and became gathering points for off-duty troops to talk with men from the plant. The Army's mission was to keep the plant in production. As Assistant Secretary McCloy had said, the task would have been the same if production had been stopped by a fire or if a flood had shut it down. We were not there to decide any issue between management and labor, but to keep production going, and we were very much concerned about getting people back to work. If management wanted to cooperate, we would welcome it, but if they did not, we would have to go on without them. Production must continue, and, if necessary, the plant would be run by the Army. Those were our orders, and it was up to us to see that they were carried out.

None of Colonel Branshaw's staff had ever been involved in an operation like this before. Nor had those who were guiding us from Washington any previous experience in this line. Every problem was a new one. We did our best to solve them as they arose, and we eventually succeeded. After a few days, most of the employees returned to work, and production proceeded, with the aircraft company carrying on as the representative of Colonel Branshaw. No solution was attempted of the basic union-management issue, but after production was in full swing and a strike was no longer threatened, the dispute was resolved— but the Army took no part in it. That was the job of the civilian authorities, and, eventually, this sort of work was handled by the War Labor Board.

The North American case provided important precedents for

later take-overs. Thus, because lawyers like precedents, we continued to use the take-over order that I hastily scrawled that morning. These situations were rare, but when they did arise, the need was great and the Army had to move in. Although the job was essential to our defense effort, it was never an easy one. At various times the Army was called on to operate the country's railroads, bus lines and transportation facilities of the City Transit System in Philadelphia, and even Montgomery Ward—a preposterous case—which the White House ordered the Army to take over because it had acquired the know-how and had developed an expert team prepared for emergencies.* These men included our chief labor adviser, former Assistant Secretary of Labor Edward F. McGrady, James P. Mitchell, who later became Secretary of Labor, and William J. Brennan, now a Justice of the Supreme Court, as well as an extraordinarily able public servant, John H. Ohly, and A. H. Raskin of the New York *Times*.

In September of 1940, largely as a result of the efforts of Grenville Clark and Stimson right after Stimson became Secretary of War, Congress had passed a "Selective Training and Service Act," but it extended only for one year, and in the summer of

---

* Because Secretary Stimson strenuously opposed using the Army for this purpose, the President designated the Secretary of Commerce to take over. Jesse Jones dodged the job by letting the Attorney General handle it, and it was during this regime that Sewall Avery, the president of Montgomery Ward, was escorted out of his office by two soldiers called in to help. A photograph of the incident had tremendous circulation and gave the false impression that the Army was conducting this operation while Avery was being ejected. In his book *In Brief Authority*, Francis Biddle, the Attorney General, gracefully takes the blame for this "unnecessarily melodramatic" action, which had the quality of *"opéra bouffe."* Over its objection, the Army was later compelled to take over Montgomery Ward, and succeeded in getting a court order to sustain this operation (*U.S.* v. *Montgomery Ward & Co.*, 150 F. 2d 369). All the other Army take-overs were essential to war production, including those plants where management and not labor refused compliance with a Labor Board order. President Truman tried to extend this extraordinary wartime power by taking over the country's steel mills during the Korean crisis, but the Supreme Court set this aside in the record-breaking time of seven weeks after the executive order was issued (*Youngstown Sheet & Tube Co.* v. *Sawyer*, 343 U.S. 579). Neither the federal nor state governments have yet solved the problem of how to halt strikes that cripple the production or distribution of necessities.

1941 the draft was about to expire. It was very unpopular—
people wanted to know what the soldiers were being drafted
for—and in this respect it was very like the Viet Nam situation.
The extension of the law was accomplished only after much
hard work by Stimson and Patterson, who urged the President
to tell the country that all who served in the Armed Forces
would get the benefits of what later became the G.I. Bill of
Rights. The President did so, and the draft extension barely
squeaked through—by one vote in the House. Maybe the President's promise of a G.I. Bill of Rights had gotten that one vote.
But for a long time nothing was done to get the bill introduced.
My side-kick, Howard C. Petersen, and I had a conscience on
the point and started needling. Patterson encouraged us to keep
at it. And I guess because I continued to pester him about it,
Steve Early, the President's secretary, finally told me to send
him "another" copy of what the President had said about the
G.I. Bill of Rights. This made me believe that he couldn't find
one. Since everybody else at the White House had plenty of
more urgent things to do, I took the opportunity of sending with
the copy a draft of what we thought the President might say
now to get Congress to act. General Frederick H. Osborn and
Petersen drafted a darn good statement, which was shipped over
to Early. Not long after, the President issued it. My wife happened to be in New York around then, and some of our intellectual friends pointed out to her just what the President meant
when he had used certain words in his statement, and explained
just why he hadn't used some other words instead. She knew
how the statement had been prepared, but said nothing. This
has since often helped me understand explanations given with
such positiveness by people on things about which I have such
uncertainty.

At about the same time Congress amended the National De-
fense Act, changing Patterson's position to Undersecretary of
War and creating the offices of Assistant Secretary and Assistant
Secretary for Air.

The summer of 1941 in Washington was a hot one, particularly so in the Munitions Building, where air conditioning was
unheard of. The lend-lease program was getting bigger and

bigger; so was everything else. Space was at a premium, and emergency offices were continually being moved from one location to another. Indeed, this "rotation" process was said to be a Government device to have one outfit constantly housed on trucks. The Army's need for space was increasing, and it was given the elegant new building on Virginia Avenue that the State Department had built but had not yet occupied, just across the street from the Munitions Building. When Major General James H. Burns, executive officer to Undersecretary Patterson, entered it, he looked around downstairs and said, "I'll take just one drink, but I won't go upstairs!" Secretary Stimson decided to stay in the Munitions Building. We moved into this new State Department building, and the Undersecretary's offices and the Engineers occupied the whole building. Lend-lease was housed in an office building across the street on Virginia Avenue. Its head was Harry Hopkins, with Edward Stettinius, Jr., and General Burns in charge of operations. General Henry Aurand was in charge of lend-lease for the Army. He had been working with me on what would be done on lend-lease if we should go to war. Obviously, the arrangements would have to be vastly different, since our own Army and Navy would need the huge quantity of planes and other war matériel that were going into lend-lease. We had prepared an order for the President to sign if we went to war, and kept it in my safe for Patterson to bring to the President if the occasion arose.

On a Friday afternoon in late November, General Aurand asked me if I was going to the Army-Navy football game in Philadelphia the next day. He was greatly relieved when I told him I wasn't. The next Friday, December 5th, he again asked me if I would be in Washington over the weekend. I told him that I would be. On Sunday afternoon, I went to the Washington Redskins football game with my sister, Grace. During the first half, there were calls on the loud-speaker for Admiral This and Captain That to report to their offices immediately. These calls made me jumpy, and Grace and I left for home. As soon as we got to Twenty-ninth Street, my wife told me of the Pearl Harbor attack—news which had just come over the radio—and that I was wanted at my office. There, General Aurand was waiting for me, and wanted to know where the hell I had been. (I never did know why he had expected action on these weekends, but he surely did. His son was in the Navy at Pearl Harbor that day.) We got the lend-lease order from the safe, gave it to Judge Patterson, and President Roosevelt signed it. That night General Aurand spent with Mr. Stettinius, transferring hundreds of millions of dollars' worth of lend-lease matériel back to the Army and the Navy.

The next morning when we came to work in the new War Department building, we all wore our uniforms and continued to wear them for years. Armed guards were at the entrance. We were now at war.

IX

DAY AFTER DAY AFTER DAY

NEXT day I learned how staggering our losses had been. We no longer had a Pacific fleet. Before I could continue with my work, I had to go out and walk around in the park by myself. I was trying to digest it all and to get my bearings. But I couldn't. The atmosphere had suddenly become electric. We were at war. No one talked about anything else. Hundreds of people—good ones—phoned, wrote, came to the office. They all wanted to work in Patterson's office. Everyone wanted to get into the war. Up till now, people had been lethargic, uninspired, almost indifferent. Now it all changed.

But after this first spurt, the work in our office went along much as it had before. For six days each week for more than a year we had been going at full speed. There was no let-down after Pearl Harbor. Gneisenau, the Prussian general in the wars against Napoleon, had said, "Lost ground can always be regained; but lost time, never." I had written this out and had it in my desk. It continued to be my motto.

The National Defense Act of 1920 had provided that the supply services report directly to the Assistant Secretary's Office. This placed many operations under him. Our office had grown tremendously, and the whole War Department had been expanding in every direction. A conflict that had always existed in the Army between the supply arms and services and the military had never been resolved, and the seeds of real trouble were germinating. The cleavage between the military and civilian was only one part of this problem. G-4, which was part of the regular General Staff, had charge of requirements and planning for the military, but the actual procurement, manufacture and delivery of arms, and the supply of them to troops was taken care of by another branch of the Army. That was the part that was under Patterson.

By February of 1942, plans were under way to reorganize the Army into three commands: the Army Ground Forces, the Army Air Forces, and the Army Service Forces. The latter was to be under the command of General Brehon B. Somervell of the Army Engineers, but would still be under the direction of the Undersecretary, as would be procurement for the Army Air Forces, which was under the command of General Henry H. ("Hap") Arnold. We conferred on the reorganization and met with General Somervell and his new team. An Engineer officer whose adjutant general's card had shown superior ratings since his graduation from West Point, one Major Lucius D. Clay, was a member of this team. He was a most attractive man, and I was immediately taken with him. My liking for him was much increased when I discovered that he had made the same point to Somervell that I had made to Patterson about one feature of the proposed plan. When I was directed to take this up with Somervell's office, I was told to see Clay. I then found out that Clay had already worked out the details in a proposal that Somervell had vetoed. This plan was finally adopted.

Nearly all the officers on duty in Patterson's office were transferred to Army Service Forces. It was Patterson's direction that our staff, which then occupied most of the War Department building on Virginia Avenue, be cut to about 120, including all officers and civilian personnel, and it remained at this level all through the war.

Not very long after the reorganization, the European-theater headquarters in England were being organized for the invasion of the Continent. The operation was called "Bolero," and General Eisenhower, whom I had then never heard of, was to command.* McCloy asked me if I'd like to meet him. I said I would, and McCloy suggested a fishing trip. But this was the weekend before Eisenhower was scheduled to go, and, as I expected, Eisenhower had other ideas for his last weekend at home.

General Somervell was planning the supply for this operation and picked me to head the legal division. It was an exciting and important job, but I had the feeling that Somervell had picked me principally to get me out of Washington. Stimson okayed my appointment, and I got leave to go up to Martha's Vineyard for a few days. Walking along the beach, I told my wife that I was going, but as it turned out, I didn't go. Patterson was overseas when I was assigned, and when he came back, Somervell told me that Patterson had vetoed it, although he never said a word to me about it. In my place Colonel George A. Spiegelberg was sent, and his plane crashed into the river at Lisbon. George was bitten by rats while in the water and was hospitalized for many months. I always felt guilty about George's injuries.†

In the Pentagon, Somervell's office was right next to Patterson's, with a door communicating between the two. He was in and out all the time. I was made a brigadier general and became Patterson's executive officer.‡ Patterson and Somervell were

---

* Eisenhower was known as "the Major" in the Patterson office, where he had served years before. Later, when the surrender of Italy was to be announced, I sent word around that all would be welcome in my office to hear his broadcast. I found out that this was announced to the staff in a memo reading: "The General invites everybody to his office at 1100 to hear the Major speak."

† Later I was again requested for an overseas assignment. This time it was by Lieutenant General William H. Simpson, who commanded the Ninth Army. I had gotten to know him slightly, and admired him greatly, on several trips I had made to his headquarters while he was training troops down South. He was ordered to the Pentagon to organize the staff for the army that he was to form and command. It gave me a tremendous kick to be asked by him to join that staff. But although he made the request directly of Patterson, it was again turned down.

‡ Since Patterson's job included the Army's relations with the civilian popu-

amazingly alike in many respects, but quite different in others. Somervell's principal objection to Patterson was Patterson's complete disregard of military channels. When Patterson wanted to find out something, he just sent for the guy who knew about it. That's just what Somervell did, but he got wild when Patterson did it. He insisted that Patterson should get the information through him. One day I was with Somervell while Somervell was again complaining to me about this. His phone rang, and the General carried on a conversation with a captain at the other end about an ordnance weapon and got a lot of information as to the status of its production. When he hung up, I innocently said, "I guess General Campbell (then Chief of Ordnance) will hear all about this conversation, won't he?" Somervell grinned and said, "That's a dirty crack!" Anyway, we worked out a scheme so that Patterson could continue just what he had been doing—since I knew he couldn't be changed. And Somervell was to get a copy of every memorandum and every letter that went from Patterson's office to any member of the Army Service Forces.

As a result of this almost daily association, I got to know Somervell well, and acquired not only a vast admiration but a very real liking for him. He had a delicious sense of humor, while Patterson had none. Once, I told him of a letter that I had received from a soldier I knew, telling me that the main trouble in his outfit came from the fact that some privates first class were "drunk with power." A few days later, at one of his staff meetings, Somervell told his two-star chiefs of service about this letter, adding with a deadpan look that he knew others with an even higher rank who also suffered from the disease of being "drunk with power."

When he was away on trips, I would make notes for him covering the high spots of what had happened while he was

---

lation, this brought many daily contacts with the Hill. The time I had to devote to this was much increased by the fact that the United States Government Manual, published by the Office of War Information, listed my name directly beneath the names of Secretary Stimson and Patterson. Naturally it was much easier for Congressmen, their secretaries, or anyone else to call me.

away. During one of his absences an airplane had crashed into the New York Empire State Building in a fog, and the Army public-relations people did what they could to keep it out of the paper. Believe it or not, the front-page story in the New York *Times* the next day quoted an Air Force general whose name could not be mentioned as saying, "The Army wants no publicity about this entire matter." It was this type of item that Somervell wanted to hear about, and his comments on them were plenty strong.

On his return from another trip that included a visit to the China-Burma-India theater, he sent me the name and serial number of an Air Force lieutenant who had been flying the Hump, with a request that he be transferred to the Army Service Forces. Somervell was a bit peeved when I insisted on knowing the reason for the transfer. He showed me a photograph of this officer, taken in Assam beside his plane, with the name *My Assam Dragon* painted on it, and told me that the Lieutenant was the one who named it, and that anyone with that good a sense of humor should be with the ASF and not with the AAF. When I didn't get the transfer through, he was quite mad at me.

Somervell was a hard-driving, efficient master who demanded perfection from everyone under him. His principal subordinates were the chiefs of service, many of whom held statutory offices. Once a week they all met, and Patterson and I were always invited. At one meeting everyone immediately noticed that a new person was sitting in the Chief Signal Officer's chair. That was a bombshell, but the only remark in reference to it was made by General Somervell, who said, "I guess you all know Dad, who's sitting in the Chief Signal Officer's place. He'll be there from now on." This was equivalent to saying, "Any of you who doesn't measure up will get out of here." And that's the way it was. He was a tough leader, but an able one.

Several days before each meeting the chief of each service had to submit a little booklet showing how each item on his production schedule was doing. Compilation of these lists showed how over-all production stood. Before the meeting, Somervell got the summary from General Clinton Robinson of his Control Division, and these meetings were largely devoted to a discussion

of the items that were behind schedule. At one meeting a chief
of service called attention to items on his list which were ahead
of schedule—and he wanted to talk about them. Somervell cut
him short, saying that he had no time now, but after the war
we'd devote a full evening to those very items.

After at least a year of close daily contact, Major General
Wilhelm D. Styer, the Chief of Staff, paid me what he considered a compliment by remarking, "Why I never knew that
you were a lawyer!"

All engineering was to be overseen by Patterson, but there
was no one in the office qualified to assume its direction. One
Sunday evening at his home, Patterson was talking about this
and asked me who was Robert Moses' chief engineer. I had
known Bob Moses for many years and said that M. J. ("Jack")
Madigan, whom I knew only by reputation, was the man.
Patterson sent for him, and he became a dollar-a-year, seven-
day-a-week consultant who never wrote a memorandum.*
Madigan was an amazing, brilliant engineer, with little regard
for anyone on the staff, a complete unwillingness to observe
any rules, and an uncanny feel for the realities of what was
happening. He had a farm in Vermont, where a foal was born
that he christened "General Somervell." When he told the
General, he was very pleased. Soon after, Madigan told him
that it was amazing how much acumen he had shown in the
name he had picked. When pressed to explain, he said that
the other day he had seen the little colt running with its mother,
get ahead, and then "kick its own mother right in her puss."
Somervell told him to get out and stay out. It was Madigan's
self-imposed role to walk around the building—first on Virginia
Avenue and then in the Pentagon—from office to office, with an
unlit cigar in his mouth, listening to everything and saying little.

We couldn't have done without Madigan. He was invaluable

---

* This is not technically correct. Madigan did send out one memorandum.
I had suggested he send one asking for the information that he wandered
around to get. He sent the memo, signed "By direction of the Undersecretary." A few days later he came into my office, showed me the
memorandum, and pointed to the third endorsement, which read, "Referred to Mr. Madigan for reply." There were no more Madigan memos.

on camp construction, the Caribbean bases, the production of gasoline, the Pentagon Building, Manhattan District, and all sorts of other problems.

Senator Harry S. Truman was chairman of a Senate committee examining the conduct of the war. The inquiry could have been very troublesome, but Patterson, who was a real authority on the Civil War, explained to Truman on a couple of airplane trips arranged to visit Army camps the great damage that a similar Senate committee had done during the Civil War. Truman, having read the history of the Civil War himself, understood, and never went into war plans as far as I know. Indeed, I don't think he even had any information about the atomic bomb until after he became President.

One of Madigan's first jobs was to attend the hearings of the Truman committee, which was then investigating camp construction. It was a rare treat to listen to him regale us back at the office in the late afternoon with a report of the day's doings and to hear the plan for tomorrow's show. A girl clerk at Camp Meade was getting $140 a week, and her highest previous pay had been $55 a week in a beauty parlor in Baltimore. A truck was being leased at Camp Edwards on the Cape in Massachusetts, and the rent paid to date was already nearly as much as the truck cost. This stuff, and many similar items, had been fed to the committee regularly by Madigan at its executive sessions, usually the day before the testimony was given. Madigan had just annexed himself to the staff and drifted into their meetings. Finally someone asked him what he was doing there and he was ejected. From then on, he was kept out of the meetings, and we did not know what was coming out next day.

The sort of questions we were afraid of were along these lines: Why was a three-shift, round-the-clock operation needed to finish a camp when it would have been impossible to fill it with soldiers by the time the camp was scheduled to be built? For example, suppose Camp Meade was to be ready for 80,000 troops by February 1st, how many troops did we have ready to go in when the camp was opened? Would it have been possible for us to get that many troops there on opening day?

If not, why in the world did we have to speed up the construction of the camp? Fortunately for the Army, none of these questions ever was asked.

During one of the Churchill visits to this country, Isador Lubin called from the White House to tell me that a member of Winston Churchill's party wanted to go to Aberdeen Proving Grounds, and asked if I could arrange it for tomorrow. General Harris, who had been the Deputy Chief of Ordnance, was then commanding general at Aberdeen and we set it up. I called for the visiting fireman at the Wardman Park Hotel, which was the quaint name of his hotel. He was about six feet three, wore a fascinating bowler hat, and looked exactly the way a British lord ought to look. That is what he was, and his name was Lord Cherwell. I took him over. I didn't know anything about him except that he was interested in hollow charges, which means rockets, and he apparently knew a lot about ordnance. General Harris showed him what he wanted, and we spent most of the day looking at rocket material and other ordnance material, including his first view of a bazooka, which interested him very much. I observed that he was extremely knowledgeable on these subjects, although I didn't yet know that he was a famous professor from Oxford. By the time we flew back to Washington, we were becoming good friends. I told him a story that was going around in the Army then, and he enjoyed it immensely. It was really a very funny, dirty story, but for the life of me I can't think now what it was, and my failure to remember it is the main reason why I so regret that I did not keep a diary.

That night I bumped into Joe Alsop, the newspaper columnist, at the opening of the National Gallery. He said, "Well, Eddie, I hear you've been hobnobbing with royalty all day." Apparently he knew all about my day with Lord Cherwell, so I asked him to tell me about him. He was astounded that I didn't know who he was and informed me that he was, among other things, "a combination of Jim Farley, Bernie Baruch, and Van Bush." I found out that that was a pretty good description of Milord, and learned that the P.M. and Lord Cherwell had spent every day together during the preceding year, as they were doing right now. It was around Christmastime, and

Cherwell told me that his mathematics students at Oxford had given him a wonderful Christmas present—a solution to the following problem: Exactly what will the score be if one plays backgammon every night for 365 successive nights? It had been Lord Cherwell's fate to play this game with the P.M. every night in the previous year before they went to bed. Sometimes this would be as late as two or three o'clock in the morning, and His Lordship told me that he was good and sick of it, but Churchill never tired of the game. When he showed Churchill his Christmas present and tried to explain it to him, Churchill, although he didn't understand a thing about it, immediately pulled a note out of his pocket and said, "Here's a pound that says it's wrong," Cherwell said this meant not only that he would have to play the game every night, but that he would have to check and see how wrong the total was after 365 games.

A few days later I was again asked by the White House if I would take His Lordship to Monmouth, where he wanted to see what was going on in radar. We went there, but since I had no special relationships with the people in charge—and radar was then highly classified—I found it a little difficult getting him cleared at the post for the things he wanted to see. But if he didn't find out much that day about radar, he certainly learned a lot about how an American camp was run, and in contrast to the lunch we had at the Officers' Club at Aberdeen, here we ate on the line in the mess hall. To my horror, I saw His Nibs carrying his tray to the end of the line after he had thoroughly enjoyed picking out different items of food. I ran up and sneaked in the ninety-seven cents which paid for his lunch. The Signal Corps officers who were showing him around all called him "Lord," and he was grinning from ear to ear; I think he learned more about the camp in one day than most Washington inspectors could find out in a week. Anyway, on the plane going back to Washington, he asked me if I had any more stories. I told him I didn't, and he seemed very disappointed. He then said that after our last trip, he had told the P.M. the story that I had told him (the one I can't remember), and the P.M. thought it was the best story he heard in this country. Indeed, I felt that Lord Cherwell made up the trip to

Monmouth in order to see if he could get another good story out of me!

A few days later, on December 26, 1941, the Prime Minister made his famous stirring speech before a joint session of Congress in which he said: "What kind of a people do they think we are? Is it possible that they do not realize that we shall never cease to persevere against them until they have been taught a lesson which they and the world will never forget?"

Cherwell had told me about the birth pains that Churchill went through before he made a speech. He would be up a good part of the night before, writing and rewriting, and then had that brilliant facility of giving the speech as though he were making it up impromptu as he went along. He certainly gave me that impression the day he made the speech; yet I could see from where I was sitting (rather near him) that everything had been written out. He threw the pages away one at a time, and when it was all over he seemed quite mad when someone tried to pick up the pages from the floor. Churchill managed to get all of them back in his possession. Later we invited Cherwell to our little apartment, where some friends came in to meet him. There he told my wife of the terrible thing that had happened to him—namely, that he had not been in England to meet me when I was there on a visit during the war.

One day soon after that Judge Patterson sent for me and introduced me to two representatives of the State Department who told him that General de Gaulle was expected in Washington next week and that the Army was to act as his host. The Judge said that Colonel Stimson had previously told him that he would be out-of-town, so that the Judge would have to handle it. With this brief résumé, he shook hands with the State Department representatives and a G-2 officer who accompanied them and turned them all over to me. From now on, this project was mine. I took them into my room and decided that I might as well grin and bear it.

The first question the State Department representatives took up with me was the salute. They wanted to know how many guns I thought should be given to General de Gaulle when he arrived, adding that General Giraud had been there the preceding week and that he was a major general, but the State Department had said that both the generals should get the same honors. The G-2 officer then asked me whether General de Gaulle could have as his aide a certain colonel who had just come back from serving in Vichy, France, and who spoke excellent French. The State Department representatives suggested that the first dinner should be given by the Secretary of State, that the following night one should be given by Undersecretary Patterson, and, if we wanted, they would be glad to make all arrangements for both of these dinners. At this point, I was about ready to conk out and suggested that they come back the following day.

When they returned next day, I told the State Department boys—to their horror—that we would have the same number of guns for General de Gaulle as we had had for General Giraud. I said that it wouldn't make the slightest difference, and that nobody would pay any attention to it, anyway. The G-2 boy was then told that the colonel they had suggested would not fill the bill, and that he should come back with another suggestion.

The following day they arrived again, and the G-2 boy asked for permission to see the Undersecretary and discuss with him, not with me, the subject of the aide to General de Gaulle, because, with the greatest respect for me, they still thought that the colonel they had suggested would be just the right man. I immediately got up, told them to wait a minute, that I would go in to see the Undersecretary, and try to arrange for them to see him. I told Judge Patterson about the aide business and he agreed with me, but at the same time told me that he wanted to show them a draft of a *"la belle France"* speech that he was writing for the dinner and which he would deliver in French. I went back and told them the Judge was ready to see them and mentioned his proposed speech. This caused an immediate crisis, resulting in their withdrawing their request for a meeting, saying they didn't want to see the Judge and urging me to urge him to make his speech in English. (Later I succeeded in doing this.)

Several days later General de Gaulle arrived. He wasn't so

bad at all. He made out that he couldn't speak any English, but I suspected he understood everything we said. He had a Chief of Staff who spoke perfect English and was most pleasant. He wanted to know all the plans for the General's visit and exchanged various courtesies with us.

Then the Secretary of State's party was held. The following morning, Mr. McCloy asked me to come up to his office right away. He told me that it had been the worst party he or anyone else had ever attended; that nobody sat next to anyone else who could understand a word of the same language. He gave me as an illustration a running conversation between Secretary of State Hull and General de Gaulle. The Secretary wanted to know if the General wanted a piece of *"le pain."* The General said he had plenty *"du pain"* and held up his bread to prove that he didn't want any more. Five minutes later, Secretary Hull asked the General whether he wanted a glass of *"l'eau."* The General thanked him and said he didn't need any *"eau,"* pointing to his glass of water, which was still full. The same conversation took place about *"le beurre,"* and McCloy said that was the type of gay table talk that was going on all around the room. At about 9:20, when everybody had toasted everybody else, everybody shook hands with everybody, said good night, and the party was over.

McCloy said we couldn't perpetrate anything like that to-night. I asked him what he thought we should do. He said the first thing was to get French-speaking Americans seated next to the French who couldn't understand any English. We had to do that, come hell or high water, whether the State Department approved it or not. He said that, in addition, I would have to go to the Signal Corps and pick out a movie that was darned good. I spent the rest of the morning look-ing for a picture like the one in which Betty Hutton sang "Mur-der, He Says." Then I got hold of some pleasant French-speaking young American officers. The State Department had arranged the cards for the seating at the table that evening. We rearranged them, putting in our added starters, all of whom spoke perfect French and were most attractive. That evening, when the State Department representatives walked into the room and saw what had happened, they nearly died, but they couldn't do anything about it because everyone was already walking to the seats. The party was really almost jovial! Everybody had a good time, and I even saw General de Gaulle laughing several times. The speeches began with Judge Patterson's speech (in English), and he put everybody at ease. Everyone liked the movie. No diplomatic relations were broken. The General's Chief of Staff, however, did ask me to point out to him all of the Americans on our list, and I noticed that he was checking them against a list he had of those who had attended General Giraud's party.

I'll admit I felt very much better when the General's plane took off the next day.

But entertaining foreign visitors was only an occasional diversion. Most of the days were spent on more exacting chores, and those problems continued to increase.

Military justice was one of the areas assigned to Patterson. It was a difficult responsibility that required much work and thought.

When a man becomes a soldier, he is at once subject to military law. The Constitution provides that his conduct is to be governed by "military justice," and he may be tried by the military for doing something that was not even an offense for him the day before. For instance, if he stays away from camp, instead of just being absent from a job he is now guilty of an offense and is subject to court-martial for it. If he doesn't do what his corporal tells him to do, or doesn't show proper respect for his sergeant, he may also be court-martialed. This is necessary because the Army has to maintain discipline. But it is obviously very difficult for an enlisted man, who is not used to having his freedom interfered with, nor is it easy for the Army, which has to carry out an equitable system of military justice. The Army's very existence depends on the method by which this is done.

The rules governing the administration of justice in the Army are contained in the Articles of War. They are enacted by Congress on authority given by the Constitution, and basically they are older than the Constitution itself. The first Articles of War were prepared by George Washington. They were adopted by the Continental Congress in 1775, and have been amended from time to time by Congress to meet changing needs and conditions. They form a legal code set up by civilian authority for the government of the Army.

The Articles of War specify the offenses for which a soldier may be punished. They prescribe the manner of trial. They set up safeguards to protect the accused. They incorporate not only the basic rights of any accused person given in the Bill of Rights, but also include additional safeguards and protection not available to persons tried before civilian courts. The Articles of War provide for three different types of courts-martial. The first is the summary court, with one officer, which can give sentences of up to one month. Then comes the special court, which can give sentences of up to six months and must have three officers serving on it. The highest type of court-martial, the general court-martial, must include no fewer than five officers, and can give any sentence, including death. Although punishment of offenses in the Army is much more severe than in civil life, clemency procedures are far more liberal. One reason, of course, is because of the Army's strong desire to get men back on duty at the earliest possible moment.

The Army realizes that the Articles of War are not self-executing, and charges its officers with acquiring a complete knowledge of military law and the practice of military courts. For many years Army regulations have stressed that "the discipline and reputation of the Army are deeply involved in the manner in which military courts are conducted and justice administered." And the Army makes its officers keenly aware of this and trains them to meet the responsibility.

Supervising the administration of military justice in the Army was not easy. Judge Patterson and his staff paid a great deal of attention to it, and my experience in World War I and, since then, in the Judge Advocate General's Department helped me in my involvement with this work. As the war went on, the number of our military prisoners increased. This was inevitable because more and more men were coming into the Army. In these abnormal times it was natural that the crime rate would be higher than usual; and since 80 per cent of those who commit crimes are between eighteen and forty, many of these crime-prone characters were in the Army, and the Army had to contend with them. In addition, there were many offenses which became crimes, although they hadn't existed as crimes in peacetime.

One of the responsibilities of Undersecretary Patterson's Office was to review, within six months, all cases serving general court-martial sentences and to re-examine every man's case within the next year. (This was not dependent on any action on the prisoner's part; it was automatic.) With troops in our huge Army serving all over the world, it was a tremendous task to supervise this work. The complexity of the job is illustrated by the wide variety of offenses we dealt with in World War II. Here are a few actual cases:

A soldier from Tennessee in Algiers kills an Arab. A sergeant from Pennsylvania extracts money from the mail of his fellow soldiers in Liverpool. A corporal from Florida holds up a lunch counter in Denver. A private from New York shoots a companion in a crap game in New Caledonia. A captain from Massachusetts engages in black-market operations in Casablanca. An Army Air Force lieutenant from Illinois overstays his leave from the Lincoln Air Base in Arizona, leaving a trail of bad checks.

After trial and approval by a judge advocate in the field and then by the Judge Advocate General, these cases ultimately came to the Undersecretary's Office. A clemency board was set up in the office to handle them, and James P. Hendrick, a lieutenant colonel who had been a lawyer in Secretary Stimson's New York law office, was put in charge. He was assisted by other lawyer-soldiers, including some who had served abroad in combat. Later, a Harvard Law School classmate of Secretary Patterson's, Raymond S. Wilkins, now Chief Justice of the Massachusetts Supreme Judicial Court, volunteered to help; he was followed by former United States Supreme Court Justice Sherman Minton. Another Supreme Court Justice, Owen J. Roberts, became chairman of the board that worked on these cases after the war.

The supervision of the operation of military prisons was probably an even more difficult task. Because a man in the guardhouse is no asset to the Army, it did everything in its power to restore convicted men to duty as soldiers. To aid in this process, a board of consultants was assembled from leading penologists throughout the country. Among them were Austin H. McCormack, former Commissioner of Corrections in New York; James V. Bennett, former Director of the Federal Bureau of Prisons; Sanford Bates, former Commissioner in New Jersey; and Edward R. Cass, former Secretary of the American Prison Association. This outstanding group of men helped to establish rehabilitation centers, whose purpose was to get the prisoners back on duty at the earliest possible moment. We had nine of these centers during the war, and Colonel F. Lovell Bixby, who had been warden of the Federal Reformatory at Chillicothe, Ohio, rendered valuable service to this work. One of the rehabilitation methods experimented with at this time was group therapy, which proved immensely helpful to the Army and is now being used extensively throughout the country.

Toward the end of the war, when the Army had more than 31,000 prisoners, we began to think of the tremendous burden the Army would still have in caring for these prisoners after the war, as was the case after World War I. I spoke to Jim Bennett about this, reminding him that after five years of war the number of prisoners in the federal prisons had dropped considerably and suggesting that after the war the Government take care of our long-term prisoners. His immediate response indicated that he had thought this problem through and had already come to a number of conclusions. He said that he would not accept any prisoners who had been convicted of military crimes, and that of the nonmilitary prisoners he would only take those screened by him. He said he would think over the problem and give us a final answer. He did so and, later, the federal prisons took thousands of our prisoners, saving the Army huge sums of money and great responsibility for the care of these men and their guards.

I do not think it is too much to say that the Army's record in handling its military prisoners was an outstanding one. Indeed, the way in which the Army Correction Division was set up indicates the Army's exceptional ability to put plans in operation promptly and effectively. After careful study of the problem, McCormack and I presented our ideas for a Correction Division to Patterson one morning. He made certain changes in our proposed draft, and asked General Somervell to come into the room. After making other suggestions as to the Army procedure, Somervell sent for General Styer, his Chief of Staff. Within an hour an order was drafted, which was soon signed, and the Army's Correction Division was in existence that afternoon. McCormack, who was then working full-time with us, was astounded when he saw how quickly this was done. He remarked that in civilian life it would have taken months and months of planning, followed by approval by some state bureau, and then, after months more of debate, passage by the state legislature, and, ultimately, approval by the Governor—and not until then would it have been put into effect. This had all been accomplished within a day. McCormack also felt that civilian agencies could learn a lot from studying the Army's methods. He referred to the Army's treatment of the individual after sentence and said, "This has been done more thoroughly than any civilian institution has ever been able to do it." About 24,000 prisoners were transferred to Rehabilitation Centers, and over half of these were restored to duty as soldiers and earned honorable discharges. Not a bad record.

X

MORE AND MORE PROBLEMS

On Pearl Harbor Day, a civilian high up in the War Department telephoned to ask me whether the battleship *Arizona* had been sunk. He was calling because someone from his home town had asked him to inquire whether his son, an ensign on the ship, was all right. The high-up civilian got mad when I told him that I was sorry, but this information could not be given to him over the phone. He never understood why.

Security continued to be a troublesome matter in the Undersecretary's Office, but our troubles were usually related only to the rules of the game as played by G-2. One move of the game was for them to turn up some classified papers ("Secret," "Confidential," or "Restricted") left loose in a Pentagon office overnight—this was a point for G-2. Their technique was to go through unlocked drawers and other likely spots and, when a restricted paper was uncovered, immediately to phone that office's security officer and make him come down to the Pentagon Building, even if it were 3:27 A.M. Then they made him bring down the man in whose office it had been discovered. Howard Petersen of our office hated this game and devised a countermove. As soon as he was called, he would ask for a description

162

of the paper. Then he would immediately declassify it. He had the right to do this, and the paper could then be left exactly where it was—in the unlocked drawer. But this left undecided the fine point as to whether G-2 had scored anything on this move.

Tapping phones was also a part of the game, and at rather frequent but irregular intervals, G-2 got around to us. The only trouble for G-2 was that they did it awfully clumsily. My very attractive and popular secretary, Miss Petersilia, loved to play this game. Whenever the wire was being tapped, she would immediately phone me, and her advice ran like this: "Watch out, General, be very careful. They are on again." With this and similar remarks she hoped to drive G-2 wild. I guess she did. Once we really scored big. It was just before the North African invasion. Because of the part he was to play in the invasion, we had been alerted against using Robert Murphy's name on the phone. One day when the wire was being tapped, the incoming call to me mentioned the tabooed name several times. Sure enough, shortly after this I was very respectfully asked by a captain in G-2 if I would be kind enough to step down to the G-2 office immediately on a matter of vital importance. I did so, and the Captain and a young lieutenant began questioning me. With considerable diffidence, coupled with the joyful anticipation of expectant fishermen, they brought the interrogation around to the name of Robert Murphy. They asked me if I was familiar with the taboo on the use of that name. After I said I was, they came to their big point and asked me whether that name was used in a conversation over my wire that morning. I said yes, and was then asked if it had happened more than once. I said, "Yes, several times." They were through, but I asked them if they were interested in finding out to whom I had been talking—who had used that terrible name. They admitted they might like to know. In answer I pointed to the door at the end of their room. It was the office of G-2 himself, and I told them that it was he who had phoned me and used the name. They were much disturbed when I got up to leave. They were nice boys and I felt a bit sorry for them, so I asked them if they would like it if I went in and told G-2 about our interview. They seemed much relieved and said they would appreciate it. Rather enjoying myself, I went in to G-2.

A very high-ranking "eyes only" report was circulated daily. It had to be signed for and delivered personally to Judge Patterson's secretary, Lucille Mundy, or to me. Then it went right into the safe until Judge Patterson saw it, and then back into the safe until returned to G-2 the next day for incineration (that means destruction). There were very few copies of this paper—one for Secretary Stimson, one for General Marshall, and the copy for Patterson, plus maybe one or two others. It was an awful responsibility, a terrible nuisance and a daily problem. I came to the conclusion that we shouldn't get it any more, and asked Judge Patterson whether I could request that they stop delivering it to us. I reminded him that he rarely looked at it, that he already knew of the things that he had to know about, and I would much rather not know about the other items. I asked to be relieved of this daily responsibility. He agreed, and I went to G-2 to ask them to stop delivering these reports. That interview was something! You would think that we were the worst possible subversives. It was the hottest stuff circulating in the building, and here we were telling them that we didn't want to see it any more. They were particularly bothered when I explained that we would rather not know about much of this stuff, and that what we had to know about, we knew about anyway. After quite a tussle, we won out and were taken off the list. But G-2 couldn't understand it. I am sure they felt there was something subversive and sinister about our conduct on the whole business.

There is nothing that I have said by which I intend in any way to underrate the importance of security, nor the value of its proper use.

Soon after the War Production Board was born, its different branches began finding things to do. The public-relations section was no exception, and published an information booklet that you could get just by asking for it. The Army didn't like this at all because it felt the booklet told too much. WPB brushed aside the Army's objections. Newspapers wrote up the disagreement and began to pick on the Army. Arthur Krock of

the New York *Times* joined in by making fun of the Army objections. I asked Arthur Krock over to the War Department and
gave him a copy of the controversial booklet with some items
underscored for his attention. A typical item was the number
of parkas (hooded winter overcoats) needed by a given date
on the West Coast. At the same time I handed him several
questions which I had typed out. For instance, how many troops
are to be used in an action scheduled for the Aleutian Islands
in October? It was a simple task for a man like Krock to figure
out a definitive answer to this and to many other similar questions. Krock immediately saw the point and promptly ran a
column explaining why the Army was opposed to this publication. In effect, he said that it was absurd for the Government
to compile and publish in a neat little package what amounted
to vital war information for the benefit of the enemy. Even
though everything in the booklet was public information, the
enemy would have had to put in a great deal of effort and
money to obtain these facts—and they would have had no
guarantee of the accuracy of their information.

A similar situation arose in connection with the widespread
criticism of the Army for not having a second front. In 1942
and 1943 the Army was very much in the doghouse for not
having started an invasion of Europe, and even the most reliable
and skilled war correspondents, including one of the best, Mark
Watson of the Baltimore *Sun*, were kicking up a fuss. At that
time I had been working on this subject and had prepared a
memorandum to be sent to the General Staff. I asked Judge
Patterson for permission to send for Mark Watson and show him
my memorandum and some supporting documents, all of which
were classified as "Top Secret," on his agreement that he would
never use the information. Because of our complete faith in
Watson, Patterson agreed. I sent for him, gave him this material,
and left him alone in a room with it for several hours. He never
joined in the criticism thereafter. The material I had given
him indicated as accurately as we could pinpoint it the rate of
sinking of our ships by submarines, the present rate of production, and the number of tons of supplies that were needed per
month to support each man for a year overseas. The only con-

clusion that one could draw from these figures was unambig-
uous. It was absolutely impossible for us to send enough supplies abroad to support the number of men we needed for a year.
First we had to reduce the rate of sinkings and increase the
available shipping space. Mark Watson understood.

As the war went on and gasoline rationing continued, Congress became irritated at what it felt were abuses in the use of
cars and took extreme and arbitrary action forbidding anyone
except the Secretary of War and the Chief of Staff from having
an Army car assigned to him. After this law had been passed
and just before it was to be effective, Secretary Stimson asked
me for a legal opinion as to whether it was all right for an Army
chauffeur to operate a privately owned car. If so, he wanted to
transfer a car he owned to Undersecretary Patterson and one
that his sister owned to General Somervell. After I got an
opinion from the Judge Advocate General that it could be
done, Stimson's aide gave me two automobile registrations, transferring the cars. Stimson's only instructions were that neither
of the men should know that the cars came from him. Stimson
preferred this way of handling the matter, rather than dignifying
Congress' action by opposing it publicly.

The work went on day after day, and I'm talking about every
day, seven days a week. That was what it had become. The
hours were long and hard. The only way that a person could
take it was by not thinking beyond next week, and by not per-
mitting oneself to think of one's personal life. Thousands and
thousands did the same throughout the war. People in and out
of uniform, in Washington and elsewhere. Many of them did
heroic work, but they were heroes to nobody. Early one New
Year's Eve my wife suggested that it would be nice to invite
some Army friends who were alone to come over and celebrate
the New Year with us at midnight. I thought this a fine idea
and we made up a list. The first one I phoned was a good Williams friend, Colonel John P. Loomis. He immediately said,
"Swell!" and then asked, "When is New Year's Eve?"

During the summer of 1944, it looked as if Germany could
not last much longer. D day, followed by General Patton's dash
across France and other thrilling victories, made the end seem
near. We were working on plans for the discharge of many of

our troops. But we would still have to carry on a very full-scale war against Japan, which presented us with a huge problem. We could discharge only those whom we would not need for the Japanese victory, and we had to discharge not only all the men we could spare, but all the men who had been in long enough, fought hard enough, or had done enough to make it seem unfair to keep them longer. Moreover, we did not want to discharge units wholesale, since some of the personnel were entitled to a discharge and others were clearly not. These and kindred problems were a task of the General Staff and gave rise to the "point system," which became the basis of our discharge plan. The plan provided a formula by which every soldier's discharge status could be readily determined. Points were assigned for each month of service, more points for months spent abroad, more for combat time, as well as points for decorations and points for various other services; points were also given based on a soldier's home conditions, including marriage, parenthood, and other factors. The plan needed to be explained to the G-1 (personnel) officers in the field. At several meetings in the States, I discussed the plan, while it was still tentative, with various officers. The response of the listener was always the same: careful attention, jotting figures on a sheet of paper, keeping count on fingers, adding up, a puzzled expression, and then always the same question, "How many points are needed for discharge?" Even though they never asked, "How many points do I need?" every officer was doing the same thing—seeing how he made out. But there was to be no announcement of the required number of points until later. After the plan was finally approved in Washington, I, accompanied by an officer who had had a great deal to do with drafting it, was sent to the European theater to explain it to the G-1's. And the response when we explained the plan abroad was just about the same. Everyone wanted to know first how many points he had, and then he'd be ready to talk business. Reaction to the plan was almost always favorable. First, it was good to be talking about getting out, and, then too, the plan itself, which had been given a great deal of thought before it was set up, seemed fair and reasonable to most people.

The trip gave me a good opportunity for some glimpses of

Europe during the war: Scotland and England, ports in Wales, then Paris, which we saw soon after its liberation, a side trip to Omaha and Utah beaches, and back to London via Cherbourg. Then to Naples via North Africa, on up to Rome, Florence, and the line above, flying over France to England, up to Scotland, and back home on the *Queen Mary* with a shipful of wounded soldiers and some notables including Bing Crosby and Fred Astaire.

Another job that the Undersecretary's Office was involved in began several years earlier when, after returning from the White House, Patterson sent for me and told me that we would have to use some of our Expediting Production Funds * for a secret purpose that was not to be disclosed to anyone, and that whenever money was requested by General Leslie R. Groves, it was to be given to him with no questions asked. He said that this was all he could tell me, and he didn't have any idea how much money it would be. He wanted to know if I could carry out these instructions. I said that if he could give me permission to tell the officer in charge of the Expediting Production Funds account as much as I had just been told, I thought it could be managed. He gave me this permission.

General Groves came frequently to our office and he often brought with him a young lawyer, Colonel John Lansdale, Jr., his security officer. They discussed many things with me, but I never asked any questions. The following gives an idea of the kind of matters that they brought up with me:

A complaint was made by a very distinguished scientist who had been working for this project that he was fired and no reasons were given for it. The project, which had the innocuous name of Manhattan District, was known among scientists as being a very sensitive operation, and if a man was fired from it, it was a serious reflection on him and would probably mean that he could not get any other position involving war work. I was told by Colonel Lansdale that there had been good and sufficient reason for firing this man, but there was nothing what-

---

* Expediting Production Funds were an item in the budget which the Undersecretary could spend in such manner as he deemed proper.

ever against his character or his loyalty and that they just could not give any reason for his discharge. I was not satisfied and wanted further information. Finally, I was told that he had been fired because, as head of a division, he had completely ignored all security regulations, in spite of being told time and again that he had to comply, thus making it impossible throughout his unit to have security enforced at all. I thought this over for a long time and felt that the reason was probably a good and sufficient one, but I felt that the man ought to be given something he could use to protect his reputation. Accordingly, he did receive a letter which said that not only was he a man of great distinction, but was of undoubted loyalty, and that his leaving Manhattan District should not prevent his being employed in other war work.

The National Labor Relations Board had been looking into a labor dispute at the Manhattan District plant in Oak Ridge, Tennessee. Groves was protesting violently against the ordering of a plant-wide election there. He felt very strongly that it was important from a security angle to keep operations separate, and if there were an election on a plant-wide basis, this would inevitably mean that everybody would know about everybody else's business. I agreed with him, but felt that this did not give the NLRB any excuse for not carrying out the law. Nor did I think it was wise for General Groves to go before the NLRB. He just knew too much he couldn't tell them. Finally, I thought of a plan: the President, acting under the War Powers Act, should designate someone other than the NLRB to decide all labor matters relating to Manhattan District work. If the NLRB wanted to, it could discuss this with the President. But, of course, I had to get authority before suggesting this to the NLRB. I asked Jonathan Daniels in the Office of the President for permission to present this to the NLRB. Daniels told me that I could go ahead. I then showed the NLRB a draft of a proposed executive order naming Daniels in place of the NLRB to handle the matter under the War Powers Act. The NLRB finally agreed to do nothing.

After we had given Groves $1,700,000,000 (*sic*), he told me that I would be glad to learn that that was all he needed. But

before I was finished breathing a great sigh of relief, he was
back again. He was sorry, but he had found he would need just
a little bit more—$300,000,000—to finish the work at Hanford,
in the State of Washington. I had followed the President's instructions and given Groves everything he asked for without
any questions, but this seemed a little bit steep to me, and so I
told him to come back tomorrow. I spoke to Patterson about it,
and he asked whether I could get the money. When I said that
I thought I could, he told me to go ahead and give it to Groves.
Still troubled about it, I thought that we should do something
to check up, and suggested to Patterson that we send Madigan
out to Hanford to investigate. Patterson reluctantly agreed, and
I asked Madigan to go. Within three or four days he was back
in the office, cigar in mouth as usual. I yelled at him and
asked him why he hadn't gone. He said that he had been there
and back, and was now ready to report. I asked for the report,
but he said he wanted to give it to Patterson, not to me. I said
that he couldn't see Patterson until four o'clock, and he said he
couldn't wait. He wouldn't tell me anything, so I made arrangements for him to see Patterson right away. Patterson asked what
he had found out, and then came his reply, in these immortal
words: "If it works, you have *nothing* to worry about. If it
doesn't work, you have *nothing else* to worry about." When
asked to repeat this he did so, adding that he had looked around
at Hanford, saw miles and miles of buildings, different kinds of
buildings of all sorts. He said he could assemble a crew of
engineers, assign them to various parts of the project, and after
weeks and maybe months of study, he could assemble their
reports. They would be bound in thick books with lots of tabs
sticking out at the ends, and all these reports would be submitted to other, even bigger engineers back here in Washington.
And what would they say? Nothing. Or maybe, if the project
should fail—and we could show that even if we had given them
that extra $300,000,000 it would have failed just the same—the
study would show that Greenbaum was right; all that the project
would then have cost us was the measly sum of ONE BILLION,
SEVEN HUNDRED MILLION DOLLARS. Patterson listened
very carefully and very thoughtfully, and then said without a

smile, "Oh, get out of here!" He knew Madigan was right, and so did I.

The morning after President Roosevelt died, Patterson sent for me. He told me that Secretary Stimson had asked to see me and I should go in to him right away. I asked him what it was about, and he said Stimson would tell me and that it was all right to do what he would ask me. As soon as I was in his office, Stimson handed me a letter to read from F.D.R., saying that he had just received it. Roosevelt wrote that he had read Stimson's memorandum endorsing the Corps of Engineers' disapproval of the MVA (Missouri Valley Authority) and asked Stimson to reconsider his position and advise F.D.R. personally.

Stimson said that the letter had greatly disturbed him and wanted to know whether I had ever studied the MVA project. When I told him I had not, he asked if I could get away from my work for several days, look into the problem, and give him my own views without talking to anyone else about it. I told him that I would and left his office much upset. He wanted someone to share with him the great responsibility he felt. I felt sorry for him. I could very well understand how troubled he was by this message from his dead chief, and it made me again realize what a tremendous burden he had been carrying. I studied the problem carefully and gave Stimson my report, in which I reluctantly agreed with him.

A short time after that we learned that the atomic-bomb test had been successful at Alamogordo. Then came the big news of Hiroshima. I phoned my wife at her studio in Washington, told her what had happened, and arranged to meet her for lunch. I was so happy and excited that I could hardly speak. She was excited, too, but had tears in her eyes. She had known nothing whatever about Manhattan District or Alamogordo, nor anything at all concerning the project. But she understood much better than I did what lay ahead. All I could think of was that the war was going to be over—and we could go home.

I've often thought back to that since. Why wasn't I horrified? I knew what had happened. We had dropped one of those Manhattan District things from the sky and a city had disap-

peared. Thousands of its people had been incinerated, and a
few days later we did it again to another city.

War made one immune to this type of thing, I guess. It had
been going on for years. You squeezed the trigger of a rifle, and
someone died; you fired a shell, and more people were killed.
That's what war was doing all the time. That's what war was
always about.

While the Japanese envoys had been meeting with us in
Washington back in December, 1941, to prevent war, their planes
had suddenly dropped bombs killing the men having breakfast
at Hickam Field or on their ships at Pearl Harbor. Before that,
London, Coventry, and so many other cities in England had
been bombed by the Germans, and then other bombs were
launched at them from the Continent. For years we had lived
with the fear that the Germans might succeed in their efforts
to do the same thing to us with atomic bombs.

In August, 1939, Dr. Albert Einstein had warned the President
that "extremely powerful bombs of a new type" might be con-
structed, and advised that we look into this. We had enlisted
the services of our leading scientists, under the leadership of
Dr. James B. Conant, president of Harvard, and Dr. Vannevar
Bush. We had spent two billion dollars to build a bomb—and
now we had succeeded. As Secretary Stimson pointed out in the
article which he published in the February, 1947, issue of
Harper's Magazine, "It was a common objective, throughout the
war, to be the first to produce an atomic weapon and use it."

In 1945 it was no longer necessary to fear that Germany
would use the bomb against us. The country had surrendered
and we were meeting in Berlin with our Allies when news of
Alamogordo was received. Our new President, who had been
told about Manhattan District by Secretary Stimson just after
he had assumed office, was now in command. He had to make
the decision.

We still had the gigantic task of defeating Japan. In order to
do it we would have to land in Japan and then fight our way
to final victory against a military strength, which, although
weakened, was then estimated at five million men. Our war
plan told us that it would cost us one million casualties to do

this, and we would have to commit troops who had already been through years of devastating fighting in Europe. Our war-weary economy on the home front would have to be told that it must still go forward. And we were prepared to do just that. The operation was to be launched on November 1st. To support it, our people would have to endure the agonies of having millions of husbands, fathers, and sons shipped to the Far East for this hazardous undertaking.

All of this, Secretary Stimson believed, could be avoided by using the bomb. He had given months of soul-searching study to the problem, and he finally recommended that we use the bomb. On July 26th, 1945, our Allies joined in issuing the Potsdam Declaration telling the Japanese that if they continued the war, it would mean "the inevitable and complete destruction of the Japanese armed forces" and "the utter devastation of the Japanese homeland." Two days later the Premier of Japan responded to this warning, saying it was "unworthy of public notice." * This response was tantamount to rejection and Hiro-

---

* It should be noted that the reaction to the Potsdam Declaration was many days before the Hiroshima bomb. The exact meaning that the Japanese wanted to give when they turned down the Potsdam ultimatum has been subject to quite a little discussion. In Herbert Feis's book *The Atomic Bomb and the End of World War II,* he implies that the Japanese official reaction to the Potsdam ultimatum was "withholding comment." In Toshikazu Kase's *Journey to the Missouri,* the author says that the Japanese Army at first opposed a publication of the Potsdam Declaration, "but was finally prevailed upon by the Foreign Office to agree to it," although the part about allowing the Japanese Army to return to "peaceful and productive lives" and the statement that the Japanese were not to be "enslaved as a race or destroyed as a nation" were suppressed. The Emperor and many others wanted to accept this proposition outright, but the opposition, the members of the Supreme War Council and others, and the aged Prime Minister, Suzuki, "told the press it was the policy of the government to ignore the Proclamation [sic] entirely." Suzuki's statement was printed, and it was published in America. The book goes on to say: "The punishment came swiftly. An atomic bomb was dropped on Hiroshima on August 6th by the Allies who were led by Suzuki's outrageous statement into the belief that our government had refused to accept the Potsdam Proclamation." Kase continues: "Had Suzuki been more steadfast or his advisers less stupid, we might have been spared the atomic attack." Then he adds: "To state expressly that we would ignore the Proclamation was entirely contrary to the purpose of the decision."

shima was bombed on August 6th and then Nagasaki on August 9th.

This was not an irresponsible act. Maybe if we had not dropped the bomb, our casualties would have been fewer than one million. Maybe the Japanese would soon have given up without losing many more thousands of lives. But nobody knows the answers to these things—except those of the younger generation who loosely give answers for everything. Who knows which of them would be alive today if the bomb had not been dropped and their fathers had not been recalled from the attack on Japan? And who knows that we would now be free from the problems of atomic warfare if we had not dropped the bomb?

For many years it will be debated whether those who dropped the bomb should be condemned or defended. The debate may be useless, but it will persist. It cannot be denied that many more lives would have been lost by the continuance of the war. Dropping the two bombs saved many times the number of lives that incendiary bombs would have destroyed, and, says Vannevar Bush, certainly ended the war "under such conditions that we were free to begin the rehabilitation of the Japanese people rather than forced to undertake the conquest of a starving desert inhabited by a broken lot of physical and mental wrecks." *

Secretary of War Stimson, who had the initial responsibility for this awesome decision, said later, "The bombs dropped on Hiroshima and Nagasaki ended a war. They also made it wholly clear that we must never have another war. This is the lesson men and leaders everywhere must learn, and I believe that when they learn it, they will find a way to lasting peace. There is no other choice." No one can fairly and honestly criticize Secretary Stimson for using the weapon that instantly stopped a further and enormous loss of life, both Japanese and American. Not to use it would have been "irresponsibility so flagrant as to deserve condign punishment." †

---

* See *Modern Arms and Free Men.*

† See *On Active Service in Peace and War,* by Henry L. Stimson and McGeorge Bundy.

The first few days after Hiroshima and Nagasaki were hectic ones. Peace was expected at any moment. Messages went back and forth to Japan. Early one morning we heard on the radio that New York was celebrating the end of the war. To share in Washington's celebration, my wife and I got up and went for breakfast to the Hotel Washington, which is right opposite the Treasury Department, very near the White House. But the dining room wasn't open, and everything was quiet in the streets. Finally we got breakfast, but we were the only ones in the dining room. Then we walked to Lafayette Park, just across from the White House. There were three or four strollers around. But nothing happened, nothing at all. After a while, I decided that I had better go to the office, but my wife stayed there. She waited for hours, but no announcement came. It was just a normal day in Washington.

At the office, too, everything was normal. We were expecting a message from the Japanese that we hoped would be accepted as the final surrender. During the afternoon, McCloy sent for me and showed me a message which had come to the Swiss Embassy. The War Department, knowing the code, had it already, and Stimson had seen it and thought it was O.K., but wanted Patterson's opinion. I brought it to Patterson, who agreed with Stimson. Then we waited and waited and waited to hear from the White House. Nothing. At about six o'clock, we had still heard nothing and I went home. I had scarcely gotten there before everything exploded. The message had just come over the air. The White House announced that the war was over. Whistles started blowing, automobile horns were tooting, the whole world suddenly turned right side up. With my wife, we drove down toward the White House. So did everyone else. They came in cars or on foot, dancing, singing, yelling and screaming, arm in arm, three abreast, five abreast, columns of ten, twenty, soldiers, sailors, girls, boys, everybody. They were all there. Dancing, kissing, singing and shouting. It was wonderful!

Next morning at the office, I said that Washington had put on the greatest show ever. Later I was told that Mrs. Esther Rice, one of our most respected civilian employees, had said

when she heard this, "The General wasn't here the night the
Senators won the pennant!" That put me in my place.

Why did it take so long from the time we had seen the
message in the Pentagon until the White House made its
announcement? I was told that the Swiss Embassy had sent
the message over to the White House by a Western Union
boy who went on a bicycle. Rounding DuPont Circle he was
picked up for speeding, and that had to be cleared up before
he could complete his delivery. I will not vouch for this, and
don't see how a bicycle would be charged with speeding, but
he might have made a wrong turn—or something. In view of
the orderly way in which things must be done in Washington,
it seems very likely that a traffic violation would have to be
disposed of before a message to the White House could be
delivered.

Termination notices on nearly all our contracts had been
drafted to go out right after the happening of this blessed event.
Lines of officers crowded into my office to get clearance, and
hordes of others had to get approval for this, that, and the other
thing. At the height of the hubbub, Madigan wandered in and
stood watching. When he heard me say something about the
headaches we were all having, he listened with disgust, then
turned to leave, muttering, "The executive officer of the Secretary
of War of Japan. Has *he* got a headache tonight!"

There had been much concern as to what an economic disaster
would strike the country when peace came. Estimates had been
made that unemployment figures would increase by 20,000,000.
The lowest estimates were 12,000,000. All the economists had
predicted dire consequences. Their estimates were supported by
studies and by unanswerable argument. The distinction of these
experts and the plausibility of their arguments seemed to make
it certain that the country would be in for a pretty tough time.
The Committee on Economic Development, headed by Paul Hoffman, seemed to be the only outfit to disagree. Its prediction was
that there would be very little unemployment. This was based on
a plant-by-plant study which showed that peacetime production
was looked forward to in nearly all the plants and that most of
them had actually worked out plans for effecting a prompt re-

conversion. Peace came. No disruption took place. The country was still standing, and the period of our greatest prosperity began. Without a blush, the economists explained all this and showed, for reasons I never understood, that their predictions were sound.

Stimson resigned. The General Officers, assembled down at the airport to see him off, formed two lines. The Secretary and Mrs. Stimson walked between us onto the plane. He waved farewell and he was gone. The war was really over we now knew.

Patterson was appointed Secretary of War in his place. A few days before, Patterson had come back from the White House and asked me to come into his office. He said that President Truman had offered to appoint him Secretary of War or Supreme Court Justice, asking which he preferred. He had replied that he did not care which. The following day Patterson was sent for by Justice Byrnes, who was then Secretary of State. When he returned, he told me that Byrnes had asked him if he actually didn't care which job he took. Patterson said that was correct. Naturally, he was appointed Secretary of War. My feeling is that it really was a matter of indifference to Patterson. He never planned things for himself, and he respected and honored the position that Stimson had held and was proud to serve in it.

They wanted to put on a big show when Patterson was to be sworn in as Secretary, and I was told to make the arrangements. I knew very well that he would not want this, but I did ask who he would like to swear him in as Secretary. He said any notary public would do. I thought we ought to do a little better than that, and having heard that Judge Learned Hand was in town, I asked Patterson whether he would want to ask Hand to swear him in—and he did. Some time after that, Judge Hand referred to himself as Patterson's favorite notary public.

Patterson moved into the Secretary's Office, and my wife, as she had done for him on previous occasions, supervised fixing up the room. The days following Patterson's swearing in continued to be long and hard. We were in the process of unwinding—and there was a lot to unwind. Everybody, of course, wanted to get out of the Army, but on the whole, the process of discharge went fairly smoothly under our system of points.

At last the time came, toward the end of November, when I felt I could leave. I spoke to Patterson and asked him whether he didn't agree. He said he did, but he wanted to know whether I would remain and be his Undersecretary. I thanked him, but said I would like to get back to my law office, and soon my discharge came through.

We had a goodbye in his office. I had a big lump in my throat and found that I couldn't say anything. Neither could he. I had tears in my eyes. So did he. We shook hands and I left. Afterward I got a wonderful letter from him. No one ever had a finer boss. It was not until after he was killed several years later in a senseless airplane accident in Elizabeth, New Jersey, that I realized that I had been serving under a truly great man.

I had had very little time off during my period of service, so I had accumulated quite a lot of leave. We needed a holiday and decided to go to Santa Fe. Leaving Washington in a third-hand Ford, we headed west. Driving through our newly peaceful land was quite an experience. We spent the nights at different Army posts along the way, including a stop at the Command School at Fort Leavenworth, where I gave a talk on the work of the Undersecretary's Office. There they discovered that I had bursitis in my left shoulder, and I was scared I'd be kept at Leavenworth. (I was finally allowed to leave after agreeing to report for treatment at the General Hospital in Santa Fe.) At a prisoner-of-war camp on the way, we were warned that a big snowstorm was coming and were advised to hurry along. The old Ford coughed its way over the Cimarron Pass. No one had warned me about the effects of high altitude on a low-grade car. After a long, awful drive, with batteries run down and dim headlights that barely picked out "Danger Ahead" and "Bad Curves" on the signs, we finally got into Taos late at night. The next morning was a glorious one; snow was falling at a great rate. I got up and found our car completely covered with snow and supported by two flat tires. What timing! We stayed at the Bishop's Lodge near Santa Fe until just before Christmas and then returned to New York.

I received a letter from Arthur Sulzberger, in which he said that it had always been his thought that we could work together and that now I must be thinking of coming back to civilian life and he wanted me to come and work at the *Times*. I was very flattered, not only because of my affection for him and respect for the New York *Times,* but because I had always felt that working on a newspaper was the best job anyone could ever have—except, of course, being a lawyer. I never seriously considered Arthur's offer, but I admit I liked it! Although I didn't take the job at the *Times,* I'm glad to say that I've spent a lot of my time working as a lawyer on New York *Times* problems for the majority-stock ownership, both before and after I got his letter. One of my younger partners, Wirth Koenig, has now taken over a great deal of this work.

The firm was still located at 285 Madison Avenue. But during the war we had sold (practically "given away," according to my wife) our home at 162 East Seventy-fourth Street. We had to live in a hotel, and were trying to get what we called "re-adjusted." This included getting a suit of clothes, for I hadn't worn any civilian clothes for over five years and had nothing I could wear. It was literally true that it took me over a week before I could buy a suit. I finally managed it, though, and when it was delivered to the office, I changed in the washroom on the twenty-second floor. I felt very strange when I put the new suit on. But I went back to my own room and nobody noticed that I had changed! After work, I went home in the bus in my new civilian clothes, standing all the way. Nobody noticed what I was wearing. Now I was a civilian again.

But people still called me "General." They seemed to like to. As a friend (Adlai Stevenson) put it, "During the war everybody called the General 'Eddie.' Now everybody calls Eddie 'the General.'"

XI

OUT OF THE ARMY

It wasn't too difficult getting back to being a civilian lawyer. Although I hadn't looked at a law book for over five years, I didn't find myself out of practice. At first I was bored—for the first time since I started to practice law. For a while everything seemed much less exciting than the work that I had just been doing. Anyway, I discovered that other friends, when they came out of service, had the same deflationary experience. But it didn't last long with me, and I was soon just as excited about my law practice as ever.

For the first few months, about half of each day was spent at the New York *Times* on a special legal job, and the rest of my time was devoted to the work of other clients. In a surprisingly short time, I was working as hard as ever and in much the same way as before. But I found I was being asked to do more and more jobs of a public sort. One evening about six, just before I was leaving the office, the Chief of Staff phoned from Washington. He was General Joseph L. Collins and he wanted to know if he could send a general from the Medical Department to see me in my office in the morning about a case that was coming up in the New York courts. The General came

with a captain as his assistant, and told me quite a story. If the
case were to be tried, it was likely to lead to the publication of
material that could be blown up into a story that would give
the Army a black eye far worse than the actual facts justified.
The thing to do, it seemed to me, was to tell the whole story
to the District Attorney and trust that this frank disclosure
would result in a guilty plea and a suspended sentence. That's
what was done, and a one-day inside-page news story was the
the end of the matter. It had taken quite a bit of time, but it
was good to feel that I could still be of assistance to the Army
in an emergency.

One of the things that had always troubled me was the
awful language that lawyers use when they write. I found
when I got back to my practice that this bothered me even
more than before. Taking advantage of the G.I. Bill of Rights,
I took a course on "Clear Writing," taught by Dr. Rudolf
Flesch, at New York University in its General Education
Department. Each week we were asked to write about some
current news subject, and the following week the paper was given
back. My brother-in-law Bennett Epstein, who after his retirement
reviewed books for several periodicals and entertained his friends
and family with his biting and humorous skits, asked me to show
him what I had written, and I gave him the week's piece. It
was about General William S. Knudsen, who had just died.
Bennett read it and said, "Why don't you sell it?" I asked to
whom, and he replied, deadpan, "To *The Saturday Evening
Post.*" I mailed the piece in, and to his horror and my amazement, a few weeks later I received a check for $500.* Because
I didn't want to lose the distinction of having *The Saturday
Evening Post* accept everything that I ever sent, I never sent
them anything again!

Lloyd Garrison, who was chairman of a Bar Association committee on lectures asked me to give a talk about drafting wills,
trusts, mortgages, or something or other. I didn't do it, but told
him that he should have a talk about how lawyers wrote. This
resulted in his arranging a debate between me and Charles P.

---

* "This Was Bill Knudsen," *The Saturday Evening Post,* June 26, 1948.

Curtis of Boston. My side was entitled "Lawyers Talk Too Much," and I suppose his side was that they didn't talk enough. Anyway, his talk was much more erudite than mine, and a much better job.

My paper was later published,* and I got a letter about the article from a humorless friend of mine who was a judge. It was complimentary, but he was disappointed by the 136-word last sentence, in which, he said, I had shown that I had not learned my own lesson. He didn't know that I was kidding, and told me to practice what I preached. I never answered this letter. I didn't know how. The article appears in the Appendix (pp. 229–36), and if you read it, I hope you won't take the last sentence too literally.

Coming back to the law office made me realize how much work habits had changed during the war. Hours were shorter. Offices were generally closed on Saturday. Holidays were much more frequent. When Bob Patterson got out of the service, he remarked on this to me and asked me how we ever got any work done. Incidentally, he also complained about the fact that it was hard to get a meal in a restaurant. Everything was so crowded. I asked him why he hadn't rejoined the Lawyers' Club. He said that it took three or four years on account of the long waiting list. When I got back to my office, I called up Whitney North Seymour, who was on the Nominating Committee, and told him of this conversation. In a few days, the former Secretary of War phoned to me to tell me that he had just been re-elected to the Lawyers' Club. He was delighted and asked me down to have lunch with him the next day.

Patterson was made president of the Association of the Bar of the City of New York, and because I had urged his election I was asked to remain as its vice president. This enabled me to renew our wartime relationship, and once again I was spending considerable time with him.

Because of several bad accidents on the Long Island Rail Road, Governor Thomas E. Dewey appointed Patterson as chairman of a commission to investigate the railroad. The other mem-

---

* "Lawyers Talk Too Much," 19 *Federal Rules Decisions,* October, 1956.

bers were Bob Moses and Judge Charles C. Lockwood of Brooklyn. I was appointed counsel, and we soon assembled an outstanding staff. When he appointed this commission, the Governor instructed us to get our report in within three months. We
met the deadline, but the staff, including its lawyers and engineers, really had to work hard to make this time limit. My work
covered the whole railroad, including Montauk, Greenport, and
spending the night in the L.I.R.R.'s Special Working Car at
Jamaica. We recommended that an "Authority" be created to take
over the L.I.R.R., since the railroad was an essential service and
could never be successfully operated as a money-making ven-
ture. But the Governor wouldn't buy our recommendation. Such
action wouldn't have helped him get the hoped-for nomination
for President next spring. Now, more than twenty years later,
the State of New York has come to the same conclusion as the
Commission did, and the Long Island Rail Road is run by an
Authority. How it will work remains to be seen.

Another job I was asked to do was to be a member of the
United States delegation to the United Nations. It was 1956
and a particularly tough time because of the Suez Canal problems and Hungary. John Foster Dulles was the Secretary of
State, and he asked me to serve as a delegate. He explained
that it would be a full-time job for about four months, including
a good deal of time in the evenings for social activities. He said
that while he was a member of his law firm, he had served, and
hoped that I would do so. He wanted me to let him know the
following day. I told him the answer would then have to be
no, but that if he would give me a few more days it might be
different. He did. Besides having doubts as to whether I was
qualified for the job, I wondered whether I should again pull
away from my firm, even for four months. I asked George F.
Kennan for his advice, since he had previously talked about
the United Nations with me. He again told me that our foreign
affairs should be conducted by professionals and that an individual member of the United Nations delegation could really
do nothing. But instead of advising me not to accept, he strongly
urged me to serve. He thought it was important that we have
delegates from this country who were not merely political ap-

pointees, and after talking it over with my wife and partners, I agreed to serve. The ten statutory members consisted of the two permanent representatives, Henry Cabot Lodge and James J. Wadsworth; two Congressional members, Senators William F. Knowland and Hubert H. Humphrey; and six other delegates, who seemed to be selected to get a representative cross section. I was chosen, I presume, because I was a Democrat and a Jew.

Most of the delegates' work was done in the committees. Generally speaking, every item on the Assembly's agenda went to one of its standing committees. For example, one of the areas assigned to me was the law of the sea, and this was handled by Committee No. 6, the legal committee. The Special Political Committee took care of such matters as Vietnam and Korea, which were also assigned to me. Every country is represented on each committee, and the representatives are seated alphabetically by countries. On my left was the delegate from the United Kingdom, and on my right was the delegate from Uruguay. The U.S.S.R. was close by. At one of my first meetings, my eyes suddenly rested on the sign just in front of me—"United States of America"—and I found myself wondering idly who represented our country. Then it suddenly dawned on me—and I got a chill. In that moment, I realized the responsibility of my assignment. When I spoke, it was the United States that was speaking.

Our delegation lived at the Hotel Vanderbilt on Park Avenue at Thirty-fourth Street. We had offices in a building to the south on the west side of Park Avenue. Each day began and ended at the office there. My office was next to that of my fellow delegate Paul Hoffman. Most days started with a meeting of the ten members of the delegation sitting around a table and about thirty professionals from the State Department assigned to the Mission to help us in our work. Ambassador Lodge presided and asked each delegate for his views before the next item on the agenda was taken up.

The day usually ended with a round of social activities, and, when there was enough money in the Mission's coffers, included a lunch that we would give for a group of delegates. The parties were usually either at the U.N. or at some hotel. They were amazingly alike, but it was a good way to get acquainted with delegates from other countries. I varied it a bit by giving a dinner near the end of the session at the Williams Club, followed by a visit to the New York *Times,* where the guests were given an informal briefing by the *Times* editor Turner Catledge on how tomorrow's paper had been prepared and an opportunity to see it come rolling off the presses. I think that it was an interesting evening, and the *Times* followed it up by holding similar meetings for other groups of delegates.

During that session, Japan was admitted to membership in the United Nations and I got to know Ambassador Toshikazu Kase, who was an Amherst man. This acquaintanceship gave me the extremely pleasant opportunity of being with him in Tokyo years later. Other friends that I made at the U.N. included Lady Kay Eliot, now a member of the House of Lords, whom we have visited several times at her home in Hawick, Scotland, and Sir Kenneth Bailey, who was the Solicitor General of Australia, and became one of my close friends. George Kennan was certainly right, and as far as I am concerned, it has meant a great deal to me to have been able to meet and know such persons. They have, I believe, given me greater understanding of the problems of their countries and people.

Before the last meeting of our delegation, I prepared a somewhat unorthodox resolution and offered it on behalf of my colleagues. Although it was a bit irregular, our delegation passed it. Here's what it said, in authentic United Nations language:

KNOWLAND, HUMPHREY, GREENBAUM, HOFFMAN, JONES, NASH and LORD,

Recalling the pre-Krishna era before we became members of this Delegation,

Recognizing that since then we have learned much and suffered more, and participated in quite a rat race,

Abstaining from a more appropriate and accurate description thereof,

Bearing in mind how much more we would have suffered without the aid and encouragement of Ambassadors Henry Cabot Lodge, Jr., James J. Wadsworth and their able staff,

Appreciating the confidence they have shown in us by unfailingly and completely leaving each of us to paddle our own canoes through the tricky waters of responsibility allocated to each,

Noting that our sentences are about to expire . . .

We then went on to

Express our deep appreciation (a) To the State Department for the
instruction it has given us in the use of words, phrases, colons, semi-
colons and even the commas, to so confuse, bewilder and mystify
that no one can possibly understand what is meant or even implied,
(b) To the staff of the Mission for interpreting the instructions of
the Department so ably that occasionally a glimmer of understanding
penetrated the foggy minds of the delegates and otherwise making
it possible for us to carry out instructions of the Department,

Commend Ambassadors Lodge and Wadsworth for the extraordinary
and superhuman brilliancy which gives them the power to survive
bushels of draft resolutions, buckets of canned canapés, stale olives
and diluted liquor.

I'm glad that I served. It was a real education for me and
allowed me to participate firsthand in one phase of the handling
of our foreign affairs. Although I cannot truly say that our delegation contributed anything much to the welfare of nations, I
feel strongly that without the United Nations, the world would
be much worse off.

As the flow of new countries continues and membership in-
creases, changing the U.N.'s internal regulatory procedure has
become a necessity. The General Assembly was not created for
a membership of its present size (122 nations). The U.N.
has grown tremendously since it was organized, including the
recent admission of the Maldive Islands, which have the same
voting rights in the General Assembly as the United States and
the Soviet Union. (I have to admit that I had never even heard
of that nation before it became a member.)

It is doubtful whether the General Assembly can long exist
unless some action is taken to meet this situation. New nations
should be welcomed and a place found for them without strain-
ing the machinery originally designed for a constituency of
much smaller size. Real statesmanship is required to let these
new nations belong without giving them rights and obligations
far in excess of what is needed and far beyond what they are
capable of fulfilling.* Maybe the Security Council should be

---

* See "The U.N. Needs Family Planning," by Francis T. P. Plimpton, in *The
New York Times Magazine*, September 18, 1966.

given the right to take certain steps which presently require action by the General Assembly.

It was characteristic of most work in the legal profession that when my term in the General Assembly was up, I returned to my law office, and the United Nations was out of my life. I no longer have anything whatever to do with it. It still fascinates me, and I would have been very interested in continuing to work on problems there, but I was back at the office again, working full-time on other matters, and not too much later found myself busily engaged in another public-service assignment.

Not too long after the war we had moved down to Princeton, New Jersey, and I began commuting. After renting there for a short time, we bought a house with a studio and became New Jersey residents. Governor Robert E. Meyner asked me to be a member of a group he was appointing to study and make recommendations about the operation of the Department of Institutions and Agencies, the largest department in the state, which included all prisons, mental health institutions and social work agencies throughout New Jersey. Because I felt I should contribute some public service to my new state, and because I thought this would give me a good opportunity to see the state and learn something about it, I accepted.

We were to take a look at the work that had been started in 1918 on the recommendations of a commission under Governor Dwight W. Morrow. At that time each of the prisons, mental institutions, and other agencies was put under the authority of a board appointed by the Governor, with statutory power "to manage, direct and control" their respective organizations. But since then a full-time commission with a professional status had been set up to run the department. Most of the local board members were the highest type of citizens, and the boards did good work. But in the past forty years many things had changed in New Jersey, as they had throughout the country. No longer was it either desirable or possible for a local board to run its own prison, hospital, or agency. Personnel was under civil service; food, clothing, and equipment were centrally purchased. The program of each organization could no longer be locally determined, and many other things were necessarily controlled by the state central office. Yet each board was still charged with the responsibility for running its own organization and "managing, directing and controlling" its affairs. This seemed to me a glaring inconsistency that required correction, and I felt that was why the Governor had appointed our group to look into it. Most of the local boards knew little about the details of what was going on in similar institutions elsewhere. What to do about this situation? It was a difficult problem because there were so many local loyalties and cross-currents to take into account. Four of our commissioners felt that the changes that had taken place in the past forty years made it necessary to change the functions of the local boards. Their present statutory powers had been steadily eroded by the practical daily needs of the system. Common standards, common procedures and integrated programs were now essential. The twenty-two local boards could no longer operate independently. We felt that these board members should be relieved of local housekeeping duties and charged with broader state-wide responsibilities. But we ended up by filing a divided, four-to-two report, which naturally contributed little, if anything, to a solution of the problem. But it was an interesting task and I learned a great deal about the department and the state from my service on the commission.

At about this time, my partner Morris Ernst was asked to represent Trujillo on charges that he caused Jesús de Galíndez, a Columbia professor, to be kidnaped and then murdered. Morris' acceptance of the job was widely denounced—particularly because he was well known as a liberal lawyer. How could any lawyer defend Trujillo? Because one of our partners agreed with this view, our firm did not represent him; we never take a case when a partner objects. That did not relieve our firm of criticism when Morris decided to undertake the job in his own name. He did not know whether Trujillo was guilty of the Galíndez charge, but he thought the charge deserved a thorough, unbiased investigation. He agreed to do it on the understanding that he could withdraw if any witness was not made available, and that he could publish the report whether the client liked it or not. He made a thorough investigation, felt that his client disclosed all the facts, and then published his report giving the material facts.

One question, it seemed to me, was this: Does the fact that Trujillo was a ruthless dictator and probably guilty of many charges preclude a lawyer from defending him on other charges? If he was not guilty of them, it appeared shocking to me to deny him the right to have a lawyer. If we deny an innocent man the right to have counsel, aren't we really nullifying our whole system of justice?

But, I believe, the question is broader than that. Right to counsel should not be dependent on the party's guilt or innocence. When this situation arose, in 1958, I tried to answer one of the critical letters I received by writing this in my reply to a client whom I had defended gratis in a loyalty case:

We should bear in mind the necessity for having honest legal representation for all who are accused, those whom we loathe and abhor as well as those we admire and respect, those who can pay as well as those who cannot, those who are guilty as well as those who are innocent. This concept was obliterated in Nazi Germany, is unknown in Soviet Russia and for all I know in the Dominican Republic. But it is basic with us and indeed essential for the survival of our form of government. It is our way of seeking the truth. This concept is in accord with the highest tradition of our profession. It led John Adams to defend the British soldiers after the Boston massacre. And more recently it has led many—but not enough—devoted lawyers to represent Communists and victims of McCarthyism, in spite of the abuse that has been heaped upon them. Unfortunately, the American public's failure to appreciate the necessity for honest representation of the unpopular has frightened many lawyers from this difficult and unpleasant task.

If the right to have a lawyer is made dependent upon the man's innocence of what is charged, then our system becomes unworkable. If the right to a lawyer is dependent upon whether he is guilty of something else, then obviously no one may have a lawyer unless he is free from prior taint. The adoption of such a standard would, in effect, be the acceptance of the Russian system of having a trial only for those whose guilt has already been determined, or, putting it another way, to determine guilt without trial. For, under the Russian system, no one can be tried whose guilt has not already been established. That means that the trial is merely the procedure for publicly proclaiming someone's guilt, and clearly that is best done by confession.

While I was still in the Army, I got word that Justice Robert
H. Jackson wanted some books sent to him at Nuremberg describing our system of determining the guilt of an accused. When
he got back, I found out that before the trial started, he had
been discussing the question as to who should be tried with
General I. T. Nikitchenko, the young Russian major general who
was a member of the court. Nikitchenko could not understand
why the Western powers were insisting on trying anyone whose
guilt had not yet been determined. Jackson had asked how one
knew someone was guilty until he had been tried. The Russian
felt it was barbaric and cruel to subject a man to a trial, where
he had to suffer and face the public, and then find out he was
not guilty. Jackson made a similar point in the Preface to
his book *The Nürnberg Case* and in an address delivered to the
Institute on the Teaching of International and Comparative Law.
In it he referred to the view of the Soviet representative at the
Nuremberg trial: "That the Nazi leaders are criminals has already been established. The task of the tribunal is only to determine the measure of the guilt of each particular person and mete
out the necessary punishment—the sentences." But the doctrine
that the tribunal was bound by the declaration of guilt by the
heads of the governments was finally rejected, and the Soviets
agreed that the tribunal would decide independently. But I
wonder what General Nikitchenko thought about all this. Like
so many other arguments, it arose from mutual misunderstand-
ing, based on different fundamental approaches to the same
subject.

In England, no obloquy attaches to a lawyer who defends a
man who is unpopular for any reason, whether he is a Communist, a Fascist, or just a scoundrel. But here it takes a brave man
to defend anyone whose cause is unpopular, whether he is a
Negro in Alabama, a Communist (or one suspected of being
such) in the McCarthy days, or a Trujillo at any time.

Nor can the criticism of Morris for taking the case be justified
simply because Trujillo had not been indicted or otherwise
charged in the courts in this country. The fact was that the
charges against him were made in newspapers, magazines, on
the radio and TV. They were voiced everywhere, in Con-

gress and other high places. How could the charges be
answered? What is wrong about a lawyer's agreeing to
investigate the charges, examine the witnesses, and publish
his findings, whatever they may be? Some claimed that the work
was undertaken for the purpose of disproving the charges, and
that the report would be but a brief for the client. If that were
true, it would, of course, be hard to justify. But if the work was
undertaken honestly and performed in a conscientious, lawyer-
like way, then I submit that the report could not be subject to
any legitimate criticism. In this case few, if any, of the critics
read the report. The investigations were conducted by competent, reputable people, including a distinguished former New
York Supreme Court justice, William Munson, and other able
lawyers. Putting it mildly, the report leaves the fair-minded
reader in grave doubt as to whether Trujillo was guilty of the
kidnaping or the murder of Galíndez. Indeed, the reader is left
in considerable doubt about Galíndez. Was he just the college
professor he was said to be or was he a secret agent engaged on
a Government mission, with plenty of funds at his disposal?

Maybe the question really is whether the person responsible
for the report should be commended rather than censured for
undertaking it. At the outset, it was obvious that considerable
criticism would result. It often takes courage to uphold the
highest standards of our profession. Maybe this was one of those
times.

Service to the Dominican Republic in the Galíndez case, or
to the State of New Jersey on the Governor's commission, or to
New York State in regard to the Long Island Rail Road, or to
the United States at the United Nations are outside the ordinary
work of the office—but they are all part of a lawyer's job.

There were also some extremely interesting by-products of
the normal work that I did for clients. One grew out of work
with a college classmate of mine, Dean Langmuir. He was an
extremely original character, with a most intriguing mind, and
was our class valedictorian when we graduated. He became
investment counsel for our firm. My brother-in-law will always
remember him for a breakfast at the Williams Inn early in their
acquaintanceship. Dean was a bit overweight and was dieting.

After his orange juice and baked apple, cornflakes and buck-
wheat cakes, he was just starting his scrambled eggs when he
suddenly discovered that he had no saccharine to put in his
coffee. He had fits, but nothing compared with my brother-in-
law.

Some friends of mine had unique investment problems, which
were presented to me as their lawyer. I naturally turned to Dean.
Through an inheritance, my friends had acquired a rather sizable
pile, and the money had become quite a problem for them.
They did not want it to overwhelm their lives; nor did they
just want to give to the normal run of charities and become
Lord and Lady Bountiful. Years of careful work with them and
Dean produced a record of many generous anonymous gifts to
a lot of liberal causes, but each year also ended with a rather
sour record—the fund got bigger and bigger.

Dean suddenly died. We had really solved nothing. We had
the same problem all over again—with lots more money. Dean's
brother, Irving Langmuir, the Nobel Prize winner from General
Electric, came to see me one day about something concerning
Dean's estate. During our conversation, he talked of his interest
in a project to find the structure of a protein. The idea, which
I couldn't really understand, was to isolate the elements from
the atom by experimenting with diffraction from crystals. If this
could be accomplished, Irving Langmuir thought it would lead
us to the very line that divided living matter from that which
was no longer living. He attached the greatest significance to
this investigation and told me that he considered it even more
important than splitting the atom. He said that the people at
the Rockefeller Foundation believed as he did, and that he had
an assistant at G.E., Dr. David Harker, who felt the same way
and was ready to resign from the company and devote the next
ten years of his life to this work.

I told Irving about my clients who had become so attached
to Dean, and indicated that they might be willing to do something in his memory. He became quite excited and introduced
me to Warren Weaver, who was the director of scientific research at the Rockefeller Foundation. Weaver was just as en-
thusiastic about what might result from the project and what

my clients might contribute toward it. But again I didn't understand. All they could contribute was money, and while it was
a lot, it was only peanuts compared with the Rockefeller money.
He told me that this was not so, that they had something much
more to give if they were willing to do so. When I asked what
that was, he said their interest, their support, their sponsorship.
Then he explained to me something I had never thought of
before, which became very useful to me in connection with my
work with other foundations. Every project has three essential
prerequisites. First, of course, it has to be worthwhile and have
real validity. Second, it needs enough money to support it for
a minimum projected time. And third, it must have someone,
some person or organization other than the people operating it,
who cares enough about it to contribute to it financially and
support it in other ways.

If, he said, my people could supply this third prerequisite,
the Rockefeller Foundation would also contribute funds for its
support. I talked to my clients, and while obviously I could not
explain the project very intelligently, they understood enough
and agreed. But they didn't even want their names known to the
Rockefeller people. This became a bit of a problem, but when
I discussed the situation with Vanderbilt Webb, the counsel to
the Foundation (Bob Patterson's partner, whom I had known
for years), he solved it by suggesting that I write a letter saying
that in my opinion anything that my unnamed clients agreed to
would be carried out. So we made a contract, providing what
my clients would give for each of the next ten years, and the
Rockefeller Foundation agreed to give a like amount.

David Harker soon started the Protein Structure Project at
Brooklyn Polytechnic Institute, assembled a staff, and obtained
the right to use IBM computer facilities in New York. Years of
experimentation and hard work followed. A vast amount of trial
and error tested Harker's resourcefulness as well as the tremendous patience of both Harker and his sponsors. At the end
of ten years, Dr. Harker and his project moved to Roswell Park
at Rochester, where his perseverance and enthusiasm continued.
After six more years of hard work, success was finally achieved.
In a front-page story on January 22, 1967, the New York *Times*

announced the results of the project as a "momentous discovery." Deciphering the structure of ribonuclease, the enzyme that had been chosen by Harker, enabled him to learn the contents of a substance that is crucial to all living cells. It can be thought of as one of the regulators of life, which start, stop, speed, and slow all living tissue and play a part in the process of direction of reproduction. The discovery has aroused much interest not only among chemists, but also in the field of health and medicine. It has been suggested that ribonuclease, which controls cell growth, may possibly be of vital importance in the study of cancer, as well as of certain mental diseases.

It may be that the minor role that I played in this situation was more important than anything else I ever did.

XII

AFTER MORE THAN FIFTY YEARS

I USED TO drop in on Sunday afternoons at C. C. Burlingham's. On one of these occasions, Judge Augustus N. Hand, Otto Wierum, and a Harvard Law School classmate of C.C.B.'s were visiting. He was then almost totally blind and could not hear you unless he held his hearing aid right up to your mouth. When a newcomer entered, this is what C.C.B. did to find out who he was. When I told him, he immediately said, "Thank God you came. You brought the average age down to eighty-seven."

Although I've not yet reached that average age, I'm only ten years away and feel that I've earned the right to reflect about the law.

A while back I said that the machinery of our courts in almost every phase, including the manner in which our judges are chosen, lacks efficiency, operates clumsily, and cries out for improvement. Judges are chosen mostly for political reasons, courts are administered by antique methods, and the whole administrative procedure operates in total disregard and ignorance of modern methods. The result is inordinate delay, excessive cost, and bewildering uncertainty (see p. 213). That was true when I started out to practice law, and it is true today.

Because my father was a judge, I knew from a very young age that courts were in existence to decide disputes between people, and to decide whether a person was guilty or innocent and whether he should be free or go to jail. As a boy I assumed that because courts were so important, they were necessarily well run. But I soon found out that they weren't. The way the courts were run was so primitive that it seemed as if they were operating in a different world. The simplest cases turned into big, time-consuming productions. It was not only the delay but the red tape. Even after a case was tried, it could be reversed— sometimes, it seemed to me, for totally unimportant and unnecessary reasons. Nobody seemed to mind this; most lawyers didn't appear to notice it. Even my father, when I spoke to him about it, wasn't the least bit disturbed and was a little bothered by why I was paying attention to this. He really wasn't interested. Neither was Judge Cardozo when I once spoke to him about it.

But for some reason I was much interested in the unbusinesslike way in which the courts were run, and I was continually clipping articles pointing up the problems—and still do. C.C.B. was one of the only people who knew what I was talking about. He was always working on ideas of his own for court reform and always encouraged me in my interest.

In the early thirties I heard about the new Institute of Law at Johns Hopkins University and went down to Baltimore to see it. Its job was, as I understood it, to see how the courts were operating and study methods for improving their machinery. While I was there, I suggested that they conduct a survey showing how the New York courts ran, and, as I mentioned earlier, they agreed to do so under Professor Herman Oliphant. With C.C.B.'s encouragement and help, the Johns Hopkins Survey of Litigation was started in New York, and a small group of lawyers that I got together worked on it. We gathered much information from thousands of actual cases and learned a great deal. After a few years the Johns Hopkins project was forced to close up, but the work was carried on by the New York Law Society, which we organized for that purpose, and continued under Oliphant's leadership.

When F.D.R. became Governor, we had ideas about what we

wanted him to do in this direction, and I made a date over the phone to go up to Albany and discuss this with him at lunch. I thought that he said I should come up the next Wednesday at 12:30 and jotted this down in my diary, but about one o'clock the next Tuesday he phoned me and asked what better date I had gotten after he dated me up for lunch that day. He said I was the first person who had stood him up since he had become Governor. Anyway, he said I could come up the next day, which I did. But he kidded me about the broken date for quite a while after that.

F.D.R. was really interested in improving the administration of justice; he felt strongly that this was not a problem just for judges and lawyers and that it would never be solved unless non-lawyers cared about it and took an active part in it.

Beginning with his acceptance speech in 1928, he said that the law had failed to keep pace with the advances of business methods, that it was too costly, too slow, and too complex. In his first message to the state legislature, he added that we had built up a highly complicated system of judicial procedure which did "not conform to the ideals of modern efficiency and simplicity." He called for a study of the whole subject to be made by a "body of citizens representing the bench, the bar and laymen." When the legislature created a commission composed of lawyers only, he vetoed it, saying that the commission's job was to examine "the very framework and foundation of the system, which is universally regarded as archaic, expensive and inefficient," and that the remedy to these conditions was "more important to the layman than to the lawyer."

In his next annual message, he repeated his plea. Again he stressed having a commission with non-lawyers on it who would push it along. The bill creating the commission was subsequently passed. To the commission he named Robert H. Jackson (later a Supreme Court Justice) and Raymond Moley. Herman Oliphant, of the Johns Hopkins Institute of Law, became its counsel. Although they did an excellent job of investigation and filed a valuable thousand-page report, the only concrete result was a "Judicial Conference" which only had power to gather statistics and make recommendations. Roosevelt realized that the problem

of what he called "the law's injustices, delays and costs" had
risen "beyond the state of mere dissatisfaction to a public problem of major importance." * Yet he was unable to do more.

Our little New York Law Society kept working after Roosevelt moved to Washington and Oliphant was abducted by Morgenthau. We arranged for Yale Law School, under Professor
William Douglas' leadership, to steer the ship. But gradually
most of our group, starting with Douglas, went to Washington,
and many joined the services.

After the war, some of us were still afflicted with the mania
to do something about our courts. So Bethuel M. Webster,
Whitney North Seymour, Francis H. Horan and a few ardent
recruits, including Allen T. Klots and Alfred R. Connelly, were
back on the job. Bob Patterson, as the president of the Bar Association, at a public hearing said that the conditions in our courts
were "appalling and disgraceful." David W. Peck, then the Presiding Justice of the Appellate Division in New York, called for
immediate action. And nothing happened. I do not mean that
no committees were working on this. There were plenty. Each
had its own job and each did good work. There was a committee
dealing with taxation, another with matrimonial problems, one
with labor, another with discipline, and plenty more, including
art and entertainment. But none dealt with the over-all problem
of judicial administration.

In 1952 Beth Webster became president of the Association
and decided to do something about it. He appointed a "Special
Committee" to pull together all the work relating to the administration of justice. Funds were made available by the New York
Foundation and John D. Rockefeller, III, to obtain extremely
competent professional help, including Leland L. Tolman, Chief
of Business Administration of the Administrative Office of the
United States Courts. The committee worked closely with Paul
B. DeWitt, the executive director of the Bar Association, whose
appointment to that position changed the Association from being
a respectable, gloomy mausoleum to a live-wire professional or-

---

* Speech before the New York City Bar Association on March 11, 1932.

ganization (and has helped keep it that way ever since). Professor Maurice Rosenberg, the director of the Project for Effective Justice at Columbia Law School, made a most valuable third member of this triumvirate of professionals, whose new profession has not yet been given a name but whose contribution to judicial administration is already enormous.

The committee's final report, called "Bad Housekeeping," a title chosen by Frank Horan, gave facts and made recommendations which led to the establishment of a unified court system, to be directed by a Judicial Conference under the Chief Judge of the Court of Appeals. The report proved very useful in helping to achieve the judicial structure provided in the 1961 constitutional amendment which was to come.

A small group of us, including members of this Special Committee, felt that a lot could be gained by discussing matters informally among lawyers and judges in a coherent, planned manner, with the aid of Leland Tolman and the other professionals. We met in quiet and unhurried surroundings—first, with Presiding Justice Peck and then with Presiding Justice Bernard Botein of the Appellate Division—in New York and Princeton. It was pleasantly unorthodox and informal but, I hope, productive.

At Princeton we applied the most important principle that Harrison Tweed had discovered when he was president of the Bar Association—that liquid refreshment aided this work. We found that this was even more true out of New York than in the city, and learned that on-the-rocks and off-the-rocks worked equally well. Each of these meetings lasted for a couple of days, and the informal routine gradually became an established tradition. In the afternoon the group would gather at the terrace in the back of my house in Princeton for a little get-together, with my wife helping to keep the glasses full. This was followed by dinner at the Princeton Inn, then by a meeting lasting until near midnight, when the group divided for smaller talkfests. After a good night's sleep and breakfast at the Inn, we would meet at the Institute for Advanced Study in the morning and spend as much time as we needed out there until well after lunch. Whether it was the aura cast by the spirit of the late Dr. Albert Einstein or the interest of the Institute and its director, Dr.

Robert Oppenheimer, or something else, I think that we always
ended the meetings feeling that we had gotten a lot out of our
Princeton jaunt.

What did we do there? It is hard to say anything as far as a
concrete, specific program. To put it in a negative way—we did
not want the gathering to degenerate into the usual lawyers' meeting of unprepared discussion followed by undirected inaction.
We prepared for the meeting, set a specific program that we
wanted to follow and topics that we wanted to hear discussed by
those who were there. They usually included the Presiding Justice
of the Appellate Division and judges and lawyers who were
really expert in the particular areas that we talked about, such
as Chief Justice Weintraub of New Jersey and his court admin-
istrator, Edward McConnell.

These informal but thorough discussions were, I believe, of
very real benefit. One of the basic ideas that we felt was essential
was to create a court system that unified all the courts under one
head, giving him the administrative assistance needed to carry
out his responsibilities. This principle underlay the modern system which governed the New Jersey courts. It was provided for
in the new state constitution, which Justice Arthur T. Vanderbilt
had succeeded in having the citizens adopt at the polls. It was
not accomplished by the judges or the lawyers, but by those who
were not lawyers—the businessmen, the workers, the women, the
people generally—those who were most concerned.

A few of us decided to try to do the same in New York. In
March, 1955, we called a meeting at the Bar Association of some
of our leading citizens who we thought might be interested. We
explained that the courts were created not for lawyers, not for
judges, but for the citizens. The lawyers merely presented the
cases to the courts and the judges merely decided them. Whether
the cases took too long, or whether they cost too much, or
whether they were too complicated, the citizen was the one
affected. This was not a matter of primary concern to the judge
or to the lawyer, but it was to the citizen whose case was
being tried. It was he who had the greatest stake in the courts,
and he was the only one who could do something about them.
For this reason, we thought it necessary to organize a citizens

committee to do this work. We told them that no real improvement could come into the courts unless laymen took an active part. The librarian of the Bar Association had assembled reports of the many different committees that had gone into this subject during the past years. I brought down these reports from the library and showed them to the meeting. They consisted of more than 25,000 pages. These laymen understood. They cared. The Committee for Modern Courts was born. (Allen Klots thought of the name.) Edwin F. Chinlund, of R. H. Macy and Company, became the first chairman, and Lawrence Wilkinson, of the Continental Can Company, the vice-chairman; Howard Lindsay, the actor-playwright,* and others were active workers. They raised money for the committee, with a substantial contribution coming from Harold K. Hochschild, of American Metal Climax, who in his quiet and anonymous way provided the funds which started the organization. Help came from the New York Foundation and John D. Rockefeller, III, who made it possible for the committee to produce a play called *The Maze* that played throughout the state to many audiences in order to show them the need for a statewide reorganization in the Family Court.

The Committee for Modern Courts worked with the State Commission headed by Harrison Tweed. Unfortunately after years of hard work, its program met with defeat. But although it could not get the votes to pass the bills needed to modernize the courts, the citizens finally woke up and cried for reform. The cry was loud enough to force the appointment of a legislative committee and a committee of judges to undertake the task of getting a measure which would pass the legislature. In 1961 the voters got their chance. By this time, Nelson A. Rockefeller was the Governor, and the voters were ready to vote on an amendment to the judiciary article of the state constitution.

The Committee for Modern Courts, with the support of the League of Women Voters, labor groups, chambers of commerce and many other organizations throughout the state, got busy.

---

* Mr. Lindsay said that amongst the many rewarding features of his service on the Board of Directors was that he learned the difference between a "J.P." and a "P.J." (a Justice of the Peace and a Presiding Justice).

The people really went to work. They organized committees.
They held meetings. They wrote to their state assemblymen and
senators, and got bills passed by the legislature. They continued
with their meetings. They went on the air—radio and television.
They wrote pamphlets. They distributed circulars at railroad
stations. They got out the vote. They made their power felt.

As a result, a constitutional amendment to change the structure
of the judiciary in New York (most of which are usually defeated
by inertia) went through with flying colors in 1961. New York
City, for instance, voted for reorganization by the astounding
vote of 1,028,522 to 146,363. This unprecedented vote made the
political leaders realize for the first time the brand-new fact that
people really cared about their courts and were ready to do something about them.

Until the constitutional amendment was passed, each judge
in New York was the boss of his own court. No one was in charge
of all the courts. It was impossible even to find out the number
of judges we had in the state. Nor did we know the number of
cases before the courts or the amount of work that each judge did.
All we really knew was that justice was too slow, too costly, and
too uncertain. The 1961 amendment was the most important step
that had been taken in over one hundred years to modernize our
courts and to end the law's delay. The fossilized system of
sprawling courts all over the state was ended by the enactment
of a single, monumental sentence: "There shall be a unified court
system for the State."

The Chief Judge of the Court of Appeals was made the state's
chief judicial officer and chairman of a board which was given
the administrative responsibility and authority to run the courts
of the state.

But despite this great victory, the image of the courts in New
York as a place where justice is done has hardly improved since
the constitution was amended in 1961. Over forty years ago, I
wrote:

The sinister significance of the present-day attitude toward courts
and lawyers lies in the fact that this feeling of distrust has so far
permeated our consciousness as to constitute an organic part of our
national credo. Instead of merely criticizing occasional or frequent

miscarriages of justice, we expect them. It is the cynical habit of today to assume in advance that justice will be brought into further disrepute.

To justify this statement, I made a brief summary of the dozen most important cases of 1927. The result was pretty awful. Nearly every case met with public dissatisfaction.

Tests made in later years were just as bad. The dozen or so cases that occupied most newspaper space each year were hardly calculated to instill public confidence in the judicial process. Because most of those cases are long forgotten and because our interest is in what's happening today, I suggest we take a look at 1966. Here are a few of the dozen or so that got the most newspaper space in that year.

The New York Transit Strike

The first big case in 1966 was the litigation arising out of the New York transit strike. The contract with the transit workers hadn't yet expired and John V. Lindsay, the new mayor, hadn't yet taken office when the strike began. The subway stopped. The buses stopped. Those who operated them didn't go to work. But they were all city employees and the law forbade them to strike. The Condon-Wadlin law said it was illegal. So an injunction was signed forbidding the strike. The union leader tore it up on television, with everybody looking on, saying, "May the Judge in his black robes drop dead." He and the other leaders were ordered to jail.

The strike continued. The Chairman of the Transit Authority filed an affidavit saying it brought untold hardship to millions in the city and the economic losses were $100,000,000 a day. Finally the strike was settled. An agreement for increased pay was made and the injunction was canceled. Everybody seemed happy. It was now all over and the people could again take the buses and the subway to work.

But a lawyer named George Weinstein, who apparently believed in law, brought an action asking the courts: How could the Transit Authority and the other city officials make an agreement that was forbidden by law? Didn't the Condon-Wadlin law say that striking government employees couldn't get a raise for three years? When the court heard this, the judge said that, of course, that was right and the raises were illegal.

This meant the settlement agreement was illegal. What was going to happen now? Were we going to have this business all over again, with no buses and no subway? Something had to be done and at once. So it was proposed that the legislature pass a new law saying that it was all right not to pay any attention to the old law. According to the New York *Times*, the senators and assemblymen said the new law was "awful," "hypocritical," "unconstitutional," and "an outrage." But they all voted for it.

Soon another action was brought asking the court to decide that this new law was unconstitutional. The State of New York, the Mayor, the Transit Commission, the Civil Service Commission, and the unions all appeared and said that there was nothing unconstitutional about it. The judge agreed, and added that the plaintiff, merely a citizen and taxpayer, had no right to attack the law.*

Gareth Martinis

Then there was the case of Gareth Martinis. Martinis had been in an automobile accident on May 19, 1963, in which five people had been killed and another permanently injured. He had left the scene of the accident and had been arrested that night in the home of a friend on a misdemeanor charge, driving while intoxicated and leaving the scene. He was soon tried and acquitted by a three-judge court which deliberated about five minutes. Martinis' father was a judge of that court, although he did not sit on that case. More than two months later, Martinis was indicted for a felony charging vehicular homicide. Martinis' lawyer asked that the trial be stopped because he could not be tried after his acquittal. All five Appellate Court judges

---

* This problem is still facing the courts in other cases. See "Mockery on No-Strike Law," New York *Times*, March 14, 1967.

agreed that he couldn't be tried, but the Court of Appeals, the state's highest court, felt differently. It has seven judges. Three agreed, and three others didn't, but the seventh judge said that whether or not it was double jeopardy couldn't be decided until the felony case was tried.

So the felony trial was held. After a long trial and days of deliberation, the jury could not agree, as contrasted with the five-minute deliberation at the previous trial. The trial judge then dismissed the indictment because the evidence at this second trial showed that Martinis was subject to double jeopardy. The District Attorney appealed from that ruling, and the Court of Appeals decided that the original acquittal barred any further action.

Jack Ruby

Two days after President Kennedy's assassination, I, along with millions of others, watched Lee Harvey Oswald, handcuffed to a police officer, walking across my television screen. A man, just in front of him, pointed a pistol at him and he slumped to the ground. It was hard to believe that we had actually seen a murder and not just another scene from *Gunsmoke*.

But it was real all right, and soon the man who shot him, Jack Ruby, was tried and found guilty of murder in the first degree. There were motions to move the trial from Dallas, sanity hearings, and proceedings to disqualify the judge, who was writing a book about the trial. And then an appeal, and nearly three years later a court decided that Ruby was wrongfully convicted and had to be tried over again. But why?

There wasn't the slightest doubt in the world that Ruby had killed Oswald. Everyone had seen it. But the Texas Court of Criminal Appeals said that during the long trial a police officer testified that Ruby had said that in the police line-up two days before "when he saw the sarcastic sneer on Oswald's face, he had decided that if he got a chance to do so, he would kill him." The Court said that the judge should not have allowed this testimony. In effect, it was confession showing premeditation.

But why was his conviction set aside? Why did the officer's statement warrant that drastic action? Why wouldn't it have been far better, if the judgment had to be reversed, to find Ruby guilty of the lesser offense of murder without premeditation and reduce the sentence to an appropriate term of years? Wouldn't this have been a fair and proper thing to do? That's what would have happened after a trial in England or in a court-martial in the United States Army. Soon after the reversal, Ruby died.

And a Few More—

During all of 1966 and a long while before, the fabulous Congressman Adam Clayton Powell had occupied the time of the courts. It was in March, 1960, that Esther James got a judgment against him for calling her a "bag woman" on a TV program. He probably could have settled it by a small payment or an apology, but instead he totally ignored the lawsuit, and a default judgment was taken against him. As a result of his conduct he has repeatedly been held in contempt of court, the judgment against him has mounted to over $165,000, and the time of at least seventy-five judges has been consumed on busy days in trying to decide his moves to exploit the weaknesses of our judicial system. It is said that a stack of court papers over twenty feet high has been accumulated in this process. Enough material to keep a law school class busy for a full year has been gathered, I believe, on the subjects of Congressional immunity, public officers, fraudulent transfers, civil and criminal contempt, and numerous other matters. His fellow Congressmen have also been required to give much of their time attempting to reconcile his Congressional conduct with the law, morality, the color of his skin, and the right of an electorate to choose its own representative. The Powell soap opera will undoubtedly continue to supply more news for the public.

In the middle of December, Jacqueline Kennedy started her lawsuit to stop the publication by Harper & Row of William

Manchester's *The Death of a President*. She claimed a violation of a contract between the author and her brother-in-law Robert F. Kennedy, then the Attorney General, providing that the book couldn't be published without her consent. The court was also asked to stop *Look* from publishing its serialization of the book, which was scheduled to commence in early January. The defendants were ordered to appear in court on December 27th to "show cause" why the injunction should not be granted. Before that date, the case against *Look* was dropped, but Harper's was ready and submitted their papers in court. But Mrs. Kennedy chose not to go on with her motion for a temporary injunction. Then the case was put on for immediate trial at Harper's urging, and Senator Kennedy was scheduled to be examined before trial. But on January 16th, just before the case was to come on for trial, the plaintiff consented to a decree which provided that Harper & Row could publish the book as scheduled in April with several changes in the text which were agreed to by the author, and the case ended.*

The United States Supreme Court contributed to this 1966 list of cases, and the case of Dr. Sam Sheppard is high on the list. The Court set aside Dr. Sheppard's conviction for murdering his wife in 1954. This was not because the evidence of his guilt was found to be insufficient, or because there was newly discovered evidence, but solely because the Court felt that the trial had been conducted in a "carnival atmosphere" likened to a "Roman circus." Indeed, when the decision was announced, Justice Tom C. Clark is reported to have pointed out that the decision did not in any way take into consideration Sheppard's guilt or innocence.† Later in the year, Sheppard was acquitted at the new trial, with the famous F. Lee Bailey as his attorney.

If Sheppard was not guilty, why was he kept in jail all those

---

* Because my firm represented Harper & Row in this case, as we had in other matters since my partner Morris Ernst first did so many years ago, I may not have given the facts impartially, although I have tried to do so. I have reread what I have written, and it seems to me to tell the story fairly. I hope so.

† The New York *Times*, June 7, 1966.

years before he was given a new trial? His amazing book, *Endure and Conquer*, tells a lot more about the case, but leaves that question unanswered. And it should be noted that Hugo L. Black, the Court's most stalwart defender of civil liberties, dissented from the Clark opinion granting a new trial.

The Supreme Court's holding in this case, whether right or wrong, and its decisions in some other cases granting new trials either because the defendant's confession was allowed in evidence or because the defendant had no lawyer do not seem to many to justify setting aside a guilty verdict, unless in fact there was doubt of the defendant's guilt. Thus the New York *Times,* in its lead editorial ("Murderers at Large," February 23, 1967), refers to the inevitable and right community reaction of "outrage and apprehension" when a confessed murderer of his wife and five children is freed under the rules laid down by the Supreme Court. Two days later the *Times* reported the conviction in Arizona of Ernesto Miranda, whose original conviction was overturned by the Supreme Court in one of its leading confession cases.

These cases remind one of the comment of an eminent lawyer years ago that it was just as hard to predict a decision of the Supreme Court as to guess what would become of a banana tossed into a cage of chimps.* These decisions leave the man in the street wondering what is right or wrong and what is the law. This is especially true when some of the Justices of the Supreme Court register their dissent in opinions which ridicule and condemn the opinion of the majority.

Not only did 1966 show how badly some of the machinery in our courts operates, but it also gave an example of how badly New York's machinery for choosing a judge can work. This time it was a surrogate. He is the judge who sits in the court that administers estates. Each county in New York has one, except New York County, which has two. One of them was approaching age seventy and could no longer sit, so a successor had to be chosen. Supreme Court Justice Arthur G. Klein was

---

* "The Supreme Court," by George M. Martin, *Harper's Magazine,* March, 1935.

unanimously nominated by the Democratic County Executive Committee for this position, and the same day the Republicans also nominated him. That seemed to make him the next surrogate. The news of the nominations was greeted with customary indifference.

But a few days later, the indifference departed, and the apparent certainty became top news. Someone had told Senator Robert F. Kennedy about the matter. Although Klein had been legally chosen by the leaders who had the authority to do so, Kennedy said that the bosses had chosen him, and Kennedy was determined to get another candidate. He stirred up lawyers to nominate someone else. He said nothing against Klein, except that he was boss-selected. Klein had been a Congressman and a very regular Democrat for many years. He was not a Reform Democrat, as Kennedy was, and had obviously been selected with the approval of J. Raymond Jones, the organization leader whom Kennedy opposed. Kennedy put his support behind State Supreme Court Justice Samuel J. Silverman. He had been elected to the Supreme Court a few years before, while a partner of Adlai Stevenson. Edward N. Costikyan, also a member of that firm and a Reform Democrat to the precise degree that Silverman is one, had held the position of county chairman. Silverman was an able judge and thoroughly *persona grata* to Kennedy.

This started a full-fledged local campaign, with much newspaper publicity, ads in the subways and buses, campaign committees, and street-corner meetings. But nobody asked why two Supreme Court justices were willing to give up their jobs to be a surrogate. The Supreme Court is a higher court, with broad jurisdiction throughout the state, and pays an annual salary of $37,-000. The Surrogate's Court is a lower court, with local specialized jurisdiction, operating only in New York City, with the same salary.

Much to the surprise of most people, Silverman was chosen as the Democratic nominee and beat his Republican opponent, Klein, in the primary election. This settled the great issue as to which Supreme Court justice should now step down from his high court and limit his judicial duties to surrogating. In the fall election, Silverman was overwhelmingly elected over his Republican opponent, Klein. This, I feel, was in itself a matter of minor importance. However, it well points up a much larger issue—which is not only the problem of selecting judges, but the entire tangled question of court organization.

During the surrogate's campaign, the New York *Post* carried front-page stories telling of the "patronage" given to members of political clubs and others by the Surrogate's Court. After the primary, the New York *Times* published a feature story to the same effect. It told of the great difficulty its reporters had in getting the facts. The whole matter seemed clothed in secrecy. Edward Costikyan, in *Behind Closed Doors,* says that if patronage is a dirty term, "judicial patronage" is worse and "calls to mind the image of venal political lawyers living off the meager estates of widows and orphans, receiving exorbitant fees for doing nothing." But, he says, that is really not the true picture of judicial patronage. Most of the lawyers appointed are honest, most of them get very small fees, and most of them work for it. There are legitimate jobs to be done and maybe some of them should be done by regular full-time employees, but the fact is that today this work is done by those chosen by judges in specific cases. This enables the judge to give out jobs. Naturally the judges will listen to names and suggestions from political leaders and others. Moreover, some jobs carry very substantial fees and some of the chosen are far from the best lawyers. Much of the patronage given out by judges goes to those who work at the clubs of both the Democratic and Republican parties and to others whose names appear on a "list." Naming persons to positions has become a basic part of our political party system. It enables the winning party to give jobs in the executive branch to the faithful. And in the judicial branch it is convenient for the political organizations to be able to have access to these small-fee appointments, which in the aggregate make up quite a sizable number of rewards for the faithful.

At a hearing before the Joint Legislative Committee on Court Reorganization in the fall following the election, Senator Kennedy urged the abolition of the system appointing special guardians which he called "a sort of political toll booth in which estates must make a contribution." The committee heard him in silence and asked no questions. Justice Silverman urged the abolition of the Surrogate's Court and its merger into the Supreme Court. This testimony was vigorously disputed by other witnesses, including five surrogates and representatives of the Bar Associations.

The close relationship between the courts and the political parties is shown by the fact that nearly a third of the party leaders in both the Democratic and Republican parties were employed in the courts, and nearly three-quarters of these were non-lawyers in positions, such as clerks and secretaries of justices, which call for a legal background.

Among the serious afflictions borne by the citizenry as a result of bad judicial organization and administration are the interminable delays in resolving litigated matters. Articles constantly appear in newspapers and magazines telling how long it takes before a case is disposed of. Since 1932 I've been keeping clippings on this. Some of them are reproduced on page 213. News of the law's delay, of course, is no surprise, for we know what Charles Dickens wrote of the Jarndyce case, what Shakespeare said of the law's delay, and that King John was made to promise at Runnymede that prompt justice would be denied to no man.

Our own Constitution guarantees a speedy trial. But what do we do to make good our promise? Speaking generally, nothing much except to make speeches and pass resolutions. At an important meeting of a prominent group (like the American Bar Association) a leading public figure (like the Chief Justice of the United States) will make a speech. After referring to the "intolerable and unjustifiable delay" in our courts, which he says is "compromising the basic rights of thousands of Americans" and "corroding the very foundation of constitutional government," he concludes with an eloquent plea.* He asks that every lawyer and every bar association see that something is done. Gen-

---

* "Courts in Crisis," by Irving R. Kaufman, 52 American Bar Association Journal 1026, November, 1966.

erally he doesn't say what, but sometimes he says that democracy depends upon our ability to protect the rights of individuals, and if we don't do it, the Communists will win out. Therefore, we must do something—get more judges, abolish juries, settle all our cases, join with others in getting better work out of the courts—something like that. His listeners leave with a glow because they have taken part in this constructive meeting. When they come back next year, they hear another eloquent speaker tell them that they should do something, and they feel that they have again contributed.

Clearly the objectives of court reform are still a distance away. Expense, delay, confusion, and suspicion are all still very much a part of the administration of justice. But the fact is that through the hard work of many lawyers and private citizens, the foundation has been laid in New York State for real improvement. The first steps are being taken now and daylight is ahead.

Before the constitutional amendment was passed, the Tweed Commission did get through a bill in 1956 creating a Judicial Conference. This agency was given certain administrative responsibilities and, with the Chief Judge of the Court of Appeals as its chairman and with Presiding Justices of the Appellate Division among its members, it did have some responsibility for the courts but no real authority to carry out its task. Justice Peck was then the Presiding Justice in the First Department, and I was one of the lawyer members of that department's committee. When this work started, its purpose was a bit vague, and while the group was not exactly resented, there was certainly a bit of resistance to its work. Justice Peck handled the problem with restraint and discretion. Nevertheless, a feeling had been created that the work of the judiciary was no longer limited to the independent handling of each separate court working on its own. A broader concept of the judiciary as a whole was emerging, and after the constitutional amendment was passed in 1961, the Conference and its departmental committees began to take form. Now they had power. Now they could do things. Presiding Justice Botein, who was then in command, exercised his power with great restraint and then gradually had the Conference

The Law's Delay — Year After Year

N.Y. Times 1/22/32

W'S DELAYS LAID O BENCH AND BAR

cock Attacks Judicial Dis-nesty and Guthrie Scores Dilatory Motions.

N.Y. Times 7/25/32

RY CASES SWAMP IUNICIPAL COURT

Is Delayed by Defendants Defer Judgments, County Lawyers' Group Charges.

IE WAIT FOR 17 MONTHS

iry Is Urged to Identify rneys Who Hamper Justice and to Reveal Motives.

V LEGISLATION IS SOUGHT

N.Y. Times 1/13/34

URT BREAKDOWN EAR, BAR ASSERTS

eral Association Tells Leh-an Congested Calendars Here Frustrate Justice.

ALS LAG 3 TO 5 YEARS

000 Cases in Brooklyn Are heard—Governor Awaits Commission Report.

N.Y. Times 1/7/34

'POOR MAN'S COURT' URGED BY LEHMAN; 7 REFORMS ASKED

In Message He Proposes Trial Without Lawyers in Cases Under $100.

DELAYS OF 4 YEARS CITED

Judicial Council, Referees and Law Revision Body Are Also Advocated.

N.Y. Evening Sun 12/23/36

JUDGE ASSAILS COURT DELAYS

Justice Black Says Action Should Be Speeded.

HE CITES 'LEGAL TORTOISE'

Finds Moscow Insurance Case Has 'Snailed' Through Law.

N.Y. Herald Tribune 11/19/50

Leaders of Bar Starting Study Of Court Delays

Group Seeks Ways to Ease Judicial Log Jam and End Years of Awaiting Trial

N.Y. Herald Tribune 1/23/52

Peck Appoints Board to Ease Court Logjam

Settlements, Jury Waivers To Be Pushed in Backlog of 13,000 Accident Cases

N.Y. Times 2/19/55

COURT JAMS HELD THREAT TO JUSTICE

Tweed Says the Proposed Changes Are Vital to Avert a Breakdown

N.Y. Times 10/22/55

EISENHOWER BACKS 6-POINT PROGRAM TO END COURT JAM

Brownell's Plans Also Seek to Cope With Increasing Prison Population

20 NEW JUDGESHIPS SET

President Favors Outlawing of Jury Eavesdropping—Sits Up 110 Minutes

N.Y. Times 5/23/56

U. S. GROUP SET UP ON COURT DELAYS

Permanent Body to Study Congestion Is a Result of Brownell's Meeting

assume the duties and responsibilities which were contemplated by the constitutional amendment.

I will try to give a few examples of some concrete things that have been accomplished.

Probation

In 1960, following a burst of excitement about juvenile delinquency, efforts were made to deal with the problem by creating a separate probation office. Legislation was proposed in Albany by a group appointed by Governor Rockefeller. Mayor Wagner also appointed a committee. Both sought to establish a central office outside of the court system to replace the probation service in New York City's different courts.

These bills led the Judicial Conference to appoint a special committee of judges to study the problem. It opposed the suggested new extra-judicial probation system because it felt strongly that probation was and should remain a judicial function under the courts. It urged those supporting legislation to recognize this principle. Eli Whitney Debevoise was chairman of the Governor's committee. He had been one of those originally working with our New York Law Society and was sympathetic to the plan suggested by the judges committee. Agreement was reached on a measure that soon became law, establishing a new office of probation, with a director to be appointed by the courts.

As the chairman of this special committee, I saw a practical demonstration of the real usefulness of judges working together. Not only was the bill passed, but a new and effective agency came into being. The Office of Probation makes it possible to furnish auxiliary services to the courts throughout the city, and New York now has a program for probation that it may well be proud of which is part of the court system.

Among recent steps that the Probation Office has taken is the program to release prisoners without bail when investigation indicates that the prisoner will voluntarily appear in court. In six months, nearly 4,000 persons were released in this way, and it is expected that this number will increase, thereby saving the city many thousands of dollars in confinement expenses and making it unnecessary for many thousands of people to be needlessly confined in jail pending their trials.

Toward Open Hospitals

In England and some other countries mental hospitals have increasingly become "open" hospitals, but in this country these huge institutions remain places of confinement rather than places for treatment of the sick. This would seem to be more a medical than a legal problem, but its burden on the courts has been very real. Huge mental hospitals with thousands of inmates living there just because of their age, or because there is nowhere else the family can put them, have given rise to many cases where the courts are called on to inquire if the individual is improperly restrained.

An important step has recently been taken encouraging voluntary commitments, and it may well be the first step in this country toward "open" hospitals. By an amendment to the mental-hygiene law, provision has been made for easier voluntary commitments and for the creation of a Mental Health Information Service, with a director appointed by the court. He has the responsibility of investigating and reporting to the court on commitment of persons alleged to be mentally incompetent, as well as the duty to advise the incompetent and his relatives of his rights and to assist any interested person in protecting them. This has been in effect only since August 31, 1965, and it is far too early to say what will happen, but that this has all taken place quietly and with the cooperation and initiative of the courts is in itself an important fact. Here again, because I have been on the subcommittee involved, I have had an opportunity to watch this plan go through. As in England, it may become possible for a person to go to a mental institution just as he goes to an ordinary hospital today, on a completely voluntary basis and without any raised eyebrows. An incidental but tremendously important by-product of such a development should be the use of mental hospitals as *temporary* places for disturbed persons to obtain the best possible mental care. This would be substituted for the present process by which thousands and thousands are just lodged in mental hospitals and left there. Not only does this cost the community huge sums of money, but it does nothing for the disturbed individual.

Helping Juries Work

The judges committee has also been working to help citizens carry out their task of jury service. Jury panels have been consolidated and arrangements made to accommodate jurors who are willing to respond to a phone call at short notice. Yet it is a fact that many jurors still feel that they are wasting time on jury duty. Many of them sit around for days without being called on a single case. With this in mind, Presiding Justice Botein decided to produce a film to be shown to prospective jurors explaining why this was necessary. He appointed a subcommittee of judges to work out the plan for the film and then he raised the money to pay for it from the Ford Foundation. The members of the subcommittee, including me, worked with two professional organizations to produce a film which shows a man getting his jury notice, his irritation at having his day's work interfered with, and how he actually sits and serves. The narrator, E. G. Marshall, famous for his work on television in *The Defenders*, does a good job, and I think an excellent picture was produced. After sitting through many sessions in the process of production, I saw the final picture on one of the first days that it was exhibited to the jurors called in the Supreme Court. I was surprised and delighted at the effect upon this audience. It is now being regularly used in this way. It is also being shown in the public schools in New York, and is available for showing to communities throughout the country. Only time will tell how effective the picture is, but it certainly is most encouraging to know that something like this has been produced by the courts themselves.

❊   ❊   ❊

These are but a few illustrations of the innovations being made today by our courts, and they indicate the effectiveness of operating a unified court system under an administrative head instead of having each separate court run its own show in different directions. These accomplishments emphasize how very much more is still to be done.

The people who use the courts may ask why it takes three, four, or five years before a simple accident case is disposed of in this country. These questions are everybody's business, and our citizens are entitled to the answers. Do all the accident cases have to go to court? Aren't there other ways to dispose of them? Why should a man be allowed to drive his car while he has a valid claim still pending against him for injuring someone in another accident? And why should his insurance company be permitted to do business insuring others when it has failed to act reasonably to settle cases in the past? The driver is licensed by the state to run his car, and the insurance company is licensed by the state to issue its insurance policy. Before the state renews the license of the insurance carrier to do business next year, shouldn't the carrier be required to show that it has well and reasonably performed its obligations to pay the claims which it guaranteed to pay? And shouldn't the automobile owner show that he has operated his car without causing injury to others before his license is automatically renewed?

When the citizen begins to look at the court as *his* court, existing for his benefit, he will want to know why it is run more like a Donnybrook Fair than a court of law. He will inquire why so many new cases are brought each year. He will ask whether there isn't some better way by which the nearly three and a half million parking violations that go to court every year in New York City can be taken care of. He will wonder why modern business methods are not employed. He will ask what management engineers would recommend. He will be surprised to learn that for many generations the English courts have disposed of all their preliminaries through masters, in a quiet, uncrowded atmosphere, working through a calendar scheduled at fifteen-minute intervals.

There is nothing that gives the legal profession the exclusive right to decide how courts should be operated. The training of a person in business is far better geared to running the business part of a courtroom than is the training of a lawyer. The business-man and the management engineer have much more know-how in this direction. They should have their share of the responsibility for determining how best to run a courtroom. You should not take it for granted that it has to take years before your case can be reached for trial. How this process can be speeded up can be found out, if there is a real determination to find it out.

Nor should the legislature be the one to lay down the law as to just how many days should be allowed to file a bill of particulars or a notice of examination before trial. Those matters should be arranged by the court. Today's system of having the legislature pass a law each time that a change is made is fantastic. In 1966 there were 31 laws passed amending the Civil Practice Act (and 128 bills were introduced). Each bill has to go to a committee, there be considered, rejected, neglected, or passed; then the same procedure takes place in the other house. Why? The courts can determine these matters themselves. There is no need for the legislature to do so.

A Constitutional Convention started in New York in April, 1967. It could do nothing or a great deal to make our courts function properly. It could leave them unchanged, or even go back to the prehistoric conditions that we had before the 1961 constitutional amendment, when no one was in charge. It gave no indication that it had either the will or the spirit to submit to the voters a program for real improvement in the courts. Its final draft fails almost completely in improving on court administration and takes a big step backward in imposing on the Court of Appeals the administrative task so well started by the Judicial Conference and its departmental committees. Much more interest and knowledge is still needed, and it appears that the Committee for Modern Courts has a lot more educating to do before our courts will truly serve those for whom they were created—the people. If the citizens care and make their voices heard, they can make the courts do their job. A lifetime of concern with the administration of justice has persuaded me that only through popular support and hard work can the modernization of our courts be realized.

EPILOGUE

PRINCETON has now been our home for many years. There in our Victorian house on Mercer Street, a street that John Gunther described as one of the most beautiful in the United States, we have gathered together all our possessions—the odds and ends that we have brought back from our travels, the paintings and prints we bought or were given by my wife's art-school colleagues (many now well known), and all the papers and photographs that are the accumulation of our long domestic and professional lives. We stand well back from the street and in the rear of the house our grounds slope down toward the graduate college. All during the warm months I work on the back porch, and there answers to legal and other problems seem to come easier to me. The old brown carriage house is my wife's studio, now filled with modeling stands and chain hoists instead of hay and saddles. Coming here to Princeton was probably the smartest move we ever made. But for the war, we'd still be living in New York.

I'm still not able to retire. Even long after the normal retirement age, the problems of personal clients remain with me, as well as the responsibilities of a law firm that I helped to start and grew up with. Beyond these, and in spite of strong resolutions to the contrary, I still find myself working on things that intrigue me.

It's not easy for a lawyer to retire. In December, 1966, when I was approaching seventy-seven, Jacqueline Kennedy's suit against William Manchester and Harper & Row was started. My partner, Harriet Pilpel, was then doing our work for Harper. She brought me the complaint and the other papers in which Mrs. Kennedy asked the court to stop Harper from publishing Manchester's *The Death of a President*. As the litigation guy in the office I was condemned to a pretty busy time over Christmas until Mrs. Kennedy decided she didn't want to go on with her motion for an injunction. Then when Harper & Row insisted on defending the case, examining Senator Robert Kennedy and other witnesses, the lawsuit was ended, and the book was published as scheduled in April.

On the heels of this case, I became involved in another matter. One snowy evening just after my wife and I had returned home from a weekend seventy-fifth birthday party for our good friend Dan Koshland in San Francisco, the phone rang. It was George Kennan's wife, Annelise, telling me that George was sick in bed and would appreciate it if I could come right over because he wanted to see me. I did so and he told me about Stalin's daughter, Svetlana Alliluyeva, and that he was planning to go to Switzerland the next day to meet her. He told me that she was friendless, needed a lawyer, and wanted to know if my firm would help, and if I could go to Switzerland. I said we would if she wanted us to. I went home dazed and a bit knocked-out. When I told my wife, she said that I should be glad I had the chance to go. In a few days I heard from George that Svetlana did want me. The next day, after asking my young partner, Alan Schwartz, to come along with me, I went to Switzerland, and since then, with the help of another partner, Maurice Greenbaum, we've represented her. My wife was right. And it's still hard to retire.

Besides the strictly legal matters from the office, I still serve on boards of directors. I have succeeded in resigning from most of them after maneuvering to get a younger man to fill my place

—one of my younger partners, for instance. But my work still requires commuting to New York, although not every day. The time in Princeton enables me not only to enjoy our house but also to walk past Dr. Einstein's house which is only one removed from ours, down toward the Institute for Advanced Study, along the Springdale Golf Club, back by the graduate school, the Theological Seminary, and then home. It's a nice walk, but on Sunday morning I usually get a longer one, with Harold Hochschild or David Lilienthal, or both, through the woods back of the Institute. Being with them is really a liberal education. Harold not only opens my eyes to many things that I didn't know, but he also puts me on speaking terms with the problems of Zambia, Rhodesia, and other far-flung places where his knowledge is firsthand. David gives me a bird's-eye view of the TVA as well as a present view of his recent experiences in Iran, Vietnam, and elsewhere around the world.

In these surroundings, as well as in my office, I still seek solutions to some of the problems that have always plagued me. Why do I worry about them? If I didn't, I'd have more time for fun. I could loaf more, read more whodunits, go to the theater, and do more things that I enjoy. Pleasure, however, seems to be more complicated. For me, at any rate, no pleasure quite equals that of solving old problems in new times. Progress is always elusive and always possible. Working at it plays hell with retirement, but it makes for life and thus for fun.

APPENDIX

LETTER FROM GRENVILLE CLARK *

Dublin, New Hampshire
July 23, 1965

EDWARD S. GREENBAUM, Esq.
285 Madison Avenue
New York, New York 10017

DEAR MR. GREENBAUM:

As to Bob Patterson's appointment as Assistant Secretary of War in the summer of 1940, that would be quite a long story with all the detail, but very briefly the essentials are these:

Back in 1931 while H. L. Stimson was Secretary of State, he prophesied to me with amazing accuracy the coming of World War II, its probable course and eventual line-up. He said that this would unquestionably include the USA and that the length of the war would largely depend upon what preparations were made by us before our participation, which would come to pass about two years after the beginning of the war. Well remembering this, I proposed to some of the old Plattsburg group at a meeting on May 8, 1940 (after the conquest of Norway but before the big German attack in Belgium) that we advocate a peace-time selective service act. Everyone agreed and naturally appointed me to draft an act and try to get it introduced and passed. I did this with the aid of Howard

---

* Written in response to a request from me as to how Judge Patterson was appointed Assistant Secretary of War—E.S.G.

C. Petersen (later Bob Patterson's right-hand man) and William T. Stewart, both of whom were then law clerks in the Cravath firm. FDR was at first doubtful about supporting so unprecedented a measure, General Marshall strongly opposed it upon the ground that it could not pass and would interfere with other plans of his, and Secretary Woodring was strongly opposed to it. It was therefore most difficult to find good sponsorship in the two Houses of Congress and I made up my mind that the thing to do was to get a new and strong Secretary of War. At that time, however, although I knew FDR well and had worked closely with him in 1933–36, I was out of favor because of having opposed his court scheme in 1937. Therefore, I decided that I needed a collaborator in the shape of Felix Frankfurter and put the proposition to him. He agreed and in late May 1940 he and I met and made separate lists, on each of which was H. L. Stimson's name. We soon agreed on him as our nominee, but also decided that FDR was unlikely to appoint him at his then age of seventy-three unless he had a much younger and very reliable Assistant Secretary. Therefore we made a second list on which I put Bob Patterson's name and we very soon agreed on the joint ticket, which within an hour FF took over to FDR. Felix then reported to me in New York that the idea was pretty well received but that FDR wanted me to inquire about HLS's health and as to whether both would accept. I did so and got Bob's willingness to accept by phone within less than a minute. As to HLS, I had a confidential talk with his doctor (who fortunately was mine also) and got a good report. As to his acceptance, however, he laid down four very stiff conditions, any one of which would make his appointment impossible, he said. I conveyed these with my health report to FF, who in turn informed FDR. Then neither FF nor I heard anything for three weeks until on the evening of June 19, 1940, I had a phone call from Long Island from HLS to me at the Carlton Hotel where I was working to find the right sponsors for the introduction of the then completed draft of the Selective Service Act. I well remember HLS's opening words, which were "Your preposterous plot has succeeded,"

and he then went on to say that FDR had just phoned him
and asked him to be Secretary of War and when HLS replied
that FDR had evidently not heard accurately of his four conditions, FDR replied "Well, let's see" and, as HLS said, then
repeated them "almost verbatim as I gave them to you three
weeks ago." FDR then said "the conditions are all accepted
without qualification and I shall expect you at my office at
ten o'clock tomorrow morning" and HLS then added to me,
I remember, "and I shall expect to see *you* at my hotel at 9
o'clock."

One of HLS's conditions was that he should have a free
hand to support a peace-time selective service act and one of
his first moves even before he was confirmed on July 11 was
to have a meeting at his house in Washington at which
Marshall, Hershey, etc. were present together with H. C.
Petersen and me, at the end of which HLS announced that it
would be the policy of the War Department to support our
draft bill with certain minor changes.

The appointment of HLS was publicly announced on June 20
and the bill was introduced in the House that same day by
James W. Wadsworth and in the Senate by Senator Edward
R. Burke.

Although it had been firmly agreed that Patterson would
be appointed, FDR procrastinated as to that by reason of his
obligations to Louis Johnson, who was then Assistant Secretary and had expected to be Secretary if Woodring went
out. Finally after some weeks of delay HLS got tired of it
and asked me whether I agreed that something drastic must
be done. When I did agree, he wrote in his handwriting on
one sheet "I hereby appoint Robert P. Patterson Assistant
Secretary of War" with a space for the President's signature and
on another sheet attached to it "Mr. President, this appointment
should be signed today." Showing these to me, HLS asked my
opinion as to whether they were too strong medicine and when
I said that I thought them all right, he thought a while and
then said, "What would you think of my instructing the messenger who takes them to say that he was told to wait for an
answer?" I replied that this was equivalent to his resigning if

the appointment didn't come back that afternoon but that I
thought it was time to do it. Accordingly, the messenger went
with those instructions and about an hour later HLS asked me
to come to his room (at that time I had a room near his) and
as I came in merely held up the appointment with FDR's
signature on it.

As you know the combination worked out very well although
several times in the next few years I found it necessary to
speak to one or the other in order to smooth out difficulties
and misunderstandings. At the end when HLS left Washington
in September 1945 he told me that he couldn't possibly have
wished for a more loyal and steadfast partner. As you doubtless
know, he asked President Truman to appoint Bob on the
Supreme Court in the place of Justice Burton and HLS told
me that Truman entirely agreed but informed him that after
consulting members of the Senate he found it impossible because it was necessary to appoint a Republican at that time
and Bob had not only voted for FDR but had also told many
people that he had. And instead, therefore, HLS said that
Truman intended to appoint Bob as HLS's successor and then,
as you know, Petersen became Assistant Secretary, Petersen
having been recommended to Bob by me (at Bob's request
that I find him a good right-hand man) soon after Bob took
office.

This account has been longer than I thought it would be, but
gives just the main features which I think will interest you.

Sincerely yours,
GRENVILLE CLARK

ARTICLE BY EDWARD S. GREENBAUM

LAWYERS TALK TOO MUCH*

WE lawyers use too many words. Many of them are too long.
We put too many in one sentence. In short, we talk too much.
That's really all that I have to say. But, being a lawyer,
it will take me quite a while to say it.

When we talk, we lawyers are usually fairly easy to understand. Not always, but usually. But not when we write. For
some reason we then use the most awful language. We do it
even to say the simplest things. Here's how the New York
County Lawyers Association tells its members that after the
next meeting they can get together and have a glass of beer:

"The ceremonies will conclude with a collation and an
abundant opportunity will be afforded to our members for
fraternization."

Nobody talks like that.

The American Bar Association tried to do something about
this problem. The Association's announcement of its $2,500
prize essay contest for 1950 showed that it meant business. It
said:

"Clearness and brevity of expression and absence of iteration

---

* Reprinted from 19 *Federal Rules Decisions*.

or undue prolixity will be taken into favorable consideration."

This seemed to mean that the absence of both "iteration" and "undue prolixity" would not be favorably considered. So I asked about this in a letter saying:

"The Association's reluctance to move too rapidly is understandable. But it poses a difficult problem for a contestant who elects to eliminate 'iteration' and just go in for 'undue prolixity.' The instructions require him to use language over and above normal prolixity and short of iteration. A clarification of this poor contestant's dilemma would be appreciated."

The Association sent the comforting reply that "absence of either iteration or undue prolixity will count in your favor in the consideration of your essay. Favorable consideration does not depend on the absence of both."

Our legal publications feed us this kind of language all through our lives. And when we die we may rest assured our names will appear in a dignified list entitled "Necrological."

We know that our language is almost incomprehensible to the layman. But we do nothing to change it. Indeed, we do not want to change it. Why is this so? One reason is that it gives us a feeling of superiority. We, and members of other professions, seem to revel in a maze of technical expressions. They are calculated to impress the uninitiated. In his introduction to A. P. Herbert's masterpiece, *Uncommon Law*, Lord Atkin said:

"The general impression of law is too often that it is the product of a black art administered as a mystery which none but the initiates need hope to understand."

Another reason is our timidity and conservatism. Habit is not easily broken, particularly if it is deep-rooted. In 1362 Parliament passed an act forbidding the use of French in legal proceedings. But lawyers persisted in using French and Latin for nearly three centuries. This led to another Act of Parliament, in 1650, fining lawyers £20 for using any language other than English in legal documents. But lawyers had the act repealed. In 1731 Parliament finally passed an act imposing a fine of £50. That did it.

But, it is asked: "Why should we change what we have

always done? We are writing contracts, not literature. Why should we take the chance of jeopardizing our clients' interests by using language different from that approved by the courts?" The argument would be unanswerable, if it were true. The protection of our client is our first duty. But the use of clear language should not prejudice his rights. On the contrary, it should clarify and strengthen them.

The fact that a clause or provision has been judicially approved in one case does not necessarily mean that it is applicable to the facts in another. Indeed, that it had to go to court in the first place may well indicate that there was some doubt as to its meaning. Some years ago the sanity of a New York legislator was frequently questioned. He confidently asserted that he was the only member of the legislature who could prove that he was sane. He did so by proudly displaying the findings of a lunacy commission certifying to his sanity, by a 2 to 1 vote. Yet the doubt continued.

Pride in our work and pride in our profession should impel us to use simpler language. We lawyers are not popular. Our prolix circumlocution is one of the reasons for this. *The New Yorker's* examples of "The Legal Mind at Work" fairly reflect the public's attitude to what E. B. White calls lawyers' "flights of rhetorical secrecy." That other callings and professions may be equally guilty is no reason why our "learned profession" should not remove this blight. Words are the special and peculiar tools of our profession. Our use of simple and readable language would help tremendously to gain respect for our profession.

An increasing number of lawyers believe that legal documents can be made much simpler. A few specific cases will illustrate. In the first place, we should use fewer words.

On a pleasant Sunday afternoon, Henry Haddock was strolling along a road adjoining the Peaceable Valley Golf Club. He was suddenly struck by a golf ball driven from the seventh tee by Samuel Slicer. Although by Tuesday the lump on Haddock's leg had almost gone, his injured feelings had progressively increased. He decided Slicer would have to pay. Slicer's lawyer wisely told his client to settle. So they did for $50. The lawyer naturally wanted Slicer to be released from any further claims, and had Haddock sign such a release when he paid him the $50. The lawyer, like any other lawyer, had become so accustomed to legal forms that it no longer struck him as funny that the release said:

"TO ALL TO WHOM THESE PRESENTS SHALL COME or may concern, greeting: know ye, THAT I, HENRY HADDOCK, for and in consideration of the sum of Fifty Dollars ($50.00) lawful money of the United States of America, to me in hand paid by SAMUEL SLICER, the receipt whereof is hereby acknowledged, have remised, released and forever discharged and by these presents do for my heirs, executors and administrators remise, release and forever discharge the said SAMUEL SLICER, his heirs, executors and administrators, of all and from all, and all manner of action and actions, cause and causes of actions, suits, debts, dues, sums of money, accounts, reckonings, bonds, bills, specialties, covenants, contracts, controversies, agreements, promises, variances, trespasses, damages, judgments, extents, executions, claims and demands whatsoever in law or in equity, which against the said SAMUEL SLICER I ever had, now have or which my heirs, executors or administrators, hereafter can, shall or may have for, upon or by reason of any matter, cause, or thing whatsoever from the beginning of the world to the day of the date of these presents.

"IN WITNESS WHEREOF, I have hereunto set my hand and seal the 3rd day of June, nineteen hundred and fifty-five.

"Sealed and Delivered in the
Presence of
    Felix Blackstone   Henry Haddock   L.S."

This monstrosity is called a General Release. You can get it in any stationery store. The United States Circuit Court of Appeals has said: "One wonders what calamity would occur if general releases covered merely the period beginning with the year 1 A.D., or the Battle of Hastings." (Because no lawyer may quote from a case without fear of having his veracity questioned unless he cites it, I humbly refer to In re Monza Mills, 146 F.2d 161.)

An agreement usually starts like this:

"This agreement, made and entered into this 16th day of December, 1955, by and between JOSEPH ZILCH, of 35 West Amsterdam Avenue, in the Borough of Manhattan, City, County and State of New York, party of the first part, and the YORK CORPORATION, a corporation duly organized and existing under the laws of the State of New York, having its principal place of business at 120 Broadway, in the Borough of Manhattan, City, County and State of New York, party of the second part."

We could just say:

"Agreement dated December 16, 1955, between JOSEPH ZILCH (herein called Zilch) and THE YORK CORPORATION (herein called York)."

The first way took eighty-eight words, the second only eighteen words. You may say: "But you have omitted the addresses." But why include the addresses? Either party may move. And if they are included for some purpose such as giving notice, don't worry, that will all be fully provided for later in Paragraph 34, or thereabouts.

One of our greatest weaknesses is the iteration, reiteration and repetition of words meaning the same thing. Besides being irritating, it is unnecessary to say that:

"The Company has executed, acknowledged and delivered these presents and has granted, bargained, sold, conveyed, confirmed, mortgaged and set over and by these presents does grant, bargain, sell, convey, confirm, mortgage and set over to and with the Mortgagee, and his heirs, legal representatives, successors and assigns, forever, all and singular, the following . . ."

In this case the six verbs "grant, bargain, sell, convey, confirm and mortgage" here mean the same thing. Justice Oliver Wendell Holmes said "that a man who takes half a page to say what can be said in a sentence will be damned."

Consider the unnecessary language used in wills. Many of us still start off by saying that the testator is "of sound and disposing mind." But these words do not give testamentary capacity to an incompetent. Nor would their omission cast doubt on a testator's sanity.

The next clause in a will is to direct the payment of all just debts and funeral expenses. A creditor cannot be prevented from collecting his claim against an estate if this provision is not in the will. But a creditor whose claim is barred by the statute of limitations might argue that the testator waived it by directing his executors to pay "all just debts."

A will is not an easy document to prepare. It often requires painstaking work that most clients do not appreciate. The same is true of many other legal papers. The vital importance of giving them the most careful consideration and study should never be minimized. In these days, tax questions usually add greatly to the difficulties of the problem. But these problems are not solved by an overabundance of words. Indeed, our tendency to say too much often hurts rather than helps our clients' interests.

I've taken too many words to say: "We use too many words."

My next point is that the words that we use are too long. A conscious effort to use fewer words automatically tends to make us use shorter words. It will make us stop and think before using words like "collation," "reiteration," and "necrological." We may even feel a bit embarrassed to use a fancy word if a short four-letter one will do.

This does not mean that we should avoid a technical word or long word if it is the right word. Nor should we refrain from using a word just because the layman may not understand it. "Testatrix" is the right word. We should not avoid it by saying "lady will-maker." But we do not have to say "covenant" when we mean "agreed." And, of course, we don't have to say both "covenant" and "agreed." In separation agreements we need not say that the parties were "intermarried." Both of the parties thought they were merely "married" until, as we lawyers say, the "unhappy differences and disputes" arose, which led to the agreement that they would not "molest, annoy, arrest, disturb, gossip about, malign or interfere with the other in any manner whatsoever."

That is enough on my second obvious point—we should use simpler and shorter words.

We should use shorter sentences. Sentences averaging about eighteen words make easy reading. We cannot expect that low average in legal agreements. But we should remember that long sentences do not make easy reading. And more important, they do not aid our clients in getting what they are contracting for.

When Justice Holmes referred to the "man who takes half a page to say what can be said in a sentence" he overlooked something. We lawyers can make that sentence a half page long without batting an eye. Here is one. It has 286 words. It is in a lease, affectionately called "This Indenture of Lease." The sentence says that the tenant shall pay—if you'll excuse the expression I use—the taxes. But instead of saying taxes it says: "all real estate taxes, assessments, water rents and charges, and governmental impositions, duties and charges of every kind and nature whatsoever, extraordinary as well as ordinary and whether now within the contemplation of the parties or not, and each and every installment of each of them which shall or may during the term of this lease be charged, laid, levied, assessed or imposed upon, or become a lien or liens upon the demised premises or any part thereof, or upon any building or appurtenances thereto, or any part thereof, or upon any sidewalks or streets in front of or adjoining the demised premises, or which may become due and payable with respect thereto, and any and all taxes, charged, laid, levied, assessed or imposed in lieu of or in addition to the foregoing, under or by virtue of any present or future laws, rules, requirements, orders, directions, ordinances or regulations of the United States of America, or of the state, county or city government or of any other municipal, governmental or lawful authority whatsoever . . ."

Naturally, the sentence does not stop there, it goes on to provide that the tenant shall also pay for: "all gas, electricity or other service or services furnished to the demised premises or the occupants thereof during the term hereof, and all fees and charges of the state, county or city government or of any other municipal, governmental or lawful authority whatsoever, for the construction, maintenance or use during the term hereof, of any vault, passageway or space, in or over or under any street or sidewalk adjacent to the demised premises, or for the construction, maintenance or use during the term thereof, of any part of any building on the demised premises within the limits of any street."

The lease concludes with the broadminded provision that "Words of any gender in this lease shall be held to include any other gender." It contains no mention of any "he" or "she." But through the lease the party of the first part is referred to as the "landlord." The gender clause was probably inserted because it is a form lease, and the Landlord may be a lady, and some legal eagle might argue that a Landlady is not a Landlord.

Good legal draftsmanship requires skill. Most lawyers have this skill. They carefully study the law and facts necessary to enable them to do a good job. But most of them rarely give thought to the importance of using simpler language. It is significant that Professor Samuel Williston's classic eight-volume 8,500-page work on contracts has nothing to say about it.

In summary, lawyers should be urged, entreated and implored never, under any circumstances, conditions or contingencies whatsoever to repeat, iterate or reiterate, again and again and again; and never utilize, employ or otherwise make use of any word or words longer, more involved or more technical than needed, required, or deemed essential; nor to put too many of any of the aforesaid words, or any word or words used in substitution, place or stead of any of the aforesaid word or words, in one sentence in any contract, agreement, indenture or other legal document whatsoever, whether prepared by them, their partner, their office associate or clerk; and above all things never to write anything, either in the body thereof or in conclusion, containing a long, involved, intricate sentence like this, that has 136 words contained therein.

INDEX

Abbott, Nathan, 21, 22
Abrams v. Van Schaick, 78 n.
Adams, Ted C., 106, 108
agreement, unnecessary language in, 233
Alger, George W., 114
Alliluyeva, Svetlana, 220
Alsop, Joseph, 152
Amberg, Julius H., 135
American Agriculturist, 92
American Exchange National Bank, 30
American Jewish Committee, 120, 122, 124
American Locomotive Co., 131
Anti-Defamation League, 121
anti-Semitism, 120, 121, 123
Arnold, Henry H. ("Hap"), 146
Arnold, Thurman, 110
Articles of War, 53, 54, 61, 63, 157–58
Atkin, Lord, quoted, 230
Atlantic Acceptance Corp., 91
atomic bomb, 171, 172, 173 and n.
Atomic Bomb and the End of World War II, The (Feis), 173 n.
Aurand, Henry, 143, 144
Avery, Sewall, 141 n.

Backer, George, 130
Bailey, F. Lee, 207
Bailey, Kenneth, 185
Baker, Helen, 13
Baldwin Locomotive Co., 131
Bar Association, 40, 114, 115, 181, 182, 198 and n., 200, 201, 211, 229, 230
Bates, Sanford, 160
Becker, Charles, 34; trials of, 35–36
Behind Closed Doors (Costikyan), 210
Bell, J. Franklin, 50, 51, 52, 53, 54
Bennett, E. A., 30
Bennett, James V., 160
Berlin, Irving, 130
Bethel, Walter, 56, 57, 58
Biddle, Francis, 141 n.
Bill of Rights, 158
Bixby, F. Lovell, 160
Black, Hugo L., 111, 208
Blanchard, James A., 11
Blumenthal, Mark, 4
Borglum, Gutzon, 96
Botein, Bernard, 199, 212, 216
Boyle v. Semenoff, 42 n.
Brandeis, Louis D., 111
Branshaw, Charles E., 139, 140